STANDARD L

D1765532

HUMAN NATURE AND
HISTORICAL KNOWLEDGE

HUMAN NATURE

AND

HISTORICAL KNOWLEDGE

HUME, HEGEL AND VICO

LEON POMPA

Professor of Philosophy, University of Birmingham

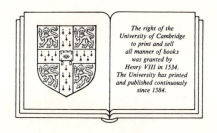

The right of the
University of Cambridge
to print and sell
all manner of books
was granted by
Henry VIII in 1534.
The University has printed
and published continuously
since 1584.

CAMBRIDGE UNIVERSITY PRESS

Cambridge
New York   Port Chester
Melbourne   Sydney

Published by the Press Syndicate of the University of Cambridge
The Pitt Building, Trumpington Street, Cambridge CB2 1RP
40 West 20th Street, New York, NY 10011, USA
10 Stamford Road, Oakleigh, Melbourne 3166, Australia

First published 1990
Printed in Great Britain at the University Press, Cambridge

British Library cataloguing in publication data
Pompa, Leon
Human nature and historical knowledge: Hume, Hegel and Vico.
1. Philosophical perspectives
I. Title
901

Library of Congress cataloguing in publication data
Pompa, Leon.
Human nature and historical knowledge: Hume, Hegel,
and Vico / Leon Pompa.
p.   cm.
ISBN 0 521 38137 1
1. History – Philosophy.   2. Philosophical anthropology.
3. Man.   4. Hegel, Georg Wilhelm Friedrich, 1770–1831.
5. Hume, David, 1711–1776.   6. Vico, Giambattista, 1668–1744.
I. Title
D16.8.P5553   1990
901–dc20   89–77374   CIP

ISBN 0 521 38137 1

CE

To J. J.

CONTENTS

INTRODUCTION

This study has two aims. The first is to offer an account of the minimal presuppositions of historical knowledge from the point of view of a particular possibility. There are many accounts of the conditions of historical knowledge available. Most of them accept, either explicitly or implicitly, that these conditions must include some general assumptions about human nature, which serve to provide historical knowledge both with a certain kind of intelligibility and with a general support for the kinds of reasoning upon which it is normally thought to depend. They thus support but, at the same time, constrain the kind of knowledge which historians can provide. It must be at least a conceptual possibility, however, that human nature itself may have changed, to a greater or lesser extent, over time. It would seem unreasonable, therefore, to pre-empt the decision whether this possibility has or has not actually occurred, simply through adopting certain limiting assumptions about human nature as a condition of historical knowledge. Whether or not, or to what degree, such changes have actually occurred ought to be a factual matter rather than one the answer to which follows from methodological considerations alone. One aim of this study, therefore, is to investigate the problem whether an account of the presuppositions of historical knowledge can be reached which will allow it to be a factual matter whether, and to what degree, human nature may have changed in the course of its history.

The second aim of the study is to offer a critical interpretation of the theories of three important philosophers which have definite implications for the first problem and, by an analysis of the difficulties which these raise, to help to clarify the problem and to see how it may be resolved. It will be seen from the list of chapter headings that I have devoted much more space to this task than to the first. The reason for this is that, although the thought of these three philosophers is directly relevant to the main issue, they did not themselves write with this problem alone in mind. In approaching their thought from the point of view of its bearing upon the central issue there is, therefore, the definite danger of misrepresenting it. I have tried, accordingly, to interpret their accounts of the nature of historical knowledge within the context of their own intentions, as well as analysing their implications for the general philosophical issue with which this book is concerned. This has involved considerable textual explication and discussion which, apart from the question of its bearing upon the central question, will, I hope, be of interest in its own right.

An initial idea of the general problem can be most easily given by noting some connections between certain widely accepted features of historical knowledge. The first is that history is essentially a factual discipline. A fundamental aim of historical knowledge, that is to say, is to establish that certain people lived and died, that certain deeds were performed, that certain events took place and so on.[1] These are,

---

[1] This is meant only as a statement of what historians purport to do. A distinction must be drawn between what most historians say that they are doing and what philosophers say that analysis shows that they can possibly do. The distinction is captured excellently by Murray G. Murphey, in the opening sentences of his book, *Our Knowledge of the Historical Past* (Indianapolis, Bobbs-Merrill, 1973), where he writes: 'Whatever their disagreements, historians as a group are agreed that history is a discipline which seeks to establish true statements about events which have occurred and objects which have existed in the past.' He then proceeds by pointing out that this claim, 'which seems so self-evident to historians', involves a number of ontological and epistemological problems, with which his book is concerned. Similarly, G. R. Elton, while disclaiming to have the expertise to enter into discussion of the philosophical problems to which it gives rise, defines history as being 'concerned with all those human sayings, thoughts, deeds and sufferings which occurred in the past and which have left present deposit; and it deals with them from the point of view of happening, change and the particular'. *The Practice of History*, The Fontana Library (London, Collins, 1969), p. 24. This does not mean, however, that all historians are satisfied that they can reach the truth. In the 1930s, for example, the American historian Charles Beard produced two essays, 'Written History as an Act of Faith' and 'That Noble Dream', in the *American Historical Review*, 39 (1934) and 41 (1935) respectively, in which he set out his reasons for believing that we could never reach an account of the past 'as it actually was'. For an analysis of Beard's arguments, see William Dray, *Perspectives on History* (London, Routledge & Kegan Paul, 1980), Chapter 2. Beard's distinguished compatriot, Carl L. Becker, expressed similar reservations in his essay, 'What Are Historical Facts?', in the *Western Political Quarterly*, 8 (1955). But the fact remains that historians normally claim that they are hoping to establish truths about the past, or at least about the

of course, not the only things with which historians are concerned. Apart from an interest in what actually happened, they are interested in explaining why such things happened, in the context within which they could happen and in the consequences of their happening. These other interests presuppose, however, that it is possible to establish, with a greater or lesser degree of security, further facts about what did or did not happen. For the distinction between, for example, an *explanans* and an *explanandum* does not normally depend upon anything intrinsic to the things brought forward as *explanans* or *explanandum*, but upon the point of view from which we are interested in the things in question. Thus something which is an *explanans* from one point of view – say, Henry VIII's dissolution of the monasteries in relation to certain features of later sixteenth-century economic trends – may be an *explanandum* from another – say, changing patterns of religious belief in the fifteenth and early sixteenth centuries. But no matter which is the focus of our interest, it will be satisfied only if further relevant facts can be established.

The second connected feature of historical knowledge is that it must be reached by valid argument based upon a body of relevant evidence. There has been considerable disagreement as to whether there is one form of argument typical of all historical reasoning or whether different forms of argument and evidence are required, dependent upon the type of history in which one is interested.[2] Despite this disagreement, however, there is almost universal agreement upon the need for some or other appropriate form of argument. For, unless this were so, in the absence of any direct or perceptual knowledge of the past, it would seem to be impossible to distinguish history from fiction. Thus, on this view, the factual character of historical knowledge is linked to the need for some adequate mode of *evidential* access to the past.

The third feature is that the evidence utilised in historical reasoning consists largely in human artefacts.[3] In many cases this might be in

human past, from some or other point of view the presence of which is not thought to preclude the possibility of their achieving their aim.

[2] For the best recent account of this debate, see C. Behan McCullagh, *Justifying Historical Descriptions* (Cambridge, Cambridge University Press, 1984), in which a wide range of different patterns of historical argument are discussed.

[3] See R. G. Collingwood's instructive comparison of the difference between the archaeologist's interpretation of a site, which depends crucially upon the fact that it is an artefact, and the work of the palaeontologist which, although it involves arranging fossils in a time-series, differs from that of the archaeologist. *The Idea of History* (Oxford, Clarendon Press, 1946; reprinted in Oxford Paperbacks, 1961), p. 212.

the form of documentary evidence, although a much larger range of kinds of documents than purely descriptive documents is involved. Moreover, as interest in the past has widened from largely political matters to include the social, economic and cultural dimensions of life, techniques have been developed to take into account a much wider range of artefacts. It is not even true, as a matter of fact, that the only relevant evidence consists in human artefacts, since the relationship between human activities and the physical environment can allow knowledge of past environments, reached on the basis of applied physical science, to act as a form of historical evidence. Nevertheless, useful though such evidence may be, it can never be more than a complement to the forms of evidence which past human artefacts comprise. For the fact that the physical environments in which human beings live may exert an influence upon the way in which they live does not remove the locus of the historian's interest from human beings to their physical context.

The overwhelming importance of the role of human artefacts in historical reasoning, however, gives rise to a further widely acknowledged feature: the need to interpret the artefacts in an appropriate way. If, for the sake of simplicity, we confine ourselves to the question of documentary evidence, it is clear that interpretation is required at a number of levels. Words, for example, differ in meaning according to the specific social context in which they are used and the purpose with which they are used. Beyond this, however, they may also change in meaning over time, according to the different historical contexts in which they are used. Thus a word which is used with a particular intention – say, to be insulting – may differ in meaning in one historical context from the same word used with the same intention in a different historical context. There is little point in making even a short list of the many well-known cases of the errors to which a failure to realise this have led. Documents of such importance as Constantine's Donation or Justinian's Code have depended for their influence upon such faults of historical interpretation.[4] Similarly, changes in the meaning of words such as 'whig' and 'tory' have

[4] For an excellent summary of the means whereby the incorrect interpretations of the Donation and of Justinian's Code were identified by Lorenzo Valla and the great French jurists, Budé, Cujas and Hotman, see B. A. Haddock, *An Introduction to Historical Thought* (London, Edward Arnold, 1980), Chapter 4.

affected historical accounts themselves, because of the possibility of misinterpretation.[5]

The need for an appropriate canon of interpretation for the language used in documentary evidence is, however, only one aspect of a general interpretative requirement. For language is used within a set of ongoing social and cultural practices, the changing content of which constitutes a continuing problem for the historian in justifying the interpretations of evidence upon which his conclusions about the past depend. Nevertheless, although language is used within this wider context of social practices, it remains our primary mode of access to knowledge of most of the specific events and occurrences which took place within them. That this is so can be seen by reflecting upon the differences between archaeological knowledge of pre-literate societies and historical knowledge of literate societies. In the former case, much can be discovered about the form of organisation of some society and of its level of technical sophistication, but hardly anything, and certainly little with any degree of specificity, about any individual deeds and actions which may have taken place within it. In the case of history, on the other hand, a great deal can be known about very detailed aspects of both larger- and smaller-scale events within an historical context, provided that some linguistic evidence is left. The problem of arriving at knowledge of *specific* facts about the activities of individuals and groups of individuals in their historical context thus presupposes a solution to that of interpreting language within the context of the changing set of social and historical practices within which it operates.

The most obvious way of meeting the difficulty of the correct interpretation of artefacts would seem to be by the utilisation of a reliable interpretative methodology. Here there are two alternatives: one is the adoption of a purely formal methodology, involving no assumptions about the general nature of the historical individuals or agents in whose activity we are interested or of the character of the society in which they inhere; the other is adoption of one which makes some such assumptions, presumably, in compliance with the principle of Occam's razor, the minimum number possible. On the face of it, the former procedure seems preferable since, in taking

[5] See Richard Pares, *King George III and the Politicians* (Oxford, Clarendon Press, 1953).

nothing for granted, it precludes no possible outcome. But, as I shall argue below,[6] this apparent virtue is a severe defect, since, in precluding no outcomes, it can neither preclude conclusions so bizarre that it would be more rational to abandon the methodology than to accept its consequences, nor produce any good reason why we should not prefer other conclusions which we may find less bizarre. A preference for the latter would, indeed, amount to recognition of the insufficiency of such a methodology. Some constraints, it seems, must therefore be introduced into the methodology, such as would be provided by the use of some limiting presuppositions.

It remains problematic, however, what these presuppositions should be and how they can be justified. If one considers the presuppositions which historians make, at least fairly close to the surface of their enquiries, the principal one appears to be that there is some degree of constancy in human nature. The people who figure in historians' accounts, individually or *en masse*, are, much like ourselves, endowed with motives and intentions, with the capacity to adjust their intentions in the light of the satisfaction of their motives in prevailing circumstances, and to translate those intentions into actions which, in many cases at least, can be seen as their successful implementation, and so on. But the nature of this constancy – in particular, whether it is purely formal, in the sense just mentioned, or whether it involves something more substantial – is more difficult to determine. For since historians are normally more interested in carrying out their investigations than in offering philosophical analyses of what these involve, they rarely offer an explicit account of the nature or justification of these more general presuppositions.[7]

Beyond this difficulty, however, lies another. If it is necessary to make some assumptions about human nature as part of the background to the interpretation and use of historical evidence, how should these be affected by the possibility that human nature may have changed over time? It hardly seems necessary, when considering this problem, to allow for the possibility that human nature, either formally or substantially, may have changed in its entirety. If there has been change of such a global nature, the historian will come

---

[6] See pp. 57–9 below.

[7] This is not to deny that in their actual research historians recognise both similarities in, and differences between, the behaviour of people in different historical cultures. But the fact remains that they show little interest in the theoretical foundations of their capacity to do so.

up against it as a limiting case, revealing itself in the fact that he will be unable to identify anything as an artefact and, hence, as even a putative piece of evidence about the human past. This would not commit him, of course, to denying that human beings may have evolved from other forms of life. But it would entail that a history of these earlier forms of life would not have the sort of intelligibility which we would expect to find in a human history involving even the minimum presuppositions about the formal character of human activity mentioned above.

The challenge presented by the possibility that *some* aspects of human nature may have changed over time cannot, however, be treated so lightly. The possibility here is not that there will be no artefacts which can be used as a basis for our knowledge of the past, but that we may not know how to interpret those that there are or, at least, that we may have no justification for the interpretative schema which we utilise. The difficulty is exacerbated by the fact that theoretically there is an indefinite number of interpretative schemata of which we may avail ourselves, giving rise to an indefinite number of different possible accounts of the past. If we are to believe that the products of any one of these is true, we must have some reason for believing that one of these schemata is superior to its rivals in its capacity to ground historical truth.

In relation to this problem, different answers follow from different conceptions of the nature of the assumptions in question. If they are thought to be purely formal, it will become a matter of historical discovery whether or not the substantial content of human nature has changed over time. But then, given the difficulties about the justification of our interpretative schemata for any substantive conclusions we may reach about human nature, we shall have considerable difficulty in justifying our belief in the conclusions reached by our adoption of one schema rather than another. If, on the other hand, the assumptions are thought to be substantial, the historian will be committed in advance to a knowledge of some core of truths about the content of human nature, possibly involving a distinction between variant and invariant aspects, for which some theoretical justification will again be required.

Conceived in these terms, I shall argue, the problem is irresolvable. The demand for the assumption of formal constancy, I shall suggest, is necessary but insufficient. It needs supplementation by further knowledge of the sort which only a substantial theory of human nature can provide. But no such theory is sustainable. Thus if knowledge of historical fact involves the satisfaction of the requirements which I have sketched above, it becomes impossible.

The answer is, plainly, to reconsider the requirements in a different way and, in particular, in a way which does not presuppose that our only access to the historical past is by means of historical argument. This would not mean that historical argument is not involved in the acquisition of historical knowledge, but it would mean that there could be no such knowledge if *argument* were our *only* mode of access to the past. If, as seems clear, historical argument has an important part to play in the production of historical knowledge, it can do so only if it is supported by a knowledge of the past derived from some other source. In the final chapter I shall try to explain and defend an account of how we might have such knowledge from a different source.

I have tried to advance towards this theory by critical interpretations of aspects of the theories of three thinkers who, for various reasons, have been sensitive to different aspects of this central problem. Since each of the three is both important and interesting in his own right, it might seem unnecessary to explain my particular choice. On the other hand, since there are many other philosophers whose work is also relevant to the main cluster of problems, it may be helpful to give my reasons for this choice.

The first is that all three philosophers were convinced of the importance of taking history seriously, partly as a problem in its own right but also because of its relevance to a philosophical understanding of human nature. In fact, as I shall argue, all three were convinced both of the need to ground historical knowledge upon a theory of human nature and also to provide such a theory on the basis of their general philosophical positions.

The second is that, as a result of the combination of their belief that historical knowledge requires a theory of human nature and of their different conceptions of philosophy, they had different conceptions of the way in which a relevant theory should be produced. Hence they arrived at three different kinds of theory which occupy, in a sense, key points on a spectrum of possible views sharing their basic assumption. At one end, Hume represents the case for thinking that a relevant theory of human nature must be empirical. At the other, Hegel is committed – or so I shall argue – to the view that it must be derived philosophically and, indeed, by a form of *a priori* reasoning.

Rather more in the centre, Vico maintains that the kind of theory in question is neither wholly empirical nor wholly philosophical, but requires a combination of empirical and philosophical elements in a mutually supportive relationship.

The third reason is that, despite what may look like, and from certain points of view are, fundamental differences between them, it is their shared assumption that historical knowledge must be *grounded* upon a theory of human nature which explains why, ultimately, the theories which they produced are incompatible with a satisfactory solution to the general philosophical problem which I have outlined above. For, given this assumption, the theory of human nature must itself be, in a certain sense, ahistorical, and such historical accounts as arise from it must share that ahistorical character. When this criticism is made explicit, and its consequences developed, the way is laid open for the different approach which I try to develop in the final chapter.

I have not chosen the three thinkers, however, simply because, as I hope to show, they make the same fundamental mistake. Their thought is much too rich for that. When the mistaken assumption is removed, there remains much of value in their views which, although I have not tried to chart it in detail, is compatible with the account which I offer in the final chapter.

Since the three philosophers are so different both in kind and in the way in which they have set out their thoughts about historical knowledge, I have treated them rather differently. It may be helpful, therefore, to outline briefly what I have tried to do in each case.

Chapter I investigates Hume's attempt to deal with two different considerations relevant to the general problem. The first is that of providing a distinction between historical fact and historical fiction. This is not the question whether we are justified in thinking that there was a past at all, although that is, I believe, problematic within the framework of Hume's philosophy. Leaving this question to one side, however, I have concentrated first upon Hume's explanation why, in relation to any specific belief about the past, we are entitled to believe that it is about a real past rather than an imaginary one. The answer which he offers is that the real past impinges causally upon the present in a way in which a fictitious past does not. In so doing, it provides material which, in conjunction with well-established causal rules, enables us to come to knowledge of the past on the basis of sound causal inferences. It will be evident that, in offering this account of our knowledge of historical fact, Hume is subscribing to the general thesis that historical knowledge must be based upon sound historical reasoning. For various reasons, which I shall not here anticipate, the theory is rejected as insufficient as an account of historical reasoning.

This part of his theory, which is advanced in his *A Treatise of Human Nature*, takes no account of the necessity to introduce principles of interpretation. In *An Enquiry Concerning the Human Understanding*, however, Hume shows himself aware that there is a problem of interpretation. To deal with it he advances two constraining assumptions. The first is the well-known thesis of the constancy of human nature. The second is a thesis to which he gave no specific name but which, because of its similarity in character to the constancy of human nature, I have called 'the constancy of human consciousness'. Both of these theses are examined and rejected as inadequate to the task in hand, on the ground that the limitations which they impose upon the historian are so severe that they would preclude him from knowledge of any changes which may have taken place in human nature during its historical career. Despite this, however, in the course of the chapter I take the opportunity to explain why I think that a methodology which makes *no assumptions whatsoever* about the content of human nature, which I call 'epistemological neutralism', would not be preferable to one invoking those made by Hume. One of the main conclusions of the chapter is, therefore, that if historical reasoning is the basis of historical knowledge, it requires *some* assumptions about human nature, although those made by Hume are unacceptable.

In Chapter 2 I consider Hegel's account of the nature of historical knowledge, assuming that this is what he intends to offer in his account of 'philosophical history'. A particular reason for discussing him in this context is that his most detailed exposition of his theory, which is given in the Introduction to his *Lectures on the Philosophy of World History*, is explicitly offered in opposition to any theory which assumes that human nature has a content which is 'fixed and constant' and which is thought to apply to 'all men, past and present'. Hegel regards any such theory as mistaken and his own is intended as a corrective, supplying principles which explain how, and in what ways, the content of human nature does change. In this sense, it stands in direct contrast to Hume's.

Because of the obscurity of Hegel's mode of expression, I have spent considerable time in this chapter in trying to present a clear, textually supportable, interpretation of his theory of historical knowledge. For this purpose, I have confined my exposition entirely to the Introduction of the *Lectures on the Philosophy of World History*, which, although it is Hegel's most detailed attempt to expound his view, is rarely the subject of a study in its own right. The conclusion which is reached is that his theory is preferable to Hume's in that it acknowledges the constitutive role of ideas in the content of human nature and does so in a way which relates social structure to subjective consciousness, while presenting historical change as a consequence of changes in certain fundamental constitutive ideas. But his account of the actual history of these changes is rejected on the ground that it cannot dispense with the restrictive idea that the changes which underlie the development of human nature, thus conceived, are determined *a priori*. As a result his theory, which *necessitates*, rather than permits, change in human nature, is just as constraining historically as Hume's.

Since Hume's and Hegel's accounts of the underlying conceptions of human nature are almost mirror images, the one imposing a constraining concept of constancy, the other an equally constraining concept of change, Chapter 3 examines Vico's attempt to establish an intermediate way in which to think of the concept of a human nature which may change over time, in relation to the problem of historical knowledge. What makes Vico interesting here is that the concept of human nature which he develops neither insists upon constancy as rigidly as Hume, nor imposes such a specific sequence of purely *rational* change on such an *a priori* basis as Hegel. The conception which he produces presents reason rather as a transformation of the imagination under the twin influences of a historically developing desire for individual self-preservation and an ever-increasing capacity to grasp the truth. He is, moreover, much more successful than either Hume or Hegel in showing how such a theory might be brought to bear upon the interpretation of evidence about the past. Nevertheless, it remains the case that he does so only by embodying this general philosophical conception in a *substantial* theory of historical development in which we are dealing not with the concept of a human nature which may have changed but with that of one which must change in a particular way. As a result, it becomes impossible for him to justify his preference for one substantial theory rather than some other, as a necessary presupposition of knowledge of historical fact.

One of the conclusions of these three chapters is that none of the three philosophers provides a satisfactory solution to the problem of historical fact because each, in his own way, constrains the historian's findings by a theory which is ahistorical, in the sense that it fails to understand the importance of the historian's own historical location in relation to the problem of knowledge of historical fact. A history written in accordance with their prescriptions would be a history written from a viewpoint external to history and by an historian who knew that human nature either must or cannot change in certain ways rather than by one for whom the question whether, and in what respect, it has changed is a factual matter.

Another conclusion, however, which seems to run counter to this, is that although, in order to interpret the evidence, the historian must assume that the past about which he writes was formally the same as the present, in the sense that it was inhabited by people who shared our formal capacities, this alone cannot provide sufficient support for his claim that the accounts which he produces on the basis of historical argument alone are accounts of historical fact. To justify the latter claim he needs some substantial knowledge of the past, rather of the sort which Hegel and Vico try to provide, but derived from some less ahistorical source. In the final chapter, therefore, I try to develop the outlines of an account, involving the concept of an historically acquired historical consciousness, which will show how this requirement can be met in respect both of specific historical actions and events and of the more general changes in conceptual schemes in the past which are reflected in changes in human nature.

HUME: THE CONSTANCY OF HUMAN NATURE

INTRODUCTION

My aim in this chapter is two-fold: to explore Hume's theory of historical knowledge and its relationship to his conception of human nature, and to develop a critique of its implications, and that of similarly orientated theories, for the possibility of such knowledge. In any discussion of Hume's philosophy, however, it is necessary to contend with the fact that his thought is both so complex and comprehensive, at least in its intentions,[1] that in very few areas of it is there much unanimity of interpretation. This is not because there are not many passages in which he appears to express himself clearly, but rather because, as a result of the variety of subjects with which he deals, the interpretation of his theories in one area is inevitably affected by apparently different remarks which he makes about them in the context of his treatment of other subjects. There is thus a continuous difficulty about how much weight to attach to what he says in those passages in which he is directly concerned with some specific topic – say causation – and how this should be modified by remarks which he makes about it in some different but connected context – in the case of causation, say, when he discusses it in connection with his theory of belief. One line of approach has been to

---

[1] In his well-known book, *Hume's Intentions*, 3rd edn (London, Duckworth, 1980), John Passmore identifies seven different themes in Hume's philosophy, each of which has, according to different interpretations by different writers, been argued to represent the most fundamental of Hume's aims. In Chapter 1 and in his Epilogue he points to the confusion and disagreement to which the presence of these seven features has, at different times, given rise. There is still no real consensus as to how to interpret Hume.

assume that he is intent upon developing a systematic programme, the logical structure of which is reflected in the order in which he sets out the main topics to be discussed. This leads to what might be called the traditional view, according to which he begins with epistemology and metaphysics, and then moves to moral philosophy, his account of which presupposes his findings in these prior areas. Another line of approach, however, which has become much more influential in the last two decades, is not to deny that he is a systematic philosopher, but to minimise the importance of the order in which he presents his doctrines and to regard the character of his philosophy as something which reveals itself only after considering his remarks upon various topics wherever they appear.[2] The difference, roughly, is between accepting that he had a philosophical programme which is reasonably well reflected in the order of his major discussions of topics, and believing that his programme can be grasped only by attempting to render coherent a very much wider range of his remarks on specific subjects, no matter where they are to be found.[3] These different

---

[2] This approach has been more widely adopted since the publication of Norman Kemp Smith's influential study, *The Philosophy of David Hume* (London, Macmillan, 1941). Kemp Smith argues that the impression given by the order in which the doctrines of the *Treatise* are set out is misleading. The order suggests that Hume's theory of ideas and impressions, of belief, of causation and so on, provides the groundwork for his views of morality. Against this, Kemp Smith claims that Hume's moral views, as presented in Books II and III of the *Treatise*, were worked out before the epistemological and metaphysical doctrines of Book I, and that the latter should be interpreted in the light of the former.

[3] Donald W. Livingston, one of the foremost exponents of this approach, applies it in his major study, *Hume's Philosophy of Common Life* (Chicago, University of Chicago Press, 1984). Drawing widely upon almost the whole of Hume's writings, and paying special attention to his actual historical works, Livingston argues that, rather than Hume having an anti-historical attitude towards the past, his 'deepest philosophical doctrines of knowledge and existence are structured by historical narrative categories' and that 'historical thinking is ... an internal part of his philosophical thought', p. 2. This interpretation is incompatible with that which will be advanced here. It is not possible within the scope of my study to explain in detail why I am not persuaded by Livingston's view. One general remark is, however, worth making at this point. Livingston claims that Hume's science of man is, despite certain affinities with the natural sciences, 'primarily a historical science', p. ix. If this is so, however, Hume ought never to have produced the theory of historical knowledge and, in particular, the account of historical inference which I ascribe to him in this chapter. Hence the incompatibility between the two views. I must leave it to the reader to decide whether the reasons for the view which I present are correct, but, if they are, the claim that historical thinking is internal to Hume's conception of philosophy must be wrong. It is perhaps worth adding that, despite his claim that Hume's science of man is an historical science, Livingston devotes almost no direct discussion to what Hume explicitly says about this science. Support for the suggestion that it is an historical science is derived from an interpretation of later

approaches have led to different results in the interpretation of his philosophy over a wide range of issues, including that of the nature of historical knowledge.

I have, as nearly as I can, adopted the former of the two approaches. It is necessary to insert the proviso 'as nearly as I can', because Hume rarely, in fact, addresses historical knowledge as a subject in its own right, discussing it most frequently as a consequence or illustration of his views of other subjects. Despite this, however, the approach gives greater significance to certain major discursive passages, while diminishing the theoretical force of remarks which he makes in other places which may appear to be inconsistent with these. This does not mean that these other remarks are to be disregarded but, rather, as will appear, that they represent views to which he was not entitled, if my account of his main theories is correct. That this is a correct way of proceeding remains, of course, to be established. This can, however, be done only by the detailed argument which I hope to provide.

As indicated in my introduction, one of the main conclusions, although not the only one, to which I shall come is that Hume's methodology forces him to rest the possibility of historical knowledge upon an essentially non-historical set of presuppositions. This is a result of the particular way in which he developed the thesis of the constancy of human nature, which, if adopted, would preclude recognition of the variety of different ways in which man *may*, at least, have thought and lived in the past. The suggestion that Hume did not have a properly historical attitude towards the past is by no means new. It has already been argued by, for example, J. B. Black, who pointed out that, like all the *philosophes*, he accepted the theme of the constancy of human nature in a particularly unhistorical form.[4] In slightly different vein, though leading to relatively similar conclusions, R. G. Collingwood has also criticised him on the grounds that he 'never showed the slightest suspicion that the human nature he is analysing in his philosophical work is the nature of a western European in the early eighteenth century and that the very same enterprise if undertaken at a widely different time or place might have yielded different results'.[5] More recently, Christopher J. Berry has also

parts of Hume's work which, if I am right, ought to be interpreted in the light of what he says about his science.

[4] *The Art of History* (London, Methuen, 1926), p. 86.
[5] *The Idea of History* (Oxford, Clarendon Press, 1946; reprinted in Oxford Paperbacks, 1961), pp. 83–4.

argued that, while sensitive to the variations of human behaviour which are exhibited in different socio-cultural contexts, Hume is committed to the constancy or uniformity of human nature, in that the influence of these contexts upon it is neither constitutive nor definitive.[6]

This sort of view has not, however, been universally endorsed. Duncan Forbes, for example, has argued forcibly that Hume's methodology can account perfectly well for the degree of diversity to be found in the practices and customs of different historical nations and that his so-called universal principles of human nature are merely an 'abstraction from the concrete variety of human (= social) experience'.[7] Donald W. Livingston has similarly rejected the criticism, arguing that 'Hume did not think that there were any genuine laws that could be expected to hold for all historical periods'.[8] Thus there is considerable disagreement about the interpretation of Hume's approach to history. In addition, however, it is necessary to take account of the fact that his view of the constancy or inconstancy of human nature is by no means his only contribution towards a theory of historical knowledge. As I shall argue, indeed, a correct assessment of the nature and value of his theory of constancy can be reached only after it is seen how this relates to prior theories which he held about the nature of historical reasoning, which sprang immediately from his theory of factual reasoning but, ultimately, from his conception of the nature of philosophy. My aim in the present chapter will therefore be to elucidate this series of relationships and to ask what we can learn of value from them, either as advanced by Hume or as developed in analogous ways.[9]

---

[6] *Hume, Hegel and Human Nature* (The Hague, Martinus Nijhoff, 1982), pp. 62ff.

[7] *Hume's Philosophical Politics* (Cambridge, Cambridge University Press, 1975), Chapter 4.

[8] Livingston, p. 225.

[9] Apart from the question of the precise interpretation of Hume's view of historical knowledge, many have defended views which are close to it. There are, for example, many similarities between it and the thesis advanced by Carl G. Hempel in his seminal article, 'The Function of General Laws in History', first published in the *Journal of Philosophy*, 39 (1942), 35–48, and developed further by himself and many supporters of the 'covering-law model' of historical explanation in the next two decades, according to which acceptable historical explanations must be supported by well-founded causal generalisations. In a different vein, W. H. Walsh has argued that the assumption of the formal constancy of human nature must be at least a necessary condition of historical understanding. See 'The Constancy of Human Nature', in *Contemporary British Philosophy*, Fourth Series, ed. by H. D. Lewis (London, George Allen & Unwin, 1976).

THE SCIENCE OF MAN

One of the most important features of Hume's philosophy is his explicitly stated intention to 'introduce the experimental method of reasoning into moral subjects'. His first philosophical work, *A Treatise of Human Nature*, is, in fact, sub-titled as 'an attempt' to do just that. There is no doubt that, in describing his enterprise in this way, he thought of himself as, in general, applying the Newtonian method to philosophy, although what he owed specifically to Newton is not so clear.[10] The principles of the general philosophical programme which follow from this are, however, set out in the Introduction to *A Treatise of Human Nature*.[11]

He begins, in a way which is fairly standard among philosophers, with a complaint about the weaknesses to be discerned in all former philosophical systems: 'Principles taken upon trust, consequences lamely deduced from them, want of coherence in the parts, and of evidence in the whole, these are everywhere to be met with in the systems of the most eminent philosophers, and seem to have drawn disgrace upon philosophy itself.'[12] No attempt is made to produce an individual justification of these various charges. Their truth, it is maintained, is revealed in the general fact that there 'is nothing which is not the subject of debate, and in which men of learning are

[10] Kemp Smith, pp. 52–61, argues that the Newtonian influence is to be seen in Hume's adoption of the method of analysis to first principles as a prelude to the synthesis of derivative conclusions, together with an unwillingness to admit hypotheses about occult causes. Peter Jones, on the other hand, has suggested that Hume's method is more speculative than his admiration for Newton would seem to imply and has pointed to Hume's readiness to employ hypotheses and thought experiments in place of, or in addition to, the accurate observations to which he pays lip-service. See *Hume's Sentiments: Their Ciceronian and French Context* (Edinburgh, Edinburgh University Press, 1982), pp. 11–19. In *Order and Artifice in Hume's Political Philosophy* (Princeton, Princeton University Press, 1985), however, Frederick G. Whelan, who attaches great importance to Hume's Science of Human Nature and extends it to include his theory of the passions, sees it as 'partly inspired by a Newtonian vision of a universe in which discrete objects subsist in observable relations to one another', p. 188. As will appear later, this is very close to my own view. There is, however, little disagreement, among otherwise disagreeing commentators, that, in adopting the 'experimental' method, Hume did not mean to suggest that he would have recourse to technical experiments. He wished mainly to emphasise that his basic principles must be supported empirically, i.e., by an appeal to experience.

[11] Hereafter referred to simply as the *Treatise* and in footnotes as *THN*. Volume I was first published in 1739. All references in what follows are to the edition by L. A. Selby-Bigge (1888; reprinted London, Oxford University Press, 1960).

[12] *THN*, p. xvii.

not of contrary opinions. The most trivial question escapes not our controversy, and in the most momentous we are not able to give any certain decision . . . Amidst all this bustle 'tis not reason, which carries the prize, but eloquence; and no man need ever despair of gaining proselytes to the most extravagant hypothesis, who has art enough to represent it in any favourable colours.'[13]

Despite the reference here to human disingenuity, the most basic reason for this unsatisfactory situation lies not in any such moral weakness but in the sheer difficulty of dealing with arguments, such as those of metaphysics, which do not belong to any particular branch of a science.[14] Nevertheless, only 'the most determined scepticism' – in which, by implication, Hume does not intend to indulge – 'can justify this aversion to metaphysics. For if truth be at all within the reach of human capacity, 'tis certain it must lie very deep and abstruse; and to hope to arrive at it without pains . . . must certainly be esteemed sufficiently vain and presumptuous. I pretend to no such advantage in the philosophy I am going to unfold, and would esteem it a strong presumption against it, were it so easy and obvious.'[15]

To resolve these difficulties, Hume introduces a thesis which is basic to his whole approach to philosophy: that all the particular sciences can be better understood and improved if we can see how, and to what extent, they are dependent upon certain features of human nature:

'Tis evident that all the sciences have a relation, greater or less, to human nature; and that however wide any of them may seem to run from it, they still return back by one passage or another. Even *Mathematics, Natural Philosophy, and Natural Religion,* are in some measure dependent on the science of MAN; since they lie under the cognizance of men and are judged of by their powers and faculties. 'Tis impossible to tell what changes and improvements we might make in these sciences were we thoroughly acquainted with the extent and force of human understanding, and cou'd explain the nature of the ideas we employ and of the operations we perform in our reasonings.[16]

The argument is that a science is a body of knowledge which, accordingly, involves judgement. But, since judgement is a human activity in which ideas are required and applied in reasoning

---

[13] *Ibid.*, p. xviii.
[14] 'By metaphysical reasonings they do not understand those on any particular branch of science, but every kind of argument, which is in any way abstruse, and requires some attention to be comprehended.' *Ibid.*, p. xviii.
[15] *Ibid.*, pp. xviii–xix.   [16] *Ibid.*, p. xix.

processes, we can come to a better understanding of the limits of, and possible degrees of improvement in, any particular science if, through a science of man, we can come to know the nature of the two component aspects of judgement. In the above passage, mathematics, natural philosophy and natural religion are mentioned as examples of sciences in which we might hope for some improvement if the thesis is correct, although their connection with human nature is not so close as to make this self-evident. In extending the claim, however, Hume suggests that there are others where we might hope for much more, since their connection with human nature 'is more close and intimate ... The sole end of logic is to explain the principles and operations of our reasoning faculty, and the nature of our ideas: morals and criticism regard our tastes and sentiments: and politics consider men as united in society, and dependent on each other. In these four sciences of *Logic, Morals, Criticism, and Politics* is comprehended almost every thing which it can in any way import us to be acquainted with, or which can tend either to the improvement or ornament of the human mind.'[17]

The suggestion, then, is that the characteristics of the four most important bodies of knowledge derive from various features of human nature, and that, once the relation between a particular science and certain features of human nature is established, knowledge of that relationship will enable us better to understand the nature and limits of the science, leading to the possibility of improvements in it. This is a bold proposal and Hume is well aware of the need to defend it, especially given his earlier remarks about the incapacity of previous systems of philosophy to provide an end to the ceaseless controversy which would seem to exist in almost every branch of knowledge:

Here then is the only expedient, from which we can hope for success in our philosophical researches, to leave the tedious lingering method, which we have hitherto followed, and instead of taking now and then a castle or village on the frontier, to march up directly to the capital or center of these sciences, to human nature itself; which being once masters of, we may every where else hope for an easy victory. From this station we may extend our conquests over all those sciences, which more intimately concern human life, and may afterwards proceed at leisure to discover more fully those, which are the objects of pure curiosity. There is no question of importance, whose decision is not compriz'd in the science of man; and there is none, which can be

17 *Ibid.*, pp. xix–xx.

decided with any certainty, before we become acquainted with that science. In pretending therefore to explain the principles of human nature, we in effect propose a compleat system of the sciences, built on a foundation almost entirely new, and the only one upon which they can stand with any security.[18]

The aim is thus to provide a foundation for 'a compleat system of the sciences', derived from a knowledge of human nature, contained in a science of man. Clearly, however, given the centrality of the science of man in the project, this aim could not be attained unless we had a reliable method of acquiring such a science. It is to this question, therefore, that Hume immediately turns: 'And as the science of man is the only solid foundation for the other sciences, so the only solid foundation we can give to this science itself must be laid on experience and observation.'[19] Thus the science of man is itself to be the product of that combination of experience and observation which, as he proceeds to point out, has for a century been successful in its application to the natural world[20] and, indeed, had begun to be applied to moral subjects by a number of philosophers in England.[21]

Given his complaints about the weaknesses to be found in previous systems of philosophy and, in particular, his charge that their principles have been 'taken on trust', it may seem obvious why Hume should want to turn to a basic science, the principles of which are to be established *empirically*. It is interesting, therefore, to note that he

[18] *Ibid.*, p. xx.
[19] *Ibid.*, p. xx. As announced, at least, the programme confirms Kemp Smith's suggestion that Hume is following Newton in advocating analysis to first principles as a prelude to the derivation of conclusions. James Noxon has noted, however, that Hume talks at times, as in the passage just quoted, as though the science of man underlies the other main sciences and, at others, as though it is identical with them, as when he asserts that in '*Logic, Morals, Criticism, and Politics* is comprehended almost every thing, which it can in any way import us to be acquainted with'. Noxon's suggested resolution of this difficulty is that Hume uses the expressions 'science of man' and 'science of human nature' ambiguously, sometimes to refer to the four sciences themselves and sometimes to one science, that of logic, upon which the others depend. In support of this interpretation, Noxon points out that in the Abstract of the *Treatise*, Hume defines the end of logic as being that of explaining the '*principles and operations of our reasoning faculty and the nature of our ideas*', a definition which coincides with that given in the *Treatise* for the science of man itself. Although Hume is undoubtedly loose in his mode of expression, nothing of consequence for the present study turns on this point, since it remains the case that, whether independent of, or identical with, logic, the science of man is intended to include an empirical study of the nature of our ideas and thought processes. See James Noxon, *Hume's Philosophical Development: A Study of his Methods* (Oxford, Clarendon Press, 1973).
[20] *THN*, p. xx.   [21] *Ibid.*, pp. xx–xxi.

proceeds by offering a further reason why his proposal should be adopted:

For to me it seems evident, that the essence of mind being equally unknown to us with that of external bodies, it must be equally impossible to form any notion of its powers and qualities otherwise than from careful and exact experiments, and the observation of those particular effects, which result from its different circumstances and situations. And tho' we must endeavour to render all our principles as universal as possible, by tracing up our experiments to the utmost, and explaining all effects from the simplest and fewest causes, 'tis still certain we cannot go beyond experience; and any hypothesis that pretends to discover the ultimate original qualities of human nature, ought at first to be rejected as presumptuous and chimerical.[22]

The point to be observed here is that the reason offered for adopting the experimental method begs the question at issue. For the claims that we cannot know whether matter exists independently of our experience of it, or whether self-identity is anything other than whatever experience and observation reveal, are conclusions which presuppose the legitimacy of the adoption of the experimental method as Hume conceives it, i.e., as involving nothing more than a careful appeal to experience and observation. They cannot therefore be reasons for its acceptance. It is not a matter of any great consequence, in the present context, that Hume should offer as a justification for the adoption of his method a reason which presupposes it. For, although it would follow that there was an inconsistency in his argument, this could easily be remedied by offering an independent justification for the experimental method and leaving the sceptical conclusions to follow – if, indeed, they do – from its application to a particular subject matter. What is of greater interest is that his mistake on this point is symptomatic of a general uncertainty which, as we shall see, runs through much of what he has to say about the relation of the science of man to human history, namely, a tendency to present certain principles contained in the former both as a presupposition and as a consequence of knowledge of the latter.[23]

It must be admitted that the programme, as thus described, is very general. Little or nothing is said, for example, about the sorts of connection which are supposed to hold between features of human

[22] *Ibid.*, p. xxi. Here, again, the Newtonian influence is to be discerned in Hume's refusal to postulate principles more ultimate than those which can be verified empirically. Cf. Kemp Smith, pp. 57–8.

[23] See below, pp. 36–7, 43.

nature and specific bodies of knowledge, or how, in virtue of establishing these connections, we may be able to effect improvements in such bodies of knowledge. Nevertheless, despite the comparative lack of detail, the main import of the programme comes over fairly clearly: bodies of knowledge are of human construction and, if we want to understand them to whatever extent is possible, we must understand the principles of human nature upon which their construction depends.

As a result of the implementation of his programme, Hume comes to two general conclusions which are basic to his treatment of historical belief: that the ideas which are used in factual reasoning – and hence, *a fortiori*, those which are used in historical reasoning – are derived, directly or indirectly, from experience;[24] and that all valid reasoning about matters of fact – and hence, *a fortiori*, reasoning about matters of historical fact – must employ knowledge of causal regularities, derived again from experience.[25] These general conclusions are applied by Hume in all the subjects with which his philosophy is concerned. I shall consider them below, however, in relationship only to their implications for his theory of the nature of historical knowledge.

[24]   *THN*, Book I, Part I, and *An Enquiry Concerning the Human Understanding*, Section II. Hereafter I shall refer to the latter work simply as the *Enquiry* and, in footnotes, as *EHU*. All references to this work in what follows are to the edition by L. A. Selby-Bigge, entitled *Enquiries Concerning the Human Understanding and Concerning the Principles Of Morals* (1893; reprinted Oxford, Clarendon Press, 1955). Livingston argues that the phenomenalist impression of these pages is misleading and presents only the internal criteria for the notion of an idea, for which Hume elsewhere adduces external criteria. He supports this claim by pointing out that in *THN* Book III Hume takes language to be a 'convention developed to satisfy the social need to communicate our sentiments, beliefs and actions. Language makes possible the many social conventions which constitute the moral [including the historical] world', p. 76. There is no need to dispute the point that, in many discussions of specific aspects of social life, Hume talks as if many ideas are conventions inculcated by teaching and education. The more important question is whether this is compatible with his specific claims about the general nature of ideas, claims which he advances not only in *THN*, Book I, but also in *EHU*, Section II. Livingston's suggestion requires that Hume's explicit statements about the nature of ideas in *THN*, Book I, Part I, should be read in the light of a conception of philosophy which Livingston derives from Hume's discussion of scepticism about the external world in *THN*, Book I, Part IV, Section II. In this case, however, it is difficult to understand why Hume did not alter his apparently identical exposition of his theory of ideas and impressions when he recast the *Treatise* in what was meant to be a more perspicuous form in the *Enquiry*, and why he there omitted the whole sequence of argument involved in the section on scepticism about the external world, upon which Livingston's claim depends.

[25]   *THN*, Book I, Part III, Sections IV–VIII and XV; *EHU*, Sections IV–V.

THE FORMAL CONDITIONS OF HISTORICAL
KNOWLEDGE

Hume's account of the formal conditions of historical knowledge is subsumed under his general account of our knowledge of matters of fact. It depends upon a distinction which he draws between two kinds of matters of fact: those which are present either to the senses or to memory; and those which are present neither to the senses nor to memory. In drawing this distinction he is not interested merely in providing a classification of kinds of fact: his intention is to argue that knowledge of the second kind of fact, which is more extensive than the first, but which is not open to direct verification from experience, is dependent upon that of the first, which *is* verifiable in the approved manner. Thus historical knowledge, which is knowledge of that which, in the main, is present neither to the senses nor to memory, will, on this account, presuppose a knowledge of things present either to the senses or to memory, such as only an observational science of man can establish that we have.

Hume thus conceives of the problem of historical knowledge as that of the move from a knowledge of something in the present, which is both direct and certain, to a knowledge of something in the past, which is indirect but nevertheless certain. The solution which he proposes is that the movement from one to the other is justifiable[26] if it is made on the basis of valid inferences which have two features: a premise concerning something in the present about which we can be certain, i.e., the existence of some piece of evidence; and further premises about causal regularities, to license the move from that which we know about the present to that which we wish to know about the past.[27] Historical knowledge consists, there-

[26] Since the notion of justification is normally taken to imply some sort of rational warrant, it may seem odd to state Hume's position in these terms, for, ultimately, he denies that there is any rational warrant for our inferences and replaces the role which is normally ascribed to such warrant by the influence of custom. Nevertheless, as has often been noted, his position is ambiguous on this point, since he also produces a series of rules 'by which to judge of causes and effects', the apparently prescriptive character of which is not easy to reconcile with his emphasis upon the influence of custom and habit. See *THN*, Book I, Part III, Section XV. It is not necessary to discuss this problem in the present context, however, since the point at issue is simply Hume's claim that the one kind of knowledge presupposes the other, and the merits of this contention can be ascertained irrespective of whether one believes that inference depends upon rational justification or upon customary belief.

[27] The comment in n. 26 above applies equally to the notion of *licensing* a move. Hume talks frequently of inferences and distinguishes between correct and

fore, in beliefs about the past reached on the basis of reliable causal inferences starting from certain knowledge of present matters of fact.

The basic principles of almost the whole of the above position are set out in a passage in Section IV of Part III of the *Treatise*, entitled 'Of the component parts of our reasonings concerning cause and effect.' Hume begins here by pointing out that in causal reasoning we go beyond what is present to the senses or memory, although we must never entirely lose our connection with the latter. He then proceeds:

> When we infer effects from causes, we must establish the existence of those causes; which we have only two ways of doing, either by an immediate perception of our senses or memory, or by an inference from other causes; which causes again we must ascertain in the same manner, either by a present impression, or by an inference from *their* causes, and so on, till we arrive at some object which we see or remember. 'Tis impossible for us to carry on our inferences *in infinitum*; and the only thing which can stop them, is an impression of the memory or senses, beyond which there is no room for doubt or enquiry.[28]

incorrect inferences. It is not necessary, in order to assess his claims in the present context of discussion, to enquire into the question whether he believes that the distinction between good and bad inferences is ultimately a distinction between inferences which arise from two kinds of custom or whether, as the rules given in *THN*, Book I, Part III, Section XV, suggest, it depends upon some more active human capacity to formulate and test claims about objective regularities in experience.

[28] *THN*, pp. 82–3. Similar examples are offered in the *Enquiry*: 'All reasonings concerning matter of fact seem to be founded on the relation of *Cause and Effect*. By means of that relation alone can we go beyond the evidence of the memory and senses. If you were to ask a man, why he believes any matter of fact, which is absent; for instance, that his friend is in the country, or in France; he would give you a reason; and this reason would be some other fact; as a letter received from him, or the knowledge of his former resolution and promises. A man finding a watch or any other machine in a desert island, would conclude that there had once been men in that island. All our reasonings concerning fact are of the same nature. And here it is constantly supposed that there is a connexion between the present fact and that which is inferred from it. Were there nothing to bind them together, the inference would be entirely precarious. The hearing of an articulate voice in the dark assures us of the presence of some person: Why? because these are the effects of the human make and fabric, and closely connected with it. If we anatomize all the other reasonings of this nature, we shall find that they are founded on the relation of cause and effect, and that this relation is either near or remote, direct or collateral. Heat and light are collateral effects of fire, and the one effect may justly be inferred from the other', pp. 26–7. It is worth remarking again that if Livingston's claim that Hume held historical knowledge to be constitutive of the beliefs of a society is correct, Hume ought not to be arguing in this manner, for to do so amounts to an implicit denial that we receive them as a result of education and teaching.

It is clear that Hume's concern here is not merely with the practical necessity to fix the basis of an inferential argument for, if this were so, he could allow for an arbitrary or accidental basis. That it is not so, however, is shown by his insistence that the basis be 'beyond doubt or enquiry' and therefore be such as can be provided only by impressions of the senses or of memory. What is required is thus an epistemological basis, or, to be more precise, a factual basis which is absolutely certain.

To illustrate this he offers an account of the reasons why we believe that Caesar was assassinated:

To give an instance of this, we may chuse any point in history, and consider for what reason we either believe or reject it. Thus we believe that CAESAR was kill'd in the senate-house on the *ides of March*; and that because this fact is established on the unanimous testimony of historians, who agree to assign this precise place and time to that event. Here are certain characters present either to our memory or senses; which characters we likewise remember to have been us'd as the signs of certain ideas; and these ideas were either in the minds of such as were immediately present at that action, and received the ideas directly from its existence; or they were deriv'd from the testimony of others, and that again from another testimony, by a visible gradation, 'till we arrive at those who were eye-witnesses and spectators of the event. 'Tis obvious all this chain of argument or connection of causes and effects, is at first founded on those characters or letters, [i.e., the documentary evidence,] which are seen or remember'd, and that without the authority either of the memory or senses our whole reasoning wou'd be chimerical and without foundation. Every link in the chain wou'd in that case hang upon another; but there wou'd not be any thing fix'd to one end of it, capable of sustaining the whole; and consequently there wou'd be no belief nor evidence. And this actually is the case with all *hypothetical* arguments, or reasonings upon a supposition; there being, neither any present impression, or belief of a real existence.[29]

A striking feature of this passage is the claim that the reasoning which supports an historical belief must start from a basis which is both existential and certain and which must therefore be given either in perception or in memory. If we attend to the last part of the paragraph, it will be seen that the argument for this is, in fact, transcendental in form. For the thesis is that, although we can distinguish between reasoning about fact and reasoning about fiction, we would be unable to do so unless our reasoning about fact

[29] *THN*, p. 83.

acquired that status by its dependence upon a premise which was both existential and certain. The account of factual reasoning given is thus asserted as a necessary condition of our capacity to distinguish historical fact from fiction.

Hume's reason for this would seem to be that, given his conception of the science of man as a contemporary empirical science, there is nothing else to which he can appeal to show that the conclusion of the inference is about a fact rather than a fiction. If all our beliefs about the past can be defended only by an appeal to that which we can currently verify empirically, the reason why we believe that Caesar was assassinated must involve the present availability of some evidence, which will serve as a fixed point to which – to adopt Hume's metaphor – our chain of reasoning can be attached. For no matter how much knowledge we may have of causal regularities in themselves, this will be in purely general terms, indicating causal relations between types of events rather than actual events. If we wish to use this knowledge to give us knowledge of particular matters of fact not presently available to us, it would appear that we can do so only if it can be tied down to some particular existent which is available to us.

Hume's insistence upon the necessity of a premise which is both certain and existential makes sense, therefore, within the framework for thinking about historical belief provided by his conception of a science of man. But it requires us to accept also the general account of historical knowledge which derives from this, i.e., that all such knowledge depends upon valid causal inferences. Since it is debate-able whether, if inference is involved, it must be causal – a point to which I shall return later – I shall disregard this question here and concentrate only upon the claim that inference is necessarily involved. For if Hume is incorrect about this, it would follow that he has failed to justify his claim that we must find a present existential premise from which the inference is to proceed.[30]

---

[30] In her article 'Hume and Julius Caesar', Miss G. E. M. Anscombe points out that there is a confusion in Hume's argument. He begins by claiming that when we 'infer effects from causes, we must establish the existence of these causes' and that, although we can make use of a number of intermediate inferences, we cannot go on with these inferences *in infinitum*; they must therefore come to rest in something seen or remembered. Here, what is seen or remembered is something which is seen or remembered *by us*. In the passage about Julius Caesar, however, which is offered in illustration of this claim, Hume believes that he is inferring effects from causes and, assuming that the intervening series of inferences cannot go on *in infinitum*, brings it to rest with something else seen or remembered. But this turns out to be

It is important to notice that the suggestion is intended to apply quite generally to all belief about the past. If it were meant to apply solely to some particular inference, it would have some *prima facie* plausibility. I cannot coherently ask myself, for example, whether it is the squirrels or the wood-pigeons which have eaten my crocuses, unless I have reason to believe, perhaps by seeing their sorry remains, that the crocuses have been eaten. But that is not how it is intended, since, as the foregoing quotation makes clear, it is meant as a statement of what is involved in all historical belief whatsoever. The account of Caesar's death is offered as characteristic of *any* example which we may choose from the past.

As an account of what is involved in all such belief, however, it becomes much less plausible. For we have many historical beliefs which are based neither upon perception, nor memory of *evidence*, nor that of others known to us. If we take Hume's own example, our belief in Caesar's assassination is not in general founded upon an inference of the sort which he maintains. We normally come across it

not something which *we* see or remember but the witnessing of Caesar's death by someone *in the past*. But this is to infer causes from effects and not effects from causes. Thus he both confuses reasoning from effects to causes with reasoning from causes to effects and fails to distinguish the terminating point of the latter, which is something now perceived, from the terminating point of the former, which is something perceived in the past. Miss Anscombe goes on to argue that, if Hume's account is to be made coherent, he needs to believe that there is a valid chain of inference both from what we perceive to Caesar's death and from Caesar's death to what we now perceive. For, without the latter, the inference from what we now perceive would be purely hypothetical. Having corrected Hume's account formally, she argues that it is still inadequate, in that it mistakes the false claim that our belief in historical facts rests upon an inference that passes *through* the links of a chain for the true claim that 'belief in recorded history is on the whole a belief *that there has been* a chain of reports and records going back to contemporary history'. See *From Parmenides to Wittgenstein: Collected Philosophical Papers*, Vol. I (Oxford, Basil Blackwell, 1981), pp. 86–92. With regard to the correction which Hume's argument needs for the sake of coherence, Miss Anscombe's claim must be accepted. Her further suggestion, that belief in recorded history is, on the whole, belief that there has been a chain of reports, etc., cannot, however, be correct, since what we believe about the past is, as Hume rightly asserts, that certain things were done or that certain events occurred. Such beliefs may presuppose a general belief that there has been a chain of reports but cannot be identified with it. In the later part of her article, in which she goes beyond the position summarised here, Miss Anscombe emphasises the role which teaching plays in historical belief, in a way which has affinities with the position for which I argue in the last chapter. She does not, however, explain how such beliefs relate to historical beliefs acquired in any other way. But it cannot be the case that all historical beliefs are a result of what we are trained to believe, otherwise there would be no such thing as the discovery of new beliefs or the revision of old ones.

as an already accepted item of knowledge. It occurs as such in the most elementary books of history and in encyclopedias; it is alluded to by political journalists; it is cited as an example of treachery or of misguided loyalty to causes rather than to persons; it is the subject of historical plays, novels and so forth. It may be, of course, that, for any given person, it is via one of these references that he *comes to learn* of Caesar's assassination, but it is not in virtue of inferences drawn from these references that it is an item of historical knowledge. For in every case, these references to Caesar's assassination are made upon the assumption that it is already generally known to be true. Indeed, were this not so, the references would themselves often fail to serve the purpose for which they have been made. It is not, therefore, in virtue of these references that the belief is generally accepted. On the contrary, the references are made because it is generally accepted.

The example of Casear's assassination is, of course, only one of an innumerable set of such beliefs. If we raise the further question why they are generally accepted, the answer would seem to be that they are part of an inherited body of public belief. Accepting them is as much a part of our general culture as is, for example, accepting that Australia is part of the British Commonwealth. Very few people could explain why they believe this simple proposition to be true. They might, if challenged, point perhaps to such things as that the Prime Minister of Australia attends meetings which are described as meetings of the leaders of the British Commonwealth countries. But this could hardly be conclusive and would amount to little more than drawing attention to other beliefs, equally challengeable, which presuppose it. It would certainly not, as Hume's account would require, amount to producing a solid inferential argument based upon premises known to be true.

These considerations do nothing, of course, to explain the nature of historical belief, discussion of which I shall defer until the final chapter. They do show, however, that Hume is wrong in his claim that the *only* way in which we can acquire a belief about the past is via our possession of a valid inferential argument and that he is wrong also, therefore, in the associated assertion that the *only* way in which our beliefs about the past can acquire a factual rather than a chimerical status is by their reliance upon a premise which is both existential and verifiable by empirical inspection. But if this is so, his transcendental argument must itself be rejected.

It seems therefore that, at the very least, Hume ought to have distinguished between a large body of historical belief which we accept because it is part of our general cultural and historical inheritance and another body to which his account might be applicable. For the sake of convenience, and without, for the moment, wishing to place any great weight upon the terms used, I shall distinguish these as *inherited* and *inferential* beliefs.

Despite the existence of a large body of inherited historical belief, it is clear that there is also a large body of historical belief which we accept upon some other basis. Historians are constantly discovering new truths about the past and, indeed, modifying some which were previously thought to be true. In some cases this may not amount to much more than a slight modification which will have little reper- cussion for any wider context of historical belief. But in others – the discovery of the Dead Sea Scrolls and the consequences of their subsequent interpretation for early Christian history might be an example here – it could have very widespread implications for our beliefs about certain periods of the past. That historians discover *new* truths cannot, therefore, seriously be doubted and, if they do, their acceptance of them cannot then be upon the same basis as that involved in inherited belief. Thus, if there is any area of historical belief to which Hume's claim should apply, this would seem to be the most obvious.

Here also, however, his analysis is vitiated by the incorrect assumption, forced upon him by his particular conception of a science of man, that historical inference must always begin from premises *about* the present, which can therefore be known to be true, if they are to result in conclusions about the past which can also be known to be true. For this conflates two very different propositions. It is true that, if an historian wishes to inspect evidence, he must do so in the present. He can, therefore, assure himself, with as much certainty as he thinks necessary,[31] that a document or some other piece of evidence now exists. But the latter proposition, which is a true assertion *about* the present, is not an item of knowledge of the sort from which alone he can arrive at certain knowledge of the past. To reach the latter he must decide how he should interpret what is contained in the document, and the justification of such a decision is not given simply

---

[31] Hume's position does not require that we have complete certainty, for he accepts that we can have doubts about our memory. It would be sufficient that the premises be certain enough to inspire us to believe them and whatever follows from them. Nevertheless, he himself does at times claim complete certainty for what we know in perception.

by the presence or availability of this or of other documents. Thus the assertions about the present which the present availability of a document can warrant are not of a sort which can justifiably give rise to certain knowledge of specific facts in the past. In order to arrive at the latter, the historian must interpret the evidence, and for this purpose he must take into account the implications of other generally accepted beliefs about the past.

What Hume has overlooked, therefore, is the necessity to interpret the evidence and the way in which this will be affected by other beliefs about the past. Thus, if it is an important part of a coherent and widely held account of some period in the past that a certain institution existed and functioned in a certain way, this belief must be taken into account should one be faced with some other document which appears to state, or imply, that the institution came into existence at a later period or that it functioned in a different way. Nothing of consequence, however, would follow from the fact that the evidence for either or both these beliefs was presently available to the historian. If there were decisive reasons for the first belief about the earlier state of affairs, the historian would use that belief as a reason for interpreting the contrary evidence in a different way. If, on the other hand, there were compelling reasons for accepting the later account, the historian would need to reconsider the interpretation of evidence on the basis of which the first account had been accepted. The point at issue could not, however, be resolved merely by a more or less direct assessment of the strength of the evidence for the competing assertions. It would need to be governed by some further knowledge of which interpretations of the evidence were historically plausible.

There is thus no one-way temporal direction involved in historical inference. Well-supported beliefs about earlier events can influence the interpretation of evidence about later events in just the same way as well-supported beliefs about later events can influence the interpretation of evidence about earlier events. The relationship between the interpretation of evidence and the conclusions to be drawn from interpreted evidence is, therefore, logical and not temporal. The fact that if the historian wishes to inspect evidence he must do so in the present thus has no bearing whatsoever upon the reasons why he should decide in favour of one set of conclusions rather than another; and it will certainly not suffice to support Hume's claim, even with regard to inferential beliefs, that these must be arrived at by inferences from truths *about* the present, based upon the present availability of evidence. The only sense in which temporal direction is relevant lies in the fact that historical knowledge is, by definition, knowledge of the past. But it does not follow from this merely logical point that historical inferences must be from a later to an earlier part of the past rather than from an earlier to a later part of it.

Hume was mistaken, therefore, in his claim that knowledge of things not present to the senses or to memory presupposes knowledge of things which are present to them. It is true, of course, that in acquiring factual knowledge – and hence, *a fortiori*, such knowledge of the past – we must *use* perception and memory. But that is quite different from the claim that one kind of knowledge is logically dependent upon the other. Hume's error is to have conflated these two propositions.

It follows from the fact that anything which might be used as an item of evidence is always open to the possibility of a number of different, incompatible interpretations, that Hume's transcendental argument fails also in respect of inferential beliefs. The claim was that we could distinguish between fact and fiction only if there were a convergence of the existential and the evidential in something available for present inspection, from which we could, with additional causal premises, justifiably infer a factual rather than a fictitious conclusion. But if the item available for inspection is always susceptible of a number of different interpretations, leading to incompatible historical conclusions, it cannot be the case that it is in virtue of the accessibility of this item, or of our knowledge that it presently exists, that we can distinguish historical fact from fiction, for under some interpretations some conclusions which we could draw from it might be wholly fictitious. The only certain assertions about the past which we can make solely upon the strength of the presence of something which may be a putative piece of evidence are those which follow *logically* from the existence of the thing in question. But these would be wholly general and would not justify belief in any particular matter of fact.

Part of the mistake in Hume's argument lies, therefore, in his having overlooked the importance of the fact that evidence always requires interpretation. To some extent, however, this arises from the circumstances in which the passage under discussion occurs. That he was not, in fact, unaware of the importance of interpreting evidence is shown by his remarks on the subject when he returns to it in

Section X of *An Enquiry Concerning the Human Understanding*.[32] In the
passage about Caesar he writes as though we have an entitlement to
rely upon the veracity of eye-witnesses and the accuracy of the
transmission of historical accounts. In the passage in the *Enquiry*,
however, he modifies this claim. The position which he now advances
is that had we not discovered that eye-witnesses and copyists were *in
general* trustworthy, their reports would not have the place in our
practical reasoning that they have. Thus, he asserts, 'our assurance
in any argument of this kind is derived from no other principle than
our observation of the veracity of human testimony and of the usual
conformity of facts to the reports of witnesses'.[33] He then proceeds to
explain this *usual* accuracy by reference to a variety of features of
human nature, such as the tenacity of memory, a common inclination to truth and probity, and an inclination to shame when
detected in a lie: 'Were not these, I say, discovered by *experience* to be
qualities, inherent in human nature, we should never repose the least
confidence in human testimony. A man delirious, or noted for
falsehood and villany, has no manner of authority with us.'[34]

Experience teaches us, indeed, not only of the existence of this
usual veracity but also of the circumstances surrounding its occa-
sional absence. Four such sets of circumstances, not meant to be
exhaustive, are mentioned: 'When the witnesses contradict each
other; when they are but few, or of doubtful character; when they
have an interest in what they affirm; when they deliver their
testimony with hesitation, or on the contrary, with too violent
asseverations'.[35] But, since experience and observation have
revealed this to us, we shall know how to proceed when dealing with
such evidence and what weight to attach to different items. Thus the
knowledge which the science of man gives us will, in effect, provide a
canon for the critical assessment of evidence via the critical assessment of its sources.

This refinement of his position, with its acknowledgement of the
need to treat sources critically, does something towards helping
Hume out of the difficulties mentioned earlier. For it allows for the
importance of the interpretation of evidence and would be compatible
with recognition of the possibility of using knowledge of earlier facts
to regulate the interpretation of evidence relating to later facts,
although Hume does not himself mention this possibility. But in

[32] *EHU*, pp. 83–4.   [33] *Ibid.*, p. 111.   [34] *Ibid.*, p. 112.
[35] *Ibid.*, pp. 112–13.

allowing for this, of course, it becomes incompatible with his account of the reasons whereby historial fact is to be distinguished from fiction, since that involved the contrary assumption that there must always be one certain interpretation of any item of evidence, available to us in virtue of the presence or potential presence of the item of evidence itself. Moreover, preferable though it is to the earlier account, the position is still limited, in so far as it involves the assumption that all that is at issue here is the question of the reliability of eye-witness or spectator testimony. Hume does not raise the question whether there may be any conceptual difficulties about the terms in which evidence should be interpreted. The way in which he states the problem and its solution, indeed, suggests that the assumption upon which he is working is that there are no major changes in human conceptual schemes in history and, hence, no problems about the terms in which the interpretation of evidence relating to past societies should be conducted. Since this is an assumption about which he is much more explicit when he advances the thesis of the constancy of human nature, I shall defer discussion of it until later in the chapter.

Hume's account of the formal conditions of historical knowledge is thus defective in two ways. The first is that it fails to distinguish between inherited and inferential knowledge and treats the question as though it were solely a matter of inferential knowledge. The second is that, even with regard to inferential knowledge, it conflates the proposition that the historian works in the present to acquire knowledge of the past with the proposition that knowledge about the present is the logical basis of knowledge of the past. As a result he is led to introduce both an unacceptable temporal directionality into the logical relationships between our various historical beliefs and, thence, to offer an incorrect account of those relationships in themselves. For, as we have seen, the historian is just as likely to use knowledge of earlier facts to enable him to establish later facts as he is to use knowledge of later facts to establish earlier ones. In part, Hume's mistake on this point is due to the fact that, given his conception of the science of man, he could see no other way in which he could find a certain basis in the present by which to distinguish between fact and fiction in history. To see what else he needed in order to provide a basis for this distinction, it is necessary to consider in more detail his account of the causal nature of historical inference.

THE CAUSAL NATURE OF HISTORICAL INFERENCE

The most striking feature of Hume's account of historical inference is the claim that the principles underlying such inference are *wholly* causal.[36] The example of the reasons for our belief in the assassination of Caesar, quoted earlier, offers a first illustration of the way in which he envisages the operation of these principles. In the passage he imagines us confronted with an historical account, given in some book or document, on the strength of which we believe the fact in question. Why, in the first place, he asks, do we believe that the characters and letters which we see express certain thoughts? Because we remember that they are used as signs of thoughts. The historian is thus expressing a thought which he either received immediately by his perception of an event, or mediately by perception of the signs of some other's thought, i.e., by reading another historical account or document. The same may be true also of that other account, but eventually the process of inference will take us back to the event itself and to those who witnessed it. Our knowledge that it occurred will then be warranted by our knowledge that their thoughts were caused by perception of the event itself. Thus, a knowledge of causal connections, based upon present experience and observation, underlies the mode of argument whereby we believe facts about the past.[37]

Hume obviously means this as no more than an illustration of his general principle. He is not committed, for example, to the view that we can know only such events in the past as were actually witnessed or recorded by a witness. He can allow that somebody might do something wholly unobserved and fail to make a record of it, as, say, in the case of a suicide, but still claim that this event can become known, sooner or later, by the use of the inferential principles which he has proposed. All that he is committed to is that the governing principles of the inference be statements of causal regularities.

This rather bare statement of the principle is elaborated and made much more plausible in a further version of it given, again, in *An Enquiry Concerning the Human Understanding*, in which two other associated requirements are added: the need to take account of the

---

[36] 'All reasonings concerning matter of fact seem to be founded on the relation of *Cause and Effect*. By means of this relation alone we can go beyond the evidence of our memory and senses.' *Ibid.*, p. 26.

[37] For a more detailed analysis and correction of this argument, see n. 30 above.

complexity of the situations in which causes operate and the need to acknowledge the invariance of the operation of the causes which are involved in these situations.

The need to allow for the complexity of the situations in which causes operate arises from the fact that, as the science of man reveals, both different people and the same people can act differently in the same circumstances. This gives rise to the problem of establishing which are the relevant causal generalisations to be used in historical inferences about the behaviour of individual agents. Hume's answer is to point to the fact that it is in an admixture of various motives and springs of action – human 'passions, mixed in various degrees'[38] – that the historical explanation of human action should be grounded. This recognition of the complexity of the causal situation is intended to enable him to overcome the difficulty created by variations in human behaviour. In the case of different people acting differently in the same situation, for example, he can point to differences in their education and customs to explain the difference in their behaviour. In the case of the same person acting differently in same situation, he can point to the operation of contrary causes, often unobserved; thus, a 'person of an obliging disposition gives a peevish answer: But he has the toothache or has not dined.'[39]

But if causes operate in clusters or combinations, it is clear that we can utilise knowledge of causal regularities only if we are assured that the same causes cannot operate differently in the same combinations or that the same combinations of causes cannot operate differently. In explaining differences in human behaviour by differences in the combinations of causes which affect this behaviour, Hume is therefore committed to the invariance, *at some level*, of the operation of the basic causal factors themselves.

For this reason he is at pains to insist that, if we make mistakes in our causal reasoning, this is due to a lack of knowledge of the total causal situation and not to a variation or contingency in the operation of the causes themselves.[40] It is at the level of the individual components of the different combinations, therefore, that the invariance requirement is meant to apply. Even here, of course, he is not claiming that it would be conceptually impossible for the causes to operate in a variable way, for it is part of his general view of the nature of causes that there is no *necessity* for any cause to produce a

[38] *EHU*, p. 83.   [39] *Ibid.*, p. 88.   [40] *Ibid.*, pp. 86–7.

particular effect or, having done so, to continue to do so. Such a variability or contingency in the cause must, on his view, always be conceivable in principle. The suggestion is not that the operation of identical causes in identical situations is necessarily invariable, but that unless we had good reason, such as the science of man offers, to believe that invariance is *in fact* the rule, we should lack any basis for our inferences.

Hume's principal argument for this is that nobody with any pretension to science has ever reasoned on any other assumption. The vulgar, he admits, 'who take things according to their first appearances, attribute the uncertainty of events to such an uncertainty in the causes as makes the latter often fail of their usual influence . . . But philosophers, observing that, almost in every part of nature, there is contained a vast variety of springs and principles, which are hid, by reason of their minuteness or remoteness, find, that it is at least possible the contrariety of effects may not proceed from any contingency in the cause, but from the secret opposition of contrary causes. This possibility is converted into certainty by further observation, when they remark that, upon a more exact scrutiny, a contrariety of effects always betrays a contrariety of causes, and proceeds from their mutual opposition.'[41] He proceeds to support this by pointing out that physicians do not regard failures of treatment as indicative of a variability in causes, but only of the operation of other unknown causes,[42] and concludes that the same must be true of 'the actions and volitions of intelligent agents'. Even when faced with the most capricious and irregular of human behaviour, the 'internal principles and motives may operate in a uniform manner, notwithstanding these seeming irregularities; in the same manner as . . . variations of the weather are supposed to be governed by steady principles; though not easily discoverable by human sagacity and enquiry . . . Thus it appears, not only that the conjunction between motive and voluntary actions is as regular as that between cause and effect in any part of nature; but that this regular conjunction has been universally recognised among mankind, and has never been the subject of dispute, either in philosophy or common life.'[43]

The concluding part of this passage plainly involves a *petito principii* similar to that mentioned earlier. If the validity of historical inference presupposes acceptance of the invariance thesis, the fact that the

---

[41] *Ibid.*, pp. 86–7.   [42] *Ibid.*, p. 87.   [43] *Ibid.*, p. 88.

conclusions of such inferences reveal no exceptions to it – reveal, that is to say, that it 'has been universally acknowledged among mankind' – is simply a logical consequence of its employment in those inferences by which we come to know of this universal acceptance. This 'universal acknowledgement' cannot therefore lend support to the claim. The same reason shows also, in fact, that the invariance thesis cannot be established, as Hume claims, by an empirical science of man. For the empirical establishment of specific causal generalisations is possible only upon the *assumption* that, at some level of specification, there are objects – the putative causes – which remain uniform in their behaviour in uniform circumstances.

Despite this, however, the claim must itself be correct: nobody could justify his confidence in the conclusion of a causal inference, if he did not accept the invariance of the operation of the causes mentioned in the inference. A general causal premise of the form 'whenever a, b, c ... then g' could not rationally be used in conjunction with the admission that there might be an indeterminacy in the operation of any of the instances of a, b or c. For this would amount, in effect, to the admission that the generalisation was not a true generalisation about things of that kind. The reason for this is not, however, as Hume suggests, that it is established by experience, but simply that it is a requirement of all valid inference that the terms should remain constant. In the case of causal inference, this means that the items designated as causes must be assumed to retain that uniformity of behaviour in uniform circumstances involved in the concept of a cause.

Hume's position is thus that historical knowledge is the product of a series of causal inferences, involving a prior knowledge of the operation of causes in various combinations and presupposing the invariance of the operation of the basic causes themselves and, hence, of their operation when combined in precisely the same clusters. It would not be misleading, particularly given his insistence, in the above passages, upon the parallels between inference in human affairs and inference in the natural sciences, to say that he conceives of history as an applied science, drawing upon causal knowledge made available by the science of man to support causal inferences about the past.

If the suggestion were only that historians must make use of *some* causal inferences in their reasoning, it would be quite acceptable, since, apart from anything else, nothing *physical* could be used as an item of evidence about the past if it were thought that it might not be a causal product of something in the past. But the claim that historical inferences are *wholly* causal is much more extreme and gives rise to serious problems.

To see what is wrong here, it is useful to commence with something with which Hume is in complete agreement: that historians are concerned to establish what happened or had objective existence in the past, i.e., what is a matter of objective fact. This means, however, that they must observe the range of constraints which permits the application of the concept of objective fact. It is true, of course, that the notion of causal interaction between things is one aspect of what is involved here. That is why if the thesis were limited to the claim that causal inferences were involved in knowledge of the objective past, it would be acceptable. But the notion of causation is by no means all that is involved in that of objective existence, and Hume's claim is defective in so far as it both disregards and implicitly denies the need for the satisfaction of any other conditions.

This can be illustrated by attending first to a simple formal feature of the concept of fact itself: that incompatible facts cannot all be true. It follows from this alone that historical methodology cannot be understood solely in terms of the gathering of evidence and the application to that evidence of knowledge of causal regularities to reach conclusions about the objective historical past. For at the very least, historians' attitudes to what is stated in these conclusions, and hence to the arguments by which they are reached, must be constrained by the requirement that the conclusions of their inferences, even if validly derived, cannot be accepted if they are incompatible with one another. If we find ourselves obliged, for whatever reason, to accept some proposition – say, that Queen Victoria was crowned in London in 1837 – this alone is sufficient to justify rejection of any incompatible statement – such as that she was crowned in some alternative place or year. In accepting this, however, historians do not need to have recourse to some further *causal* argument to the effect that she was not crowned elsewhere: they are simply acknowledging something which is involved in the concept of fact itself. To this extent, therefore, Hume's account is already formally inadequate.

Such a purely formal notion of fact, however, is insufficient to explain the range of requirements by which the historian is constrained, if he is going to construct a world of historical knowledge.

What is required, in addition, is knowledge of the conditions in virtue of which certain facts are compatible, and others incompatible, with one another, or in virtue of which some require, or are required by, others of certain sorts, and so on.

There is nothing very mysterious about this knowledge, of course, since we make use of it all the time in making statements about the world. The reason why we cannot accept the statements that Queen Victoria was crowned in London at a certain time and day and in Manchester at the same time and day is that we are here dealing with an individual event. But if we are to know which individual events we are talking about, we must make use of principles of individuation and, for this purpose, assume the uniqueness of the spatio-temporal location of events.[44] When we consider statements about such events, therefore, we can accept as fact only those which conform to this requirement.

Facts are not, of course, confined to events. They can be about people, situations, states of affairs, causes, occasions, trends, tendencies, contexts, relations and, indeed, any of the many kinds of thing which can obtain in our concept of an objective world. It would be impossible here to go through the many different requirements which must be observed if statements about all these different kinds of thing are to be accepted as true statements about the past. Fortunately, it is unnecessary to do so. For the crucial point is simply that many of the requirements are not causal, although the satisfaction of causal conditions is among the requirements. The impossibility that two different people should occupy the same space at the same time or that the same person should be in different places at the same time is metaphysical, in that it represents part of a set of inter-connected requirements which, if not observed, would make it impossible for us to utilise the notion of the self-identity of individuals, to trace the careers of, and causal transactions between, the same or different persons, and to accept these as true accounts of objective constituents of the past.

The world of fact, which is the historian's concern, is, therefore, a world subject to metaphysical requirements, of which there are many different kinds. Where an historian makes use of causal inferences in reaching his conclusions about that world, these inferences would not of themselves suffice to establish those conclusions. For the latter,

---

[44] See P. F. Strawson, *Individuals: An Essay in Descriptive Metaphysics* (London, Methuen, 1959), Part I, Chapter I.

even when validly derived, could not be accepted as statements about the world of objective fact if they failed to conform to many other conditions, the necessity for which is denied by Hume in his insistence upon the wholly causal nature of historical reasoning.

This amounts, in effect, to saying that Hume overlooks in his account of such reasoning precisely what Kant believed that he had overlooked in his philosophy in general – the conditions in virtue of which we can operate the concept of an objective world. For the conclusions about the historical world which Hume thinks would follow by the use of causal inference alone could be accepted as fact only by the use of reasoning constrained by a much more complex concept of objectivity than that which he acknowledges.

This omission in his account is the source, furthermore, of his inability to provide a satisfactory ground for the distinction between historical fact and fiction. For, by concentrating upon the importance of the concept of causation in historical reasoning, at the expense of all other considerations whatsoever, he denied himself access to the conditions which allow us to operate the concept of an objective world, which is necessary for the distinction between fact and fiction. Indeed, he would have been unable to raise the problem of the distinction between fact and fiction had he not, in his ordinary thinking, had access to a different concept of the objective world from that which, in his philosophy, he allowed himself.

There is little doubt what Hume would say in reply to the suggestion that his account of what is involved in belief in a world of objective existence in the past is insufficient. The requirements of the latter, he would have claimed, would be satisfied if, as he has insisted, among the premises of the inference, there be one which states a *present* objective fact – that a certain document is now present to one or is known to be in a certain place – which is warranted by perception or memory. As he claims in the *Treatise*,[45] it is this alone which can assure us that our chain of reasoning starts from a truth about what exists and therefore leads to a conclusion about what existed and not to one about something wholly chimerical.

But this answer is unsatisfactory. Perception may be involved in our knowing that something in the present has objective existence, but it cannot, solely and of itself, assure us that this is so. As Hume himself agrees, misperceptions can occur and ideas can be confused

[45] *THN*, p. 83.

with impressions, i.e., we can mistake the imaginary for the real. It is necessary, therefore, to decide which of our perceptions are veridical and which are not. But we can do this only if our judgements about the present conform to the same prior notion of the conditions of objective existence as are in question in the case of historical statements. Hume's reply would thus simply beg the question at issue. In addition, however, it should be noted that, if it is incorrect to hold that perception alone is sufficient to assure us of the existence of something in the objective world, by the same token it is incorrect also to claim that perception, either alone or in combination with memory, can give us knowledge of the *objective* causal regularities which Hume's account requires. Here, again, our judgements as to which of our perceptions are perceptions of *objective* causal regularities are constrained by the notion of an objective world with a structure different from that of our perceptual experience.

It follows from this, however, that, in so far as historians do make some use of causal inference as *part* of the activity of coming to conclusions about an objective past, the concept of an objective world which allows them to do so must apply both to their own present world and to the past world. For it would be invalid to use a knowledge of causal regularities which *presupposes* the notion of an objective world in order to produce conclusions about a world which did not conform to the conditions involved in that notion. It is useful, therefore, to note explicitly that it is an absolute requirement of historical knowledge that the world about which the historian wishes to establish facts must conform to exactly the same metaphysical conditions as that in which the historian finds himself. For convenience I shall label this the principle of metaphysical uniformity.

Hence causal inference, even when necessary, is never alone sufficient to establish the truth of any conclusion about particular matters of past fact. Whatever the conclusions arrived at by causal inference, they can be accepted as truths only when, in addition to being validly derived, what they assert can be placed within, and supported by their place within, the framework of a conception of the past which conforms to the principle of metaphysical uniformity.

It is a defect in Hume's account of historical reasoning, therefore, that it fails to acknowledge this and, indeed, implicitly denies it. For, if it is necessary that this principle should obtain if the conclusions of valid causal inferences are to be accepted as statements of historical fact, *that* it obtains cannot be established by acceptance of the conclusions of those same inferences. But that is the position to which Hume is committed by his insistence upon the *wholly* causal nature of historical inference.

THE UNIFORMITY OF HUMAN NATURE

It is possible now to turn to Hume's best-known contribution to the philosophy of history, the thesis of the uniformity of human nature. This presupposes the account of causal inference given above, but modifies it in such a way as to make it applicable to specifically human history, rather than to any other kind of history, such as, say, natural history. It is stated in the following well-known passage in Section VIII of *An Enquiry Concerning the Human Understanding*:

It is universally acknowledged that there is a great uniformity among the actions of men, in all nations and ages, and that human nature remains still the same, in its principles and operations. The same motives always produce the same actions: The same events follow from the same causes. Ambition, avarice, self-love, vanity, friendship, generosity, public spirit: these passions, mixed in various degrees, and distributed through society, have been, from the beginning of the world, and still are, the source of all the actions and enterprises, which have ever been observed among mankind. Would you know the sentiments, inclinations, and course of life of the Greeks and Romans? Study well the temper and actions of the French and English: You cannot go much wrong in transferring to the former *most* of the observations which you have made with regard to the latter. Mankind are so much the same, in all times and places, that history informs us of nothing new or strange in this particular. Its chief use is only to discover the constant and universal principles of human nature, by showing men in all varieties of circumstances and situations, and furnishing us with materials from which we may form our observations and become acquainted with the regular springs of human action. These records of wars, intrigues, factions and revolutions, are so many collections of experiments, by which the politician or moral philosopher fixes the principles of his science, in the same manner as the physician or natural philosopher becomes acquainted with the nature of plants, minerals, and other external objects, by experiments which he forms concerning them.[46]

The modification which Hume here introduces into his earlier account of the nature of historical inference is that he now asserts not merely that such inference must be causal, but that it must be based

[46] *EHU*, pp. 83–4.

upon knowledge of a *fixed and constant* set of causal principles by which human nature is constituted. Before considering the examples which are adduced to support this claim, it should be noted that there is again a *petitio principii* in the general argument of the passage, in that Hume asserts the dependence of historical inference upon knowledge of the uniformity of human nature while also claiming that historical knowledge supports the latter thesis, by revealing nothing that is incompatible with it and, indeed, by acquainting us with these constant principles. Thus, at the start, having announced the basic thesis, that various admixtures of the same motives and desires have been 'from the beginning of the world, and still are', the causes of human actions, he proceeds to suggest that we can safely explain the actions of the Greeks and Romans by calling upon a knowledge of the springs of action which we can derive by observation of the French and English. A little later, however, he asserts, as though it is an empirical discovery, that history reveals no exceptions to this uniformity and, indeed, that its chief purpose is to acquaint us with 'the constant and universal principles of human nature'. But historical inferences cannot both depend upon a knowledge of the causal principles which govern human action, and yet produce conclusions which support our belief in those principles. Even were it thought that they did this only by revealing no exceptions to the operation of the principles in question, this would be unacceptable, since their failure to reveal any exceptions can be nothing more than a logical consequence of the fact that the inferences by which the historical beliefs are reached presuppose the principles as premises and are valid. For a valid conclusion cannot contradict the premises from which it is drawn. It is clear, therefore, that Hume cannot maintain both of these assertions. The most that he can claim – and what, indeed, he *must* claim, if the science of man is to relate to historical fact in the way suggested – is that we can, by an empirical study, derive knowledge of the fixed and constant causal constitution of human nature, which we can then use in the premises of historical inferences.

This passage has long been recognised as constituting a difficulty by those who maintain that there is nothing anti-historical in Hume's theoretical approach to history.[47] Nobody has denied that Hume considers human nature in some sense to be unchanging. The dispute

[47] Forbes, p. 117, describes it as 'unfortunate'; Livingston, p. 218, as 'notorious'.

centres solely round the questions of the level of generality at which it is meant to be unchanging, what its function is meant to be, and whether, at that level, it commits to Hume to the view that major changes in culture and society must be precluded as a condition of historical knowledge.

The most common defence against the charge that Hume's stance is anti-historical is that he is simply insisting upon the uniformity of certain underlying functional features of human nature. One view is that these are abstracted from the concrete variety of human social experience.[48] This is difficult to accept, however, since it presupposes that Hume has some independent way of gaining the knowledge of the concrete variety of social experience, particularly in its historical dimension, from which the principles are to be abstracted. It puts in doubt, moreover, the function of the abstracted principles, since the historical knowledge from which they are abstracted will have been reached without their use.

An alternative view is that human nature 'is unchanging only in the way in which the empirical laws of nature are thought to be unchanging. Human nature is not a kind of immutable substance. It consists of a set of powers, dispositions, and tendencies picked out by a uniform experience of their effects. These include the principles of association, the principles of sympathy, and a set of motives for action which depend upon these principles. Among these motives are: "ambition, avarice, self-love, vanity, friendship, generosity, public spirit ... mixed in various degrees and distributed throughout society." '[49] These again are simply abstracted from, and compatible with, the variety of human customs and practices which Hume elsewhere freely acknowledges.

This view suffers, however, from some of the same defects as the previous one. In the first place, if the principles are simply abstracted from knowledge of the variety of human historical and social practices, they cannot serve to enable us to have knowledge of that variety. They cannot, that is to say, both be a consequence and a presupposition of historical investigation. To assert both of these propositions is simply to repeat the *petitio*, noted above, which Hume himself made.

Secondly, however, the items on the list offered here cannot possibly function in the same way. Two of the principles mentioned,

---

[48] Forbes, p. 119.   [49] Livingston, p. 216.

association and sympathy, could possibly be thought of as principles of human nature which must underlie all historical knowledge, since they appear to be natural in the sense that they do not need to be learnt. On Hume's view, one does not learn to associate ideas. They associate themselves naturally as the result of some ultimate disposition of human nature. It is feasible, therefore, to think that the principle of association might be common to all men everywhere. The same could also be true of sympathy, as Hume understands it. But it cannot be true of the other examples which are given. Some people are vain, others are not; some are generous, others are not. Thus generosity and vanity cannot be presumed to be a natural part of human nature common to all societies. In the case of public spirit, moreover, the position becomes even more difficult. For public spirit is a motive which can operate only in certain specific societies, namely, those in which a sense of the public good has developed which is sufficient for people to be able to be taught, or be able to come to believe, that it should be a motive for at least some actions.

Finally, it must be observed, this cannot be an accurate reading of this passage, at least as it stands. For association and sympathy, which are the most likely candidates for principles of a human nature which might be common to all men, are not mentioned in it at all. Hume's examples all concern kinds of motives which it would not be difficult to conceive as missing in some societies.

It would be unfortunate, however, if the issue had to be resolved by concentration upon the exact wording of this one paragraph. It is of much greater importance to decide whether or not, as I have claimed, Hume's concept of a science of man commits him to the view that we can, by an empirical study, derive knowledge of the fixed and constant *causal* constitution of human nature, which can then be used as premises in historical argument. If we follow his argument a little further, we find that this is precisely what he implies when he proceeds to offer a number of examples in support of the position set out in the above passage.

In the first, which is not strictly historical, he discusses the case of a traveller who brings back reports of a race of such merit as to be unlike any we know by experience: 'men, who were entirely divested of avarice, ambition, or revenge; who knew no pleasure but friendship, generosity, and public spirit'. The incompatibility of this with what experience teaches us, we are told, is sufficient to warrant our rejection of the traveller's report 'with the same certainty as if he had stuffed his narration with stories of centaurs and dragons, miracles and prodigies'.[50] Again, there can be no 'more convincing argument' against a forgery than to prove that it involves ascribing to people actions 'directly contrary to the course of nature', to which no human motives could induce them. Finally, our acknowledgement that there is a uniformity of human motives and actions equal to that of bodily events is so strong that the 'veracity of Quintus Curtius is as much to be suspected, when he describes the supernatural courage of Alexander, by which he was hurried on singly to attack multitudes, as when he describes his supernatural force and activity, by which he was able to resist them'.[51] In these cases, a knowledge of the causes of human activity, such as the science of man can give us, is used to reject historical assertions as surely as if acceptance of the latter involved acceptance of what we know to be physically impossible.

These examples illustrate how Hume envisages the operation of the principle and lend it a certain plausibility. For it seems reasonable that we should, for example, be as sceptical of the claim that Alexander set out, single-handedly, to defeat an army, believing that he could do so, as of the claim that he managed, single-handedly, to defeat it. It must be re-emphasised, however, that the thesis represents a requirement which is additional to the earlier claim that historical inferences are causal. This follows from its principal feature: that the constitution of human nature must be the same in all parts of history, 'in all times and places', if the knowledge of it which we can acquire today is to support our knowledge of human actions in the past. To use Hume's own example, we can know 'the sentiments, inclinations and course of life of the Greeks and Romans' only because we can transfer to them *most* of our observational knowledge of 'the temper and actions of the French and English'. The suggestion is thus that we must presuppose a uniformity in a set of causes of human action throughout human history, if we are to use our present knowledge of the relation of these causes to human action to produce historical knowledge. The principle therefore goes beyond the thesis that we must suppose human actions to have causes, for it tells us that there is one, and only one, such set of causes, namely, that which now obtains, which will suffice to give us knowledge of the human past.

It is possible now to consider the thesis in its own right, i.e., as a

[50] *EHU*, p. 84.   [51] *Ibid.*, p. 84.

basic requirement of historical knowledge and of the inferences on which the latter rests. It was argued earlier that, in his initial account of historical inference, Hume was too undemanding, in so far as he failed to acknowledge the constraints which the concept of an objective world imposes on the character and use of such inferences. But if he was too undemanding in his account of what that involved, it would seem that in his new requirement he is altogether too demanding.

The first thing to be noted is that, if the uniformity of human nature is accepted as a *presupposition* of historical knowledge, then, if it were the case that human nature had either changed or developed over time, this would not be a change or development of which we could have knowledge. For, if the premises of historical inferences are to include statements about the omnipresence in human beings of the operation of a fixed set of causal principles, conclusions about the presence in earlier human beings of different principles could arise only from invalid arguments. The constancy of human nature thus precludes the possibility of a history of any changes or developments in human nature.

This result is a consequence of the fact, noted above, that the constancy principle requires us to accept not merely a causal account of human nature but one in which it is constituted by a fixed and invariant set of causes which operate throughout human history. We can see this by considering that it would be possible to offer a causal account of change and development in organisms, provided that we were allowed to introduce new causes or new combinations of causes into the *constitution* of the organisms. Thus, in evolutionary theory, for example, the wider causal context sets objective constraints upon what can exist at a certain time, while the theory of random variation within organisms accounts for the existence in some of them – those which 'develop' – of new causal properties which enable them to function in this context. It is true that much more than this is required. Nevertheless, it seems clear that, by allowing for changes in the causal constitution of an organism, its capacity to exist in an altered environment can be explained and a history of its development can be written. It is not the case, therefore, that a causal theory of the constitution of organisms is incompatible with the possibility of a history of their development.

It would seem, moreover, that if there were no objections in principle to a causal theory of human nature, an account of the above sort could be extended to human history, showing, for example, why some nations have flourished in certain economic situations in which others have declined. Here we could appeal to economic theory to provide an account of the objective constraints which the economic conditions impose – say, the constraints imposed by a scarcity of capital or of consumer goods – while random changes in the attitudes of people in different countries towards such things, as, say, work or poverty would explain the presence in some of them of characteristics which had led to their flourishing in these conditions and in others of those which had not. This, again, is obviously far too simple and much more would have to be offered for an account of this sort to be plausible. Nevertheless, it would seem that, if a causal account of human nature were acceptable, theories could be developed which would allow for its development and change in different circumstances. The restriction which Hume's theory introduces is not therefore a consequence of the fact that it is a causal theory but of the fact that it is a theory of the *fixed* causal constitution of human nature.

If Hume were merely asserting that, *as a matter of fact*, there had been no change or development in human nature, this would not of itself constitute a difficulty for his theory. The claim would be about a contingent matter and it could turn out that it was correct. The position would, in any case, at least be arguable. But this is not what he is doing. For, although his account of the constancy of human nature is said to be derived from experience and observation, the only experience and observation open to him is contemporary experience and observation since, as we have seen, his claim that history *supports* the extension of his thesis to accommodate 'all ages and notions' presupposes the point at issue. In effect, therefore, in his use of the principle he is ruling out *a priori* the very possibility of our coming to know whether there have been any changes in human nature. But since it has not been shown that there is anything incoherent in the idea that there may be such changes, and since there is certainly no obvious contradiction in such a suggestion, a theory which eliminates *a priori* the possibility of our ever coming to know of it, if it has taken place, must be unacceptable.

It might seem that this consequence could be avoided by drawing upon Hume's explicit point that it is in combinations of causes that the determinants of human action are to be found, for it could then be argued that, given a knowledge of the operation of the fixed set of causes which constitute human nature in their present combinations, we could infer their operation in the different combinations which may have obtained in the past. But this would, in fact, do nothing to strengthen his position. For the only knowledge to which we would have access would be of their operation in their present contexts, and this would license inferences only about the past operation of similar combinations in identical contexts. We would, therefore, never be able to accept an inference which concluded that a certain cause operated in a certain way in some combination in the past of which we had had no experience in the present.

THE CONSTANCY OF HUMAN CONSCIOUSNESS

The thesis of the uniformity of human nature, in its present form, thus seems to run into insurmountable difficulties. There is, however, a different way of defending it. This would involve understanding it as a way of stressing the historian's need to assume that at a certain level – the level of common sense – a particular kind of belief, i.e., certain beliefs about human nature, have been omnipresent in the past. Thus, to revert to Hume's own example, it would seem that the veracity of Quintus Curtius ought rightly 'to be suspected, when he describes the supernatural courage of Alexander by which he was hurried on singly to attack multitudes',[52] not because Alexander could not have been successful – although it is true that Hume believes that he could not have been – but because Alexander *could not have believed* that he could be successful. Hume himself makes such a point when discussing the importance of shared causal beliefs within a society:

The poorest artificer, who labours alone, expects at least the protection of the magistrate, to ensure him the enjoyment of the fruits of his labour. He also expects that, when he carries his goods to market, and offers them at a reasonable price, he shall find purchasers, and shall be able, by the money he acquires, to engage others to supply him with those commodities which are requisites for his subsistence. In proportion as men extend their dealings, and render their intercourse with others more complicated, they always comprehend, in their schemes of life, a greater variety of voluntary actions, which they expect, from the proper motives, to co-operate with their own ... In short, this experimental inference and reasoning concerning the actions of

[52] *Ibid.*, p. 84.

others enters so much into human life that no man, while awake, is ever a moment without employing it.[53]

Here, a set of shared beliefs or expectations is claimed to be present throughout the various forms of co-operation and intercourse within a society. Hume does not actually say that it is necessary for such intercourse, but, when he turns his attention to the historian and the political scientist, it becomes evident that this is his view:

Nor have philosophers ever entertained a different opinion from the people in this particular. For, not to mention that almost every action of their life supposes that opinion, there are even few of the speculative parts of learning to which it is not essential. What would become of *history*, had we not a dependence on the veracity of the historian according to the experience which we have had of mankind? How could *politics* be a science, if laws and forms of government had not a uniform influence upon society? Where would be the foundation of *morals*, if particular characters had no certain or determinate power to produce particular sentiments, and if these sentiments had no constant operation on actions? And with what pretence could we employ our *criticism* upon any poet or polite author, if we could not pronounce the conduct and sentiments of his actors either natural or unnatural to such characters, and in such circumstances? It seems almost impossible, therefore, to engage either in science or action of any kind without acknowledging ... this *inference* from motive to voluntary actions, from characters to conduct.[54]

Before considering the implications of this passage, it is worth noting that Hume is still arguing along the general lines indicated by his original idea of a science of man. Thus history would be impossible if we could not extend our *present* beliefs about the veracity of people to historians of the past. Politics could not be a science if we were not to assume that people in the past believed, *as we do*, that the law ought to be obeyed. Similarly, though perhaps less relevantly here, the sciences of morals and of criticism could not be pursued without the presumption that some beliefs which we now hold have been omnipresent in human history.

This emended version of the uniformity of human nature effectively posits the necessity for a uniformity in our beliefs about human nature, as a condition both of the pursuit of our daily affairs and of the foundation of certain sciences. For convenience I shall therefore refer to it as the constancy of human consciousness. Its implication for history is that we could not construct intelligible accounts of past

[53] *Ibid.*, p. 89.   [54] *Ibid.*, pp. 89–90.

human activity if we were not to believe that peoples and historians in the past had held the same beliefs and expectations about one another as we do and that we are therefore entitled to extend our knowledge of the latter to the former. In this form also, however, the thesis gives rise to a number of difficulties, which it is necessary to examine.

The first, and perhaps most serious, is that it still places unacceptably high constraints upon the historian. For where, in its original form, the thesis of the uniformity of human nature made it impossible for the historian to produce a history of changes or developments in human nature, or of its causal properties, the new version makes it impossible for him to produce a history of changes or developments in human consciousness. For, if acceptance of the uniformity of human consciousness is a presupposition of all inferences about human behaviour in the past, we shall have to reject as invalid any inferences the conclusion of which is that there have been changes in human consciousness.

The implausibility of the uniformity thesis, indeed, comes out more strongly in the new version than in the original. To see this, we may begin by noting that there are many ways in which we can explain human conduct in certain historical societies which are inapplicable in other historical societies. In the last two centuries, for example, the growth of nationalism has been sufficiently widespread for us to appeal to nationalist beliefs to explain a great variety of actions. We can use such beliefs, for example, to explain why some countries became involved in the Second World War while others did not, or why some countries have adopted a policy of fostering the widespread and intensive study of their native languages and customs or have peopled their administrative offices and universities with their own nationals rather than those of other countries while others have not, and so on. We do not have to go too far back in time, however, to find societies in which such beliefs are inapplicable. The medieval villein, for example, did not go to war from a sense of national duty, but because he had a legal obligation to support his lord in times of war for a fixed period of days per year. If he fought for longer than this, he did so for payment according to conditions laid down in his feudal contract and not from any sense of national solidarity.

The important point in such examples, which may be multiplied *ad infinitum* as one turns to different countries and different ages, is not that historical agents did not, *as a matter of fact*, act from motives which imply the same beliefs as we have, but that, in many cases, they *could not* have done so, for the relevant system of beliefs itself did not exist. The medieval knight, for instance, could not have gone to war to preserve the customs and traditions of a nation whose values had so permeated him that an attack upon it was felt as an attack upon himself, for he lacked any such concept of nationality. But he *could* do so, as in some of the Crusades, when it came to his religious beliefs. This is not to deny, of course, that people can and do act from religious conviction today. But there is an enormous conceptual divide between the case, for example, of a person who believes that his faith requires that he should try to ensure that certain places remain in the possession of Christian countries and that of one who believes that it requires that certain ideals of action should be preserved or promulgated. The latter could not see an attack on the Holy Lands as an attack on his religious conviction or believe that such conviction could be defended only by resisting an attack on the Holy Lands. It would thus be quite implausible to hold that somebody who fought in defence of his faith in the Crusades did so because he shared the same beliefs as someone who insisted that, for example, Christian instruction should be an obligatory part of a school curriculum. To belong to a tradition of belief, the change and development of which can be traced historically, is not the same thing as to share the same belief. Hume's view would appear, however, to imply that it was.

It might be felt that these unpalatable consequences of the uniformity of consciousness thesis could be avoided by a move parallel to that by which Hume sought to avoid similar consequences in the case of the uniformity of human nature. The crucial point there was to insist that action results from combinations of causes and to treat the agent's situation as part of a total causal combination. A cause which had one effect in one combination could thus have a different effect in a different combination. By this means differences in actual behaviour could be rendered compatible with acceptance of the general uniformity thesis. In a similar way, then, it could be held that action requires combinations of beliefs and that differences in the latter will affect the action differently. Thus, to repeat an example given just now, one country might go to war from a sense of national solidarity while another might refrain from doing so for precisely the same reason. The difference between them would be explained by an appeal to further beliefs, such as, for example, that in the first case the country believed that its identity as a nation would be strengthened if it went to war or weakened if it did not, while in the second the converse was believed. Similarly, it might be argued, the crusader and the religious educational reformer acted in the light of the same belief, the differences in their behaviour being due to some difference in the context of other beliefs which affected their actions.

This reply, however, serves only to expose a further difficulty in the basic thesis. Nobody would wish to deny, of course, that we act in the light of a number of beliefs. If a person believes that he ought to preserve his family's standard of living and that this will best be done if a certain political party comes into power, this could explain why he votes for that party. If he believes, on the contrary, that it will best be preserved if some other party comes into power, this could explain why he will vote for that one. But this type of argument can be used to save the uniformity of consciousness thesis, as Hume saw quite clearly in the case of the uniformity of human nature, only if we can isolate the constituents of the combinations and maintain that these are the same 'in all times and places'.[55]

Beliefs cannot, however, be isolated in the same way as causes in the natural world. It is true that some beliefs are independent of some others, as shown in the example given above, where a person's belief that he ought to safeguard his family's standard of living is logically independent of his belief that this will best be done by voting for one party rather than another. But no belief is independent of all others. We can see this, for example, by considering the case of somebody suffering from a persecution complex. Such a person will not simply be in possession of a conjunction of different beliefs, e.g., that the government intends to assassinate him, that a motor accident in which he was involved was a failed assassination attempt by the government, that a person who regularly passes his door is employed by the government to spy on him with a view to some further attempted assassination and so on. His state of mind cannot be understood merely as a *conjunction* of beliefs, because his belief that the government intends to assassinate him explains the construction which he puts upon the other events and the beliefs which he has about them. It would be possible, of course, for the man himself sincerely to assert that he holds only a conjunction of different beliefs, of which the belief that the government intends to assassinate him is merely one. But the real character of the latter belief lies in the way in

[55] *Ibid.*, p. 83.

which it explains his acquisition of the other associated beliefs. Thus, if one could persuade him that the government did not intend to assassinate him, he would give them up, but if one could persuade him only that the associated beliefs were false, he would not be obliged to give up his belief that the government intended to assassinate him but would simply construe further events as examples and, indeed, evidence of this intention.

Beliefs fall, therefore, into hierarchical clusters. They do not do so merely logically, in the sense that the more determinate presuppose the more general, i.e., in the sense that it would be self-contradictory to assert, for example, both that a car accident represented a failed attempt by the government to assassinate one and that the government did not intend to assassinate one. For, as illustrated above, the more general explain acquisition of the more determinate. At the same time, however, although this is so, the more general cannot be identified independently of the more determinate. For the more general are *expressed* in the more determinate, in the sense that they reveal themselves only in an overall pattern to be found in the more determinate beliefs. The only way in which we can establish that somebody has, say, a persecution complex, is by discovering that no matter how well we manage to dislodge each determinate belief, he will simply move to another symptomatic of the same general belief, and so on. If, on the other hand, the only evidence we had of someone's belief that the government wanted to assassinate him was his repeated assertion that this was so, we would, in the absence of the expression of this belief in some or other more determinate beliefs, not accept it as an operative belief, no matter how genuinely we thought it asserted by the person in question. Thus we cannot isolate a series of atomic constituent beliefs, as we can causes, and come to discover their invariable association with certain actions.

It might be argued in reply to this, however, that, although we cannot isolate individual beliefs with sufficient precision to be able to discover their invariable association with certain actions, we can isolate the hierarchical clusters and establish their invariable connections with certain actions. But this again is not so. First, we should note that the relationship between a more general belief and the more determinate beliefs in which it expresses itself is not deductive. We cannot deduce that a man who believes that a government wants to assassinate him will view a passer-by as a spy or an automobile accident as a failed attempt at his assassination. He may or may not express his general belief in *these* particular determinate beliefs, although he must express it in *some* determinate beliefs. But there is no relationship of entailment involved here. We cannot, for instance, deduce, from the premises that a man believes that the government intends to assassinate him and that a stranger is passing his house, that he believes that the stranger is a spy, or even from the premises that he believes that the government intends to assassinate him and that the passer-by is a spy, that he believes that the spy is a spy of that government.

Secondly, there is an indeterminacy in the number of determinate beliefs in which a given general belief may express itself. In one person it may do so in very few; in another, the same general belief may express itself in a very large range of determinate beliefs. Thus there are simply no pure or characteristic cases of the constitution of the hierarchical clusters which we can know with such precision and determinacy as to serve as a basis for knowledge of an invariance relation between beliefs and actions.

It is impossible therefore to isolate, either individually or in clusters, the beliefs which are supposed to be uniform in human consciousness and to provide, through their known and reliable connection with action, the basis of historical knowledge. But if this is so we cannot deal with combinations of beliefs in the way in which Hume suggested that we could deal with combinations of causes.

It may well be said, of course, that these points are drawn from an unacceptably atypical example – that of a person suffering from a persecution complex – and that they cannot hold for all belief. But the example is atypical only in the respect that such a person will not give up his controlling belief in the face of that degree of counter-evidence and rational argument normally thought to be sufficient to reveal the falsity of the belief. Even in this, however, it is not wholly atypical. Most people hold some beliefs, about religion or morality or politics, for example, which almost nothing can induce them to abandon – and certainly no argument can be *guaranteed* to induce them to abandon – which colour other more determinate beliefs and intentions in many different aspects of their lives. Moreover, even when we are dealing with beliefs which are not entrenched to quite this degree, it is nevertheless to such governing beliefs that we turn when we want to come to an understanding of behaviour and practice, be it in an individual or in a nation. For it is a methodological requirement that, when we want to reach such understanding, we must give a *prima facie* preference to accepting as operative those interpretations which ascribe to beliefs a maximal degree of coherence.

This last point can perhaps best be pursued in connection with a further difficulty which arises for the uniformity of consciousness thesis. We have seen earlier that, in his account of historical inference, Hume accorded a priority to premises known by perception, in order to provide a basis of certain knowledge of the present from which to advance to certain knowledge of the past. It was argued, however, that perception could provide no such basis. When we turn to the question of consciousness, it is even more obvious that it can provide no such basis. We neither perceive beliefs themselves, nor do we perceive actions in such a way that we can infer, with a sufficient degree of certainty, what beliefs are associated with them. If a person crosses a road at a traffic light, we cannot safely infer that he believes that it is safer to cross there rather than elsewhere: for he may just have arrived there when he decided to cross, or it may be that that is where he habitually crosses, although on other roads he may habitually cross at a point where there is no traffic light. Again, if we see a person enter a church, we cannot infer that he believes that he ought to go to church, for he may have gone to accompany his mother or to hear the choir.

Individual actions are thus over-determined by beliefs. In these circumstances the best that we can do when we want to establish people's beliefs is to accept those hypotheses which possess the maximal degree of explanatory power with regard to their actions, while structuring their beliefs into the minimum number of hierarchical clusters. This does not mean that agents' assertions of their beliefs are to be disregarded. They have a *prima facie* claim to acceptance because the assumption of truth-telling *in general* is a regulatory principle of interpretation. But agents do not always tell the truth, nor are they always correct about their own beliefs. An agent's assertion is, therefore, only one, even if a particularly important one, of the factors to be taken into account. If it cannot be encompassed within an hypothesis which, in other respects, satisfies the general criteria, the discrepancy must be accepted and some further explanation will be required for it. The hypothesis that the man who goes to church is genuinely religious should be accepted if it allows us to explain as wide a range of more determinate beliefs and, through these, of actions – why he believes that he should go to church when his mother goes and when she does not, and when the choir is on duty and when it is not and so on – in as economical a manner as possible. It would, of course, be possible to offer an individual determinate belief for each of these actions but, unless we were prepared to look for the most economical overall account, there would be no onus on us to accept even the same belief or beliefs to explain the same action each time that it occurred in the same circumstances. In that case, however, there would be no way of arriving at any reasonable certainty with regard to the explanation of any action whatsoever. Beliefs cannot, therefore, be verified in isolation but only in so far as hypotheses about them have implications for the explanation both of further beliefs and of actions and can be tested by their capacity to explain or fail to explain these.

If this is how we come to knowledge of beliefs in the present however, there would seem to be no reason for holding that our knowledge of past beliefs must be based upon their uniformity with present beliefs, since precisely the same method can be used with respect to past beliefs. For, were we to work out such inferences about past beliefs as our knowledge of present beliefs could support, we would surely reject the account which followed, if we found that it provided a more fragmented and less systematic system of beliefs than some other hypothesis which we could devise. In this case, any uniformity of consciousness involved would at best be a consequence and not a presupposition of historical research.

EPISTEMOLOGICAL NEUTRALISM

At this point, however, some justifiable misgivings may begin to arise. Even were it agreed that neither the uniformity of human nature nor that of human consciousness was a presupposition of historical knowledge, it is far from clear that the historian can adopt a position of such epistemological neutrality as is suggested above. Even if, for example, a non-causal account of the relationship between beliefs is accepted, is it possible to ascertain what a person's beliefs are solely in accordance with a methodology in which nothing is assumed and no outcome precluded? And if it were the case that *we* could not proceed in this way, how would this affect the historian's position? Hume's suggestion may involve unacceptably severe constraints, but does the opposite position, which may be termed 'epistemological neutralism', not seem too lax in its demands? If Hume rules out too much, does it not rule out too little and is there not, perhaps, a role for a modified version of one of the uniformity theses to play?

We have already come across one condition by which a full-blooded version of epistemological neutralism would need to be constrained: the presupposition of those concepts in virtue of which we can have the notion of objective fact. But these, although necessary, fall short of the requirements of the situation in which we come to know of human beliefs. For the presupposition of metaphysical uniformity comes to little more than the requirement that we treat the historical past as being peopled by agents who share our concept of an objective world. But when we ascribe beliefs to an agent, this is not the only constraint which must be observed. We are not free to ascribe to him just *any* belief, but only some belief, or cluster of beliefs, from a limited range, namely, that which obtains in the historical community in which he lives. With sufficient ingenuity, for example, we could attempt to explain all actions in the way in which the man with the persecution complex explains them. There is no ultimate logical incoherence in the supposition that all of us, with the exception of the government, may be being persecuted by the government or some other agency. Indeed, this presumably is, to a greater or lesser degree, correctly believed in countries governed by tyrannies. What prevents our accepting such an interpretation of our beliefs is not, therefore, that it could not be rendered coherent for, with an appropriate redescription of our actions, it could. The obstacle lies in the fact that it conflicts with a system of beliefs which obtains within our specific historical society. This does not mean, of course, that there is no scope for the use of different hypotheses in order to try to see *specific* situations in the most coherent way possible, but it does mean that these hypotheses must be drawn from the limited range which belongs to our own historical society. When we try to explain the various actions of an individual or of some corporate body by reference to a cluster of beliefs, trying first one then another, we do so in the knowledge that any acceptable explanation must be drawn from that range.

Epistemological neutralism is, therefore, also inadequate. Its defect lies in a failure to distinguish between a freedom to try hypotheses drawn from within a given range and a freedom to try hypotheses from a wholly unrestricted range. In effect, it must be rejected because it fails to take into account the importance of the historical situation in which beliefs exist and operate.

But if these considerations suffice to warrant rejection of epistemological neutralism, they do not serve to justify either of the uniformity theses. For if the explanation of human action must be drawn from a range of beliefs prevalent within a given historical society, it does not follow that the same range must have been available to all historical societies. Even the brief examples given earlier show that historical knowledge involves no such assumption. We can understand the beliefs which explain why the crusaders went to war without ourselves having to think that they should provide even a possible reason why we should go to war.

THE UNIFORMITY OF CONCEPTS

But this claim may still presuppose some sort of uniformity thesis. For, it could be asked, even if we do not need to share the crusaders' beliefs about religion in order to understand why they went to war, do we not need to share their concept of war? For if our concept of war is not the same as theirs, when we assert that they went to war we are asserting something which they could not have understood and, to that extent, misdescribing their understanding of their actions. Thus, even if we reject the two other uniformity theses, it would seem that we must admit a yet more basic uniformity – a uniformity of concepts.

There are, however, various ways in which this final position for the uniformity theorist can be challenged. First, as with the other two versions, if accepted, it rules out the possibility of a history of the concepts in question. If the uniformity of certain concepts is a presupposition of historical knowledge, we are precluded from accepting any conclusions which imply that these concepts may have changed over time.

Secondly, although there is no need to identify concepts with human activities and beliefs, it is difficult to see what access we could have to them other than through the things which people do, say and believe. Thus a theory of the uniformity of concepts will be utilisable only if there is a uniformity of human nature or human consciousness. But we have already found reason to reject both of these theses.

Thirdly, it should be noted that concepts stand to one another in a variety of logical relationships. According to our concept of war, if something is correctly designated a war, it will involve fighting although not all fighting constitutes a state of war. Moreover, it can be fierce or protracted but not tender or loving and so on. Thus, if there is a uniformity in *this* concept of war, there must be a uniformity in the concepts which constitute the range which can be associated with it. But in this case we shall be faced with a choice between two incompatible alternatives: either to accept uniformity over very large ranges of concepts, since all concepts stand in a relationship to many others; or to foreclose the range by severing the series of relationships, or rearranging it, according to some new and non-arbitrary principle. The first move would take us back to a full-blooded uniformity of concepts, with all the difficulties mentioned earlier. The second allows that uniformity is in many cases not required, and is thus incompatible with an insistence on it.

By far the greatest difficulty which attends all of the versions of the uniformity thesis which have been discussed is the unacceptably high level of constraint which they would impose upon the historian, which would, in effect, rule out the possibility of the history of change or development in the areas in which uniformity is presupposed. Nevertheless, it may be felt, despite the objections to the thesis, that there must be some truth in it. A large part of history is about the activities of human beings, individually or in groups, within the context of different forms of consciousness and different forms of society. Even if we want to allow for the possibility that these forms may change over time, the activities of agents within them must remain, in many ways, largely recognisable, and the accounts which historians offer of them be such that we can follow them. Hume's thesis does, at least, offer an explanation for this fact.

This is an important requirement and one which must be met even if Hume's thesis is to be rejected. This can, in fact, be done by developing a point which has so far been disregarded. The unwelcome aspects of the constraints which the uniformity thesis introduces all derive from Hume's commitment to a uniformity, at some level, in the *content* of human nature or of human consciousness. In denying this, however, one is not committed to denying a uniformity in the structure of human activity, present and past. The latter is, in fact, entailed by Hume's insistence upon the need for a uniformity in some beliefs and expectations in all societies. For, it follows from this that there must be beliefs and intentions in all societies. Nevertheless, one can deny the first of these propositions without rejecting the second. Thus, even if, as has been argued, it is necessary to reject the claim that a uniformity in the content of human nature or human belief must be presupposed throughout time, one can explain the intelligibility which we expect to find in any acceptable historical account in terms of the identity of the structure, and, hence, in the form of explanation, of human action and activity. This does not mean merely that the historian must explain human action in terms of beliefs, intentions and so on. It means also that he must assume *a priori* that explanations involving this structure have been a constant part of human intercourse in the past. In effect, he must assume that human beings have always had beliefs and intentions, which are expressed in their actions, that they have always known that they have and that they have used this knowledge in explaining one another to themselves. For unless this assumption is made, the historian would lack even a minimal notion of what it would be to be an agent in the past and, in the absence of this, he would have no idea how to use anything which currently exists as evidence for human history. In short, the enterprise of history would become impossible. It must be noted, however, that although this condition can be satisfied without introducing Humean-style constraints into the content of systems of belief in the past, this does not mean that no constraints whatsoever are required with regard to the content. The requirement for uniformity in the structure and explanation of human action does not open the way for the reintroduction of epistemological neutralism.

The requirement that the historical past be thought of as being peopled by human agents who share with us the formal properties of agency and whose actions must therefore be susceptible of explanations of the same form as ours can therefore be added to the principle of metaphysical uniformity as an *a priori* condition of human history. Nevertheless, like the principle of metaphysical uniformity, it remains a purely formal condition and does not of itself imply the need to introduce any further constraints, if we are to be justified in our accounts of the *contents* of historical systems of belief. But if the objections to epistemological neutralism are correct, some such constraints are required. I propose, however, to postpone discussion of these further constraints until the last chapter, so that it can be related to other relevant points which will arise from a discussion of Hegel's and Vico's views.

THE ONTOLOGICAL STATUS OF SOCIAL IDEAS

I shall conclude this account of Hume's views about history by considering, in much less detail, one final consequence for historical knowledge which follows from his conception of an empirical science of man. This concerns his theory of the nature of the ideas which are used in the operations of human reasoning, i.e., that the simplest or most basic ideas we have arise causally from the simplest elements in our experience. This theory has received so much general discussion that it might seem superfluous to consider it here.[56] Nevertheless there is an aspect of it which is rarely noticed, but which is too important in the present context to be disregarded.[57] It can be brought out by attending to two related points.

The first is that, although Hume claims that simple ideas are caused by experience, he treats them as though they are logically dependent upon it. He does not, of course, believe that we can have no idea of something of which we have had no experience: his distinction between simple ideas and complex ideas allows him to show how we can have complex ideas of things of which we have had no experience, as long as we have had experience of the simple components of which they are composed. This means, however, that complex ideas must always, in principle, be resolvable logically into constituents of ideas of things which we have encountered in experience. Any new idea will therefore either be derived from an increased experience of the world or be a new combination or arrangement of ideas from a

---

[56] Most commentators offering a systematic general account of Hume's philosophy begin with a discussion of this principle, taken as one of the bases of his theory of knowledge. See, for example, Barry Stroud, *Hume* (London, Routledge & Kegan Paul, 1977); Anthony Flew, *David Hume: Philosopher of Moral Science* (Oxford, Basil Blackwell, 1986). Even Kemp Smith and Livingston, both of whom believe that Hume's initial exposition of his theory of ideas and impressions is misleading, can make little headway with their revisionist accounts without, fairly early on, needing to explain how the theory of ideas and impressions ought to be understood. For present purposes, however, there is no need to discuss the problems of meaning and knowledge which are usually brought up in connection with the theory, since my concern is with a further function which ideas have, relating to a different aspect of their nature.

[57] It has, in fact, been discussed at length by Livingston, Chapters 1, 3 and 4, who takes a view almost completely opposed to that which I take here. It would be too lengthy, in the present context, to undertake an examination of Livingston's very complex position. All that I can do is to refer the reader to the general points made in n. 24 above and leave it to him, in the light of the interpretation defended in this chapter, to decide about the merits of the conflicting approaches.

limited stock of simple ideas which our previous experience of the world has given us.

It follows from this general conception of ideas that Hume must deny them any fundamental ontological status. In relation to the natural sciences – the paradigm for his conception of a science of man – this may seem to raise no difficulty. Ideas or concepts, it could be argued, are used in theories about the physical world but are not themselves part of the world which, by means of these theories, we come to know. This view, although by no means unarguable, is one which many scientific realists are happy to adopt. The important point is that, since concepts are human products, in thinking in this way we are doing little more than allow that the world of natural objects could exist in the absence of human beings and, hence, in the absence of the concepts in terms of which human beings think about it.[58]

But such a conception of the nature of ideas is unacceptable when we consider their operation in the social and historical world. Here we are dealing with social agents, and it is impossible for anybody to be a social agent without understanding the concept of the type of social agent in question.[59] One cannot, for example, be a judge or a school-teacher, unless one's conduct reveals an understanding of what one should do in the legitimate fulfilment of one's role. Indeed, the requirement is somewhat stronger than this. For not merely is it necessary to know what one's role involves, but it is necessary also to know that others know what is involved. One cannot, in other words, act as a judge unless one's conduct both conforms to a shared understanding of the role and to the knowledge that that understanding is shared. For, in the last resort, it is one's success or failure in being able to show that one has acted in accordance with what one knows to be shared that determines the legitimacy of one's actions as a judge. Acting in a social role thus presupposes possession of a social concept which one knows to be shared. This need not be something which one can explicate theoretically, but it must be such that one

---

[58] It is no objection to this that we use the concept of a natural object in order to conceive of a world in which natural objects but not concepts of natural objects exist. This simply follows from the truism that we have to be able to think in order to think about any world at all and, hence, *a fortiori*, to think about a world in which we might not be able to think.

[59] See Peter Winch, *The Idea of a Social Science and its Relation to Philosophy* (London, Routledge & Kegan Paul, 1958), Chapter 2, Part 2.

can use it, should one be challenged, in defence of one's claim to have acted legitimately in that role.

It follows from this that ideas cannot, in the social world, have only the secondary ontological status which Hume ascribes to them. For an idea to have this secondary status, it is necessary that that of which it is an idea could have existed in the absence of the idea itself. But this is not possible in the case of social agents, for to be a social agent is just to act in accordance with certain conventions and in the knowledge that those conventions are known to be shared. In the social world, therefore, consciousness of such ideas is constitutive: without it there could be no such world.

Knowledge of shared human conventions is thus fundamental to the conception of a social world. There is, however, no set of natural, psychological terms, of the sort to which Hume appeals, into which this sort of understanding can be analysed or to which it can be reduced. There is nothing which we can learn about our natural properties – our 'ambition, avarice, self-love, vanity, friendship, generosity, public spirit'[60] and the like – which can provide a basis for our shared knowledge of the world of institutional understanding in which we act and in terms of which much of our behaviour is to be explained.

This is obscured by Hume's failure to notice that the terms in which he describes the uniformities in human nature which are said to underlie explanations of human action are incomplete. It is true that we can explain a person's action by, say, his ambition, but this is acceptable only if, from the context, it is clear what is the object of his ambition – to become a soldier, a banker, a bishop, and so on – and that the kind of action in question conforms to the conventions which, in a given historical society, determine how the object can be achieved. In different historical societies, however, both the objects and the ways of achieving them may differ enormously. Here one need think only of the way in which the role of a member of parliament, and the methods of becoming a member of parliament, have changed in Great Britain in the last four centuries. The proper ambition here must be to become a certain type of social agent in a determinate historical society. A motive such as this cannot, therefore, be assumed to be a property of human nature in itself, constant and uniform through time.

[60] *EHU*, p. 83.

If this is correct, we cannot have access to adequate explanations of human activity in the past unless we recognise the importance of social consciousness and can produce acceptable accounts of the determinate contents of such consciousness in specific societies in the past. The historian does not need to rule out the theoretical possibility of a uniformity of such consciousness – although present historical knowledge renders that implausible – but if there is, at any level, such a uniformity, knowledge of it cannot be an *a priori* presupposition of historical research.

CONCLUSION

It appears that the most fundamental difficulties which arise for Hume's account of historical knowledge stem almost entirely from his desire to base it upon principles derived from his science of man, in which the concept of a science is understood in terms of the sort of science appropriate to the natural world. The concept of man as a fixed causal sub-system, operating within a wider causal system and, hence, subject to a system of universal causal laws, would leave no room for knowledge of the existence and development of bodies of belief and systems of practice specific or unique to particular historical societies, if there have been any such systems. For, as a result of the methodology employed, one of the primary features of the basic laws of the natural sciences is that they hold irrespective of time and place. It is impossible, therefore, in a science of man modelled upon such a conception, to locate and explain any characteristics of activities which may derive solely from features of an historically specific society, for it is impossible, in terms of such a science, to allow for the possibility that different forms of social consciousness may be unique to specific historical societies. The possibility of genuine historical specificity is simply eliminated *a priori*. As a result, Hume's proposal that historical knowledge should rest upon the findings of a science of man of the sort which he envisaged could not fail to produce a theory of the nature of the human past which entailed that all actual accounts of the past would be ahistorical in character, in the sense of ruling out *a priori* the possibility of knowledge of any historically specific kinds of belief and activity and prescribing *a priori* that the primary content of belief be assimilated, conceptually, to our own.

These consequences follow, however, only from the particular concept of a science of man with which Hume operated. It is certainly not necessary that all attempts to relate history to a science of man should be pursued in this way. An almost diametrically opposed conception, in fact, is developed in Hegel's notion of philosophical history, which involves a theory about the nature of the process whereby historically specific forms of social consciousness, including philosophy, develop, and how, from a position *within* it, we can produce a science of that process. For this reason it is appropriate to turn to a critical examination of this alternative conception.

2

HEGEL: THE SELF-DEVELOPMENT OF REASON

INTRODUCTION

Hegel's approach to the problems involved in the nature of historical knowledge is, like Hume's, part of an account of the nature of all knowledge whatsoever. However, the connection between history or, at least, philosophical history and philosophy, is so close in Hegel that neither can be understood without the other. For this reason, I shall not outline in advance any other aspects of his thought but will concentrate almost exclusively upon his notion of philosophical history, examining its relationship to other aspects of his philosophy as and when the relevant points arise.

Although most of Hegel's works have a very important historical dimension to them, his one principal attempt to specify his idea of history in detail is contained in his *Lectures on the Philosophy of World History* and, in particular, in the lengthy Introduction to that work, in which he explains the conceptions basic to his approach. It is a curiosity in the literature, however, that although there is no disagreement among Hegel scholars concerning the fundamental importance which he attached to history, in particular to the history of consciousness, very few studies have been based upon this text.[1] In place of a direct examination in its own right, it is usually discussed

[1] Even such a percipient and sympathetic critic as R. G. Collingwood, while acknowledging the *Lectures on the Philosophy of World History* as a 'magnificent work', judges them unsatisfactory on the grounds that ultimately they treat 'political history by itself as if it were the whole of history'. See *The Idea of History*, pp. 120–2. This is a strange criticism to comprehend and I can only think that Collingwood has overlooked the Hegelian notion of the state as that in which all aspects of spirit are united. What this means will be explained below. Certainly, however, if Collingwood's view is correct, the *Lectures on the Philosophy of World History* offer a much less valuable account of Hegel's thought than I suppose. In what follows I shall refer

indirectly because of the light which it can throw upon the importance of the historical dimension in Hegel's other works. This has resulted, however, in the comparative neglect of important aspects of Hegel's whole notion of philosophical history. For this reason, I shall concentrate upon the view which emerges from the text of the *Lectures*.[2]

to them simply as the *Lectures*, and all references and quotations will be to or from the translation by H. B. Nisbet (Cambridge, Cambridge University Press, 1975).

[2] In his Introduction to Nisbet's translation, pp. vii–ix, Duncan Forbes notes with regret the comparative neglect of this important work. Amongst the contributory factors to this state of affairs, he mentions the apparently introductory nature of the work, the fact that it is often thought of, especially in the world of analytic philosophy, as an example of what philosophy of history ought not to be, and the fact that even Hegel experts do not in general care for it, reserving their more detailed researches for Hegel's early works, up to and including the *Phenomenology of Spirit*. In this he is, I believe, right, as he is, also, in his further claim that Hegel's philosophy cannot be understood correctly unless one has a proper grasp of the relationship between logic and the historical manifestations of spirit. To concentrate on either at the expense of the other is to evade some of the most important but problematic aspects of Hegel's philosophy. In what follows, I hope to make a contribution to both of these problems, partly by concentrating upon Hegel's text itself and also by emphasising the importance of understanding the relation of the idea to the concept of its concrete manifestation in history. Unfortunately, my conclusions will, I fear, come into the category of what Forbes regards as misunderstandings of Hegel.

   In recent years, only two monographs have been devoted to the *Lectures*: George Dennis O'Brien, *Hegel on Reason and History: A Contemporary Interpretation* (Chicago, University of Chicago Press, 1975), and Burleigh Taylor Wilkins, *Hegel's Philosophy of History* (Ithaca, Cornell University Press, 1974). O'Brien's book deals with many of the issues of the present chapter and, although I disagree with his interpretation, I am much indebted to it. Despite its title, Wilkins' book does not offer an overall view of Hegel's philosophy of history but concentrates upon three crucial features in it: Hegel's conception of the relationships between non-philosophical and philosophical history, between means and end and between contingency and necessity. Some of the larger comprehensive interpretations of Hegel's philosophy in general contain substantial chapters on his philosophy of history. Among these are: Shlomo Avineri, *Hegel's Theory of the Modern State* (Cambridge, Cambridge University Press, 1972), Chapter 12; Walter Kaufmann, *Hegel: Reinterpretation, Texts and Commentary* (London, Weidenfeld & Nicolson, 1966), Chapter 6; Raymond Plant, *Hegel: An Introduction*, 2nd edn (Oxford, Basil Blackwell, 1983), Chapters 3 and 10; and Charles Taylor, *Hegel* (Cambridge, Cambridge University Press, 1975), Chapter 15. The following works, not dedicated solely to Hegel, also contain substantial discussions of the nature of his philosophy of history: Berry, *Hume, Hegel and Human Nature*, Chapter 10; Collingwood, *The Idea of History*, Part III, Section 7; William H. Dray, *Philosophy of History* (Englewood Cliffs, N.J., Prentice-Hall, 1964), Chapter 6; Karl Löwith, *Meaning in History* (Chicago, University of Chicago Press, 1949), Chapter 3; Michael Murray, *Modern Philosophy of History* (The Hague, Martinus Nijhoff, 1970), Chapter 3; Maurice Mandelbaum, *History, Man and Reason: A Study in Nineteenth Century Thought* (Baltimore, the Johns Hopkins University Press, 1971), Chapter 10, Section 3; W. H. Walsh, *An Introduction to Philosophy of History*, Hutchinson's University Library (London, Hutchinson, 1951), Chapter 7; Hayden White, *Metahistory: The Historical Imagination in Nineteenth-Century Europe* (Baltimore, the Johns Hopkins University Press, 1973), Chapter 2.

HEGEL AND THE CONSTANCY OF HUMAN NATURE

Hegel's basic thesis is that the significance of history lies in the fact that its substance is the self-development of spirit or mind. The consequences of this claim are at variance with almost all of the claims which derive from Hume's conception of a science of man, including, in particular, the constancy of human nature and of human consciousness. As a preliminary to considering the thesis, therefore, it is useful to note that, quite early in his presentation of it, Hegel makes a series of remarks which show that he was well aware of some of the problems to which Hume's claims about the constancy of human nature give rise and that he considered his theory as going some way, at least, towards offering a solution to them.

This can be done quite easily because, in introducing his argument, he refers directly to 'human nature' in terms which connect fairly clearly with something like Hume's view.[3] Thus, having announced that the spiritual sphere, which will be the main concern of history, 'encompasses everything that has concerned mankind down to the present day',[4] he asserts that this means that we must examine 'spirit in combination with nature, or human nature itself'.[5] But we must be careful how we do this, for, he continues:

The expression 'human nature' is usually taken to represent something fixed and constant. Descriptions of human nature are meant to apply to all men, past and present. The general pattern is capable of infinite modifications, but, however much it may vary, it nevertheless remains essentially the same. Reflective thought must disregard the differences and isolate the common factor which can be expected to behave in the same way and to show itself in the same light under all circumstances ... Those who look at history from this point of view will tend to emphasise that men are still the same as they always were, and that vices and virtues have remained constant despite changing circumstances.[6]

These remarks describe a view which, if not actually Hume's, is certainly very close to it, if taken to refer to the ultimate constituents of human nature.[7] Having described the doctrine in this way, Hegel proceeds to outline some of its consequences and defects:

[3] *Lectures*, pp. 44–6.   [4] *Ibid.*, p. 44.   [5] *Ibid.*, p. 44.
[6] *Ibid.*, pp. 44–5.
[7] It is not clear whether Hegel had Hume specifically in mind in these passages. He had, however, read Hume's principal works, including his *History of England*. In general he traces Hume's intellectual lineage backwards, through Locke, to Newton, whom he describes as 'the chief contributor to the philosophy of Locke or the English

Once we have accepted this, we might even say that there is no need to refer to the great theatre of world history at all. According to the well known anecdote, Caesar found in a small municipality the same ambitions and activities he had encountered in the wider context of Rome. The same motives and aspirations can be found in a small town as in the great theatre of world events. It is obvious that this way of looking at history abstracts from the content and aims of human activity. Such sovereign disregard of the objective situation is particularly common among French and English writers, who describe their work as 'philosophical history'.[8]

But such an approach is mistaken, for 'no fully informed intellect can fail to distinguish between impulses and inclinations which operate in a restricted sphere and those which are active in the conflict of interests in world history'.[9]

The first point of interest here is the suggestion that the assumption of a constant human nature abstracts from the content and aims of human activity which, by implication, are not constant. Thus it is that this kind of history can treat conflicts of interest in world history, i.e., throughout the whole range of history, as though the content and aims involved were the same as those involved in each specific period of history.

The second point is the claim that this conception of history fails to distinguish between the reasons why an individual *within* an historical community will have a certain aim – which will be provided by his identification with some cause which he finds ready to hand – and the reasons why a whole nation will have a certain aim. These cannot be treated in the same way, for an historical community does not find the content of its causes ready to hand as does an individual within a community. When it comes to the question why an individual has his particular aims, Hegel claims, an empirical answer will suffice.[10] The point here is that, if the range of the possible content of belief is known, it is an empirical question what, within that range, anybody believes. But when we come to the question how beliefs and interests themselves acquire their different content, the 'empirical approach is not adequate for our purposes, and we must pass on to the more specific question of how the spirit – i.e., the spirit

method in treating of Philosophy ...'. Not surprisingly, he is critical of what he regards as the philosophical inadequacy of Newton's conception of methodology, both in science and as applied to philosophy. See his *Lectures on the History of Philosophy*, translated by Elisabeth S. Haldane and Frances H. Simson (London, Kegan Paul, Trench, Trubner, 1892–5), Vol. III, pp. 295–313, 332–4 and 369–75.
[8] *Lectures*, p. 45.   [9] *Ibid.*, p. 45.   [10] *Ibid.*, p. 46.

as such, whether it is present in ourselves, in other individuals, or in nations as a whole – acquires such a content.'[11] When this is the question, we cannot adopt the empirical method, which is 'part of our ordinary consciousness' but require a concept 'of a completely different order'.[12]

It is clear from these introductory remarks that Hegel believes that it is a mistake to presuppose either the constancy of human nature or that of human consciousness. Not only are these propositions implausible in themselves but, when it comes to establishing and explaining the content of different systems of belief in history, the empirical method itself must be abandoned. In place of this what Hegel will advocate will be his own version of 'philosophical history', which diverges sharply from the Humean-style approaches with which he disagrees.

PRE-PHILOSOPHICAL HISTORY

Hegel approaches the conception of philosophical history by a critical examination of features of certain other kinds of history. It is useful to follow him here for, in the course of his discussion, he makes a number of points which are helpful not only in understanding in more detail his objections to the uniformity of nature thesis but also in gaining a first idea of certain requirements which, he believes, only philosophical history can satisfy. In recent years, there has been some discussion as to whether Hegel conceives of the different kinds of history which he singles out as standing to one another in a dialectical relationship. It is generally agreed that he does, although there are differences of opinion concerning the demarcation of the different dialectical moments. It is not necessary here, however, to follow this discussion in these terms. One can gain a sufficient idea of the respects in which philosophical history is meant to differ from, and be an improvement upon, the other kinds of history by a direct investigation of what he says about them.[13]

---

[11] *Ibid.*, p. 46.   [12] *Ibid.*, p. 46.

[13] It is quite clear, as we shall see, that Hegel intends philosophical history to overcome certain deficiencies in history as it has so far been practised without, however, wanting to dispense wholly with certain features of it. In some sense, therefore, his classification can be thought of as involving a dialectical progression. The main issues have been how technical is the conception of dialectic which is involved and the nature of the dialectical relationships between the different categories of history. I hope, in what follows, that the most important general

Hegel distinguishes three general kinds of history: 'original', 'reflective' and 'philosophical'. The second kind, reflective history, is further sub-divided into four forms: 'universal', 'pragmatic', 'critical' and 'specialised'.[14] Original and reflective history are explicitly described as 'other methods of dealing with history' and are introduced by way of comparison with the concept of philosophical history or, as he otherwise terms it, a philosophical history of the world.

Original history is defined as history written by authors who have 'witnessed, experienced and **lived** through the deeds, events and situations they describe, who have themselves participated in these events and in the spirit which informed them'.[15] Examples of this kind of historian are Herodotus, Thucydides, Xenophon, Polybius, Caesar, Cardinal de Retz and Frederick the Great.[16] Nothing of importance hinges upon the fact that most of the examples are drawn from the relatively distant past, for the memoirs of Cardinal de Retz, for example, are mentioned as belonging to a large class of more recent works, many of which are relatively trivial but others of which, including those of the Cardinal, are 'written by men of great ability and set in a grander and more interesting context'.[17] In fact, Hegel explicitly asserts that there are many excellent modern accounts of this sort although, for reasons to be mentioned shortly, he believes that it is more difficult to produce really good examples in a modern society.

The distinctions between 'witnessing', 'experiencing' and 'living through' the events are also of no great importance, despite the fact that most, though not all, of the examples given are of writers who were themselves actively involved in the activities described. For Hegel accepts that in all cases such writers incorporate into their accounts 'the narratives and reports of others'.[18] Witnessing, experiencing and living through deeds, events and situations are just different ways of 'participating' in them, and it is this notion which is crucial.

Before we attend to this point, two of Hegel's other remarks are worth noting. First, he claims that in writing up accounts of this sort

points can be brought out without entering these more detailed discussions. For this, see Forbes, pp. xvii–xxii; O'Brien, *Hegel on Reason and History*, Chapter 2, and 'Does Hegel Have a Philosophy of History?', *History and Theory*, Vol. 10, No. 3 (1971), 295–317; White, *Metahistory*, pp. 97–102.

[14] *Lectures*, pp. 11–24.   [15] *Ibid.*, p. 12.   [16] *Ibid.*, p. 12.
[17] *Ibid.*, p. 15.
[18] *Ibid.*, p. 12.

the original historian produces something which is necessary for any history whatsoever and, therefore, also for philosophical history: for he transfers to the realm of intellectual representation what would otherwise be a world of mere existence or happenings. One implication of this is therefore, as we shall see, that the philosophical historian must have access to the products of the original historian, if his own history is going to relate to the world of objective fact.

In producing his account, however, the original historian does more than merely provide source material for other kinds of historian. For the happenings which he transfers to the realm of the intellect were previously 'mere extraneous happenings', whereas, when he has done his work, what he produces is 'a representation of the internal and external faculties of mind'.[19] Even when they deal with the narratives and reports of others, which are the more 'scattered, subjective and fortuitous' of their raw materials, such 'historians transplant [the past] into a better and more exalted soil than the soil of transience in which it grew, into the realm of the departed but now immortal spirits ... so that their heroes now perform for ever the deeds they performed but once while they lived.'[20] The original historian thus gives expression to a mental view of things which, as a result, acquires a permanent status both as a part, and as a record, of public consciousness. The assumption here is that what has merely finite existence, what merely happened, cannot endure; but, when what has finite existence is transposed into the world of mind, it can become a constitutive part of a more enduring process. It might be thought that this transposition involved a move away from the reality of the things themselves, but this is not how Hegel regards it. Were it not to occur, the original events, or their fleeting memories, would remain in the realm of what is extraneous, i.e., extraneous to mind, and, hence, transient. The transfer to the mental is for Hegel, therefore, a first step towards, and not away from, historical reality as such. It is also a first step towards the claim that history is both possible and necessary because of the ontological primacy of social consciousness.

The second point follows directly from this: original history must exclude all legends, folksongs, and poems, for these are the products of nations whose consciousness is obscure, and such nations cannot be 'the object of the philosophical history of the world, whose end is to

---

[19] *Ibid.*, p. 12.   [20] *Ibid.*, p. 12.

attain knowledge of the Idea in history'.[21] Hegel's exclusion from philosophical history of whatever pertains to nations of obscure consciousness, i.e., to nations which have never acquired the capacity to produce intellectual representations of their activities, is one of the features which most strongly distinguishes his notion of philosophical history from Vico's.[22] Which of the two was correct in this aspect of their doctrines is a question which can be left until later. But this is an exclusion which Hegel explicitly makes and, as will become evident, he was consistent in so doing, in so far as it follows from his particular conception of philosophical history.

Participating in the spirit of the age which informs the events which he narrates, and producing an intellectual representation which expresses this, are thus two of the principal characteristics of the original historian. Hegel is insistent that this participation, or 'immersion', must be concrete or detailed. This is, in fact, his reason for claiming that it is more difficult to write such history well in a modern society: 'This unity of author and events also means [that if] the historian lives in an age in which the social classes have become more clearly differentiated [and in which] the culture and maxims of each individual are related to his social class, he will himself have to belong to the class of *statesmen, generals* and the like, whose aims, intentions and deeds are part of the political world he describes.'[23] Thus, although the original historian is writing up an account of things in the light of a consciousness which he shares with those who performed them or who participated with him in their performance, the content involved can vary according to the level of social differentiation. In societies with a markedly differentiated social structure, the original historian can express the relevant conscious-

---

[21] *Ibid.*, p. 12.

[22] White, *Metahistory*, pp. 85–7, who is mainly concerned with the tropological structures which, he claims, govern aspects of Hegel's general conception of history, points out that in his *Lectures on the Philosophy of Aesthetics*, Hegel describes poetry as an 'original, imaginative grasp of truth, a form of knowledge ...', the different characteristics of which are then explicated within Hegel's conception of the development of consciousness, including the latter as it is developed in his philosophy of history. Although this is true, it does not support White's further claim that Hegel's 'characterisation of poetry is precisely the same as Vico's', for Vico claims that there can be a wholly poetic society, of which we can have historical knowledge, whereas Hegel's comments in the *Lectures* clearly exclude the possibility of such knowledge. For a discussion of the differences between Hegel and Vico on this point, see pp. 142–7. below.

[23] *Lectures*, p. 13.

ness only if he is himself a member of the class or classes about which he is writing and thus shares the consciousness in question.

A further fundamental feature of original history is its immediate or non-reflective character. In emphasising this, Hegel does not mean to imply that skill and discernment are not among the *desiderata* of original history, for, as he notes, there are both good and bad examples of this genre. His point is that, in virtue of the consciousness which the original historian shares with his subject, i.e., of his 'immersion' in its spirit, he has no *conceptual* difficulties of understanding, meaning or explanation with which to contend. This does not mean that he may not have difficulties with the critical examination of his sources – although Hegel does not mention these – but it does mean that, at a certain stage, when he has done his work in an impartial and critical manner, the meaning of what emerges is immediately and wholly self-evident: 'the substance of his narrative and of his own culture are in equal measure the substance and consciousness of *those whose words he renders*',[24] and, because this is so, 'what he makes his characters say is not the expression of an alien consciousness *projected into* them, but of *their own culture and consciousness*'.[25]

Hegel's description of the nature of original history is thus not very different from Hume's account of that of historical knowledge *in general*, in so far as in both cases the historian is said to employ a consciousness which he shares with the subject about which he writes. The main difference, of course, is that where Hume wishes to apply this shared consciousness to all societies at all times and places, Hegel wishes to restrict its application to the specific historical society in which the original historian finds himself. The importance of this difference emerges as soon as Hegel turns to the second mode of historical writing, reflective history.

The original historian is unreflective. The fact that his work is structured by beliefs which are identical in kind with those of whom he writes makes reflection unnecessary. At the same time it also limits the temporal and historical span within which he can work. This is a serious limitation, however, for it means that, while he can use his shared consciousness in his historical accounts, he cannot give an historical account of that shared consciousness. But to achieve the latter he is faced with severe difficulties. For it requires him to contend

[24] *Ibid.*, p. 14.   [25] *Ibid.*, p. 14.

with modes of consciousness and spirit which are different from those which are unreflectively present to himself which, in virtue of being in a particular society, he can simply take for granted when writing about that society: 'everything therefore depends on the maxims, ideas and principles which the author applies both to the content of his work (i.e., to the motives behind the actions and events he describes) and to the form of his narrative'.[26]

Hegel insists that the historian cannot just apply to these other periods the consciousness in virtue of which he is unreflective in respect to his own period. At the same time, however, he does share the consciousness of his own period. There must therefore be something else available in virtue of which, while sharing the consciousness of his age, he is not so bound by it that all that he can do is unreflectively apply it to other ages in the course of his historical enquiries. Hegel's response is to introduce a distinction between that which 'was present in this or that age' and 'that which is *present in spirit*, so that its object is the past *as a whole*'.[27] This is a difficult distinction and I shall discuss it at length below. As we shall see, Hegel does not believe that any of the four forms of reflective history succeed in capturing it adequately. We may note here, however, that he is distinguishing between that which is present in determinate historical periods and something which, while also being present in these periods, nevertheless embraces the past *as a whole*. We can see the difference if we briefly return to Hume, for whom 'ambition, avarice, self-love' and so on belong to the past as a whole, in the sense of belonging, in the same way, to every determinate period within it. This view, however, loses sight of anything which could be proper and specific only to a particular historical period. In talking about the original historian, Hegel has agreed that spirit and consciousness are present differently in different determinate historical periods. In distinguishing between this and what is '*present in spirit*', and in connecting the latter with 'the past *as a whole*', he cannot, like Hume, be asserting that the principles which operate in each determinate, historical society are applicable to the whole of human history. He is saying, rather, that we must move to a viewpoint in which we can take account of something which is present throughout human history, without obliterating the distinctiveness of the consciousness of determinate historical societies. Thus he is conscious of a problem

[26] *Ibid.*, p. 16.   [27] *Ibid.*, p. 16.

of which Hume was unaware: that of finding a framework for understanding the past which, while enabling us to grasp the past as a whole, will not do so at the expense of what is specific to the consciousness of particular historical societies.

This becomes clearer as soon as we turn to some of Hegel's remarks about the four forms of reflective history. The distinction between original history and reflective history of any kind turns upon the distinction between the unreflective and the reflective. The original historian thinks about what he produces, in so far as his work is an intellectual representation of his world. His activity is not, however, reflective, for a reflective activity always, for Hegel, involves thought about thought, or what he sometimes calls 'after-thought',[28] and, as such, requires a certain kind of conceptual distancing from the original thought. The reflective historian, whose consciousness is not immediately identical with that of his subject, is in a position, therefore, to apply a different kind of thought to it.

The first form of reflective history, universal history, is the simple attempt to write a complete history of a nation, country or the world. There are various difficulties in this kind of project. In the attempt to say something about everything, as part of an overall view, the author may have to abridge so much as to be in danger of producing an abstract or dry narrative.[29] On the other hand, any attempt to write in the fuller and livelier manner of the original historian is more or less bound to be unsuccessful: 'the various ages covered by a history of this kind have widely differing cultures, as do the [original] historians on whose work the writer draws and the spirit which speaks through them in the words of the author is different from the spirit of the age he describes. When the historian tries to depict the spirit of bygone times, it is usually his own spirit which makes itself heard.'[30] The implication is clear: the universal historian's presupposition of the uniformity of human consciousness is a vice rather than a virtue.

Nevertheless, despite these difficulties, an overall view is necessary. So also, therefore, is a reflective representation, since it will be necessary to think about thoughts of societies which differ from those of one's own.[31] The other three kinds of reflective history to which Hegel now turns contain some but not all of the features which are

[28] See *Hegel's Logic*, Part I of the *Encyclopaedia of the Philosophical Sciences*, translated by William Wallace, 3rd edn (Oxford, Oxford University Press, 1975), pp. 4–7.
[29] *Lectures*, p. 18.   [30] *Ibid.*, p. 17.   [31] *Ibid.*, p. 18.

necessary for this task. Its complete achievement, he argues, is possible only in the context of a philosophical history of the world.

The first requirement arises in connection with the second species of reflective history, pragmatic history. Strictly speaking, this is not so much a kind of history as an end to which historians aspire, i.e., of providing a fully developed account of a past age and its life.[32] In the course of the attempt to fulfil this aim, however, and precisely because it is a reflective activity, a new conception of the present comes into being. For the historian is forced to look at the past in relation to present interests, and in so doing he comes to view the present in the new perspective of a relationship in which certain aspects of it stand to the past.[33]

In stressing the creation of this new perspective, Hegel does not intend to deny the existence of a past of the sort of which the original historian speaks. He cannot do this, since he has already claimed that original history provides the materials presupposed by reflective history. His point is that, in the attempt to achieve the aim of universal history, and in the course of selecting and relating the materials necessary for this, we are forced to the production of a new conception of the present. We can understand the spirit of the past only in the light of some relationship in which it stands to the spirit of the present, although we must not, as in the case of most universal historians, completely identify the two. Nevertheless, although we begin to redefine the present in the attempt to set it in its wider historical context, the principles required for this are not given in the same way as are those of original history. They cannot be given for, if they were, there would be no sense in which any *new* understanding could come into being through reflective history. On the other hand, since they are not given, there is the danger, as Hegel points out, that

---

[32] *Ibid.*, pp. 19.
[33] Because of the nature of the text, Hegel's description of pragmatic history is obscure. Wilkins claims that it is an attempt 'not only to make the past a part of the present but also, as Hegel's label suggests, to make our heightened awareness of the past useful in solving the moral and political problems of our own day', pp. 33–4. The latter suggestion seems doubtful in view of Hegel's repudiation of the value of any lessons to be drawn from comparisons of present and past institutions or events (see n. 36 below). O'Brien likens it to Dewey's contention that 'all history is necessarily written from the standpoint of the present, and is, in an inescapable sense, the history not only of the present but of that which is contemporaneously judged to be important in the present', *Hegel on Reason and History*, p. 22. But this also fails to capture the force of Hegel's point that, in the very attempt to study the past and to see its relevance to the present, a present is 'created out of the mind's own activity and bestowed upon it as a reward for its exertions', *Lectures*, p. 20.

their work can be done by the use of idiosyncratic, fanciful or fictitious concepts of the present, to which equally unacceptable accounts of the past can be related.[34]

A further contrast with Hume emerges through one of Hegel's criticisms of pragmatic history. One of Hume's claims was that history taught us that the same principles of human nature operated universally and that its main use was to acquaint us with these principles.[35] Hegel, on the other hand, is wholly opposed to this view. Attempts to derive lessons of this sort, he argues, are bound to fail because events are concretely embedded in the individual circumstances of their age. They are, consequently, unique and can bear only a superficial resemblance to the events of other ages.[36] Thus, nothing that one can learn about particular historical events will provide anything which we can legitimately use to come to knowledge of constant principles of human nature.

The considerations which have been brought forward in connection with pragmatic history clearly point towards the need to provide a ground for the conception in virtue of which the past is to be related to the present, if wholly fictitious history is to be avoided. This is one of the most important conditions which philosophical history is claimed to satisfy. Before advancing to this, however, Hegel introduces two further kinds of history.

On the third kind of reflective history, critical history, he is extremely brief. The subject matter of critical history is the history of history. What is of interest here, however, is not so much the subject matter but the methods which have been developed to deal with it: in the attempt to examine the authenticity and credibility of histories 'the author wrests new information from the narratives he examines. (He scrutinises every circumstance to test the credibility of the

---

[34] 'Accordingly, *one* reflective history gives way to *another* ; each writer has the same materials before him, each believes himself capable of arranging them and of fashioning a work out of them, and each will infuse his own spirit into them in the guise of the spirit of the age he depicts ... The French show particular ingenuity in creating an imaginary present and in relating the past to the present situation.' *Ibid.*, p. 22.

[35] 'These records of wars, intrigues, factions, and revolutions, are so many collections of experiments, by which the politician or moral philosopher fixes the principles of his science ...', *EHU*, pp. 83–4.

[36] 'No two instances are exactly alike; they are never sufficiently identical for us to say that what was best on *one* occasion will also be best on another ... In this respect, there is nothing so insipid as the constant appeals to Greek and Roman precedents we hear so often, as for example during the French revolution.' *Lectures*, p. 21.

whole.)'[37] Hegel is fairly critical of the way in which, in his own day, these techniques have been misused, leading again to the substitution of 'subjective fancies for historical data'. Nevertheless, two principles are clearly endorsed. The first is that history requires techniques of authentication, which involve coherence in the interpretation of the relation between parts and wholes in history. The second is recognition of the fact that the historical value of documents can go well beyond what is explicitly expressed in them. This is particularly important, for it introduces the notion that the historian's approach should not be confined to those aspects of the past of which the specific historical society in which he is interested was explicitly conscious. It points beyond this to the possibility of the introduction of some principle which was operative but of which the society was itself unaware. Properly grounded, this will turn out to be the Hegelian idea.

The fourth kind of reflective history is specialised history. Here historians are concerned with a single, general perspective, taken from within the wider context of the whole of national life. The sorts of examples which Hegel mentions are histories of art, religion, law, learning, property relations, constitutions and navigation. There is no doubt that he himself attaches particular importance to art, religion and law, because of the place of objective and absolute spirit within his complete philosophical system. But, setting this aside for the moment, it is clear from the examples given that the general perspectives involved concern activities which are fundamental to the life of a nation as a whole. Nevertheless, as dealt with in specialised history, they can be more or less closely related to the whole of which they are part: 'Such branches of national activity are directly related to the history of the nation as a whole, and everything depends upon whether this wider context is brought fully to light, or merely glossed over in favour of external relationships.'[38] In the latter case, the activities in question will appear as 'purely contingent national peculiarities'. But, 'if reflective history has reached the stage of adopting general perspectives', as in the case of specialised histories, 'and if these perspectives are valid ones, such activities appear not just as an external thread, a superficial sequence, but as the inward guiding spirit of the events and deeds themselves'.[39]

In referring here to the connection between a particular specialised history and the life of a nation as a whole, Hegel does not intend this

[37] *Ibid.*, p. 22.   [38] *Ibid.*, p. 23.   [39] *Ibid.*, p. 23.

connection to be understood merely synchronically. In noting the considerable increase in constitutional history, for example, he points out that 'it is already more closely related to universal history, for it has no sense or significance unless it is based on a survey of the state as a whole'.[40] Here the relation between universal history and the notion of a survey of the state as a whole shows that the latter includes the *history* of the state as a whole. Specialised history thus focuses upon, and concerns itself with, some activity which is of special importance in the history of the nation as a whole.

Specialised histories are important, then, because they deal with activities which are of fundamental importance. In fact, they express the realisation that 'spiritual determinants must also be taken into consideration'.[41] Indeed, if they could be based upon a 'valid perspective' they would reveal the inner constitution of the history of the nation. They thus provide 'a point of transition to the philosophical history of the world'. But they cannot do more than that, for they remain single aspects abstracted from the life of the nation. Philosophical history, on the other hand, will also adopt a general perspective. This will not, however, be one which is 'abstractly general', but one which is 'concrete and absolutely present; for it is the spirit which is eternally present to itself and for which there is no past'.[42]

Despite the obscurity of the final claim, which I shall discuss later, the sense of Hegel's remarks is fairly clear. Philosophical history is to be an advance upon specialised history, in so far as it will take the history of the nation as a concrete totality and will be based upon a valid perspective which will enable one to look at world history in the light of inner constitutive principles – the spiritual determinants – which will not have been consciously available to the societies or nations which have figured in it. One will thus come to see the events of world history in a new way. In view of the importance which is attached to the concept of a valid viewpoint, however, an assessment of the validity of any viewpoint adduced will obviously be crucial for an evaluation of the whole concept of philosophical history.

Despite many differences between them, it is clear that Hegel and Hume share one conviction: the impossibility that the historian can proceed without some presuppositions. For Hume, of course, these were to be empirically derived, and it was this belief which led him to the uniformity thesis. Hegel is completely opposed to this and,

[40] *Ibid.*, p. 23.　　[41] *Ibid.*, p. 23.　　[42] *Ibid.*, p. 24.

accordingly, to any Humean-style empiricism, as an adequate foundation for a correct understanding of, at least, long-term history. But he is committed nevertheless to the need for some or other presuppositions, through his insistence upon the necessity for a valid viewpoint with which to ground the claim that what philosophical history produces is objective truth rather than subjective fancy.

His first suggestion about the presupposition is that it might simply be the notion of thought itself. But, he continues, momentarily anticipating a Humean objection, 'to appeal in this way to the participation of thought in all human activities may seem inadequate, for it could be argued that thought is subordinate to being, to the data of reality, and is based upon and determined by the latter'.[43] We may, he suggests, be tempted to think that we could avoid this objection, which amounts to a restatement of the need for empirical presuppositions, by taking thought to mean philosophical thoughts, thoughts which are the product of 'pure speculation'. But the danger of proceeding in this manner would be that 'it approaches history as something to be manipulated, and does not leave it as it is, but *forces it to conform* to its preconceived notions and *constructs history a priori*'.[44] The difficulty of introducing a valid perspective as a condition of an objective understanding of history without thereby constructing history *a priori* is thus one of which Hegel is fully aware. Indeed, not only is he alive to the general difficulty, but he recognises that it may be a particular danger for the view which he intends to advance. Hence he explicitly states that the apparent contradiction cannot be allowed to stand.[45] How successful he is in resolving it must be left for later discussion, but his awareness of the need to avoid the twin dangers of an ahistorical empiricism and an *a priori* rationalism must be borne in mind as his account of the nature of philosophical history is investigated.

[43] *Ibid.*, p. 25.   [44] *Ibid.*, p. 25.
[45] 'The sole end of history is to comprehend clearly what is and what has been, the events and deeds of the past. It gains in veracity the more strictly it confines itself to what is given and ... the more exclusively it seeks to discover what actually happened. This aim seems to contradict the function of philosophy; and it is this contradiction, and the accusation that philosophy imports its own ideas into history and manipulates it accordingly, that I wish to discuss in the *Introduction* to these lectures. In other words, we must first obtain a *general definition of the philosophy of world history* and then consider its immediate implications. As a result the relationship between thought and the events should automatically appear in the correct light.' *Ibid.*, p. 26. It is difficult to see how Hegel could state more strongly his concern to show that philosophical history must conform to the requirement 'to discover what actually happened'.

PHILOSOPHICAL HISTORY

In turning to the concept of philosophical history itself, it is worth reverting briefly to the second problem with which Hume's empirical science of man left him: his inadequate conception of the ontological status of ideas, at least in the social and historical world. If, as he claimed, ideas are always derived from the world, rather than, as in the case of the social world, being partly constitutive of it, the development of the new ideas which are necessary to structure new institutions would seem to be impossible and, hence, not a part of any possible history. Here again, the thesis which Hegel introduces as central to philosophical history – 'the idea that reason governs the world, and that world history is therefore a rational process'[46] – offers the prospect of an entirely different approach to the question of the nature and role of ideas in history. For, in some sense, ideas are to be given ontological primacy and the problem which arose for Hume, as a result of the largely epistemological framework from which he viewed them, may be avoidable.

The first point to note in Hegel's development of his thesis is that it is *concrete* reason which is asserted to govern the world. This means that reason is an active force in the world or, to put the matter rather less mysteriously, that the actual forces at work in the world are rational.

Hegel offers two analogies to help clarify the suggestion. The first is the view, the discovery of which he attributes to Anaxagoras, that 'there is reason in nature or that it is governed by unalterable general laws'.[47] The second is 'the religious truth that the world is not a prey to chance and external, contingent causes, but is *governed by providence*'.[48] The first thesis contains the idea that the behaviour of

[46] *Ibid.*, p. 27. Hegel points out that from the point of view of history the proposition is a presupposition, whereas for philosophy it is not, for it can be proved by 'speculative cognition'. He then proceeds by suggesting that there are two ways in which it can be viewed. First, because philosophy has demonstrated it, it can be posited 'as demonstrated for our present purposes'. *Ibid.*, p. 28. Alternatively, since this would demand an act of faith by those who do not possess the demonstration, it can be regarded as a conclusion, the '*result* of the ensuing enquiry ... the result of our study of history'. *Ibid.*, p. 29. Plainly it is the latter method which must be utilised in history. The reason why history can prove what can also be proved in philosophy is, as Hegel remarks later, that whoever 'looks at the world rationally will find that it in turn assumes a rational aspect; the two exist in a reciprocal relationship.' *Ibid.*, p. 29. These claims will be discussed below, when the full content of the principle of reason has been examined.

[47] *Ibid.*, p. 34.   [48] *Ibid.*, p. 35.

physical phenomena is determined by some set of systematic relationships proper to nature as such. The second involves the notion that there is a 'wisdom, coupled with infinite power, which realises its ends, i.e., the absolute and rational design of the world'. This is analogous to the conception which Hegel intends to advocate, in which 'reason is freely self-determining *thought*, or what the Greeks called "nous"'.[49]

These analogies are, however, very partial. They show that the conception of reason which Hegel is going to develop is not without precedents of some sort, but both are deemed inadequate on the grounds that they are abstract and indeterminate rather than concrete and determinate.[50] This point can be clarified by attending to the analogy with the notion that the natural world is governed by unalterable laws. At first sight it might seem that Hegel's claim is based upon a misunderstanding. For, it could be argued, although it is a presupposition of natural science that the world is governed by laws, this does not entail that there is anything abstract or indeterminate about the laws which actually operate, since their content can be established by empirical appeal to the world of concrete fact. It is instructive, therefore, to note Hegel's justification for the claim that the procedures of the natural sciences do not constitute an application of the concept of reason to concrete nature. This is given via a reference to Socrates' disappointment with Anaxagoras' principle, in which he comments upon Socrates' remark that, instead of dealing with reason, Anaxagoras dealt only with external causes such as air, ether, water and the like: 'It is evident from this that what Socrates took exception to was not Anaxagoras' principle as such, but his failure to apply it adequately to concrete nature, and to interpret nature in the light of this principle; for the principle never was anything more than an *abstraction*, or more precisely, nature was not presented as a development of the principle, or as an organisation produced by it, with reason as its cause.'[51]

The important point in this paragraph is the distinction between reason characterised either as 'abstract' or as a source or cause of the development of an organisation. This may be clarified in the following way. The natural sciences proceed upon the presupposition of the above principle, with its reference to some system or structure which governs the behaviour of things. Hence, their methodology – Hegel talks as if it were solely a matter of the abstraction of laws from the

49 *Ibid.*, p. 35.   50 *Ibid.*, p. 36.   51 *Ibid.*, p. 34.

contents of the empirical world[52] – is such that the particular laws which are established empirically must conform to the presupposition. But the content of these laws is not established in such a way as to follow from anything implicit in the concrete content of the principle. Different empirical laws must conform to the fundamental presupposition of law-governedness, but their content owes nothing to the principle itself, for, understood in this way, i.e., merely as the presupposition of law-governedness, it has no concrete content. To reach a truly explanatory notion of reason, therefore, what is required is a concept with a concrete content which will make a difference, by entering into their development or organisation, to the constitution or nature of the things of which it is said to be the cause.

This point is clearly related to some of the remarks which Hegel made about the differences between even the highest form of reflective history, specialised history, and philosophical history. One defect of specialised history was that it always, to a greater or lesser extent, had to take its subject matter in some degree of abstraction from the widest context, the nation as a whole, in which it inhered. Were it to overcome this limitation and to look at the history of the nation as a whole and from a valid perspective, it would present the activities with which it was concerned 'not just as an external thread, a superficial sequence, but as the inner guiding spirit of the events and deeds themselves'.[53] In this case, of course, it would have achieved the status of philosophical history.

Philosophical history therefore requires the introduction of a concrete or determinate principle, the content of which will ground the equally determinate constitutive or internal elements in the history of the nation. When this is achieved, we should be able to dispense with merely external and contingent connections in a knowledge of philosophical history, for such knowledge will consist in tracing and following these constitutive internal relations.

It is clear, therefore, that the principle which Hegel is to introduce must have a substantive, determinate content. He would be unable to avoid his own objections to other 'abstract' approaches, if the presupposition of reason turned out to be merely the *formal* requirement that history be looked upon as rational. For although history could be written in accordance with such a presupposition, the

[52] 'It is man who abstracts the laws from empirical reality and acquires knowledge of them.' *Ibid.*, p. 34.
[53] *Ibid.*, p. 23.

content of the resulting account would remain as externally related to the presupposition as, according to Hegel, the content of empirical laws is related to the presupposition of law-governedness in the case of the natural sciences. It would therefore need to be derived in some other way – perhaps by an empirical enquiry into the relations between men's 'rational' thoughts, the *formal* characteristics of which could be deduced from the presupposition, and their actions – but would nevertheless remain, as in the case of natural laws, an abstraction from reality. Clearly, therefore, Hegel's principle must be sufficiently determinate as to be applicable to 'concrete reality' and to enable us 'to interpret [concrete] reality in terms of the principle'.[54]

Reason must therefore be a substantial constitutive principle in history. In the account which he advances Hegel utilises, with appropriate modifications, a version of the Aristotelian distinction between the efficient, final, material and formal cause.[55] In what follows, and before trying to evaluate Hegel's complex project, I shall concentrate upon elucidating the distinctions and relationships between reason as the final, efficient and material cause of historical change.

THE FINAL CAUSE

It is not possible to gain a clear understanding of Hegel's notion of the final end of history without considering it in relation to his basic thesis about the course of world history: that world history is the process of spirit's self-development towards a final end. The end to be reached is its actualisation in a state which exemplifies or, indeed, constitutes the fullest development of the idea of freedom, i.e., one in which the form and content of the state is determined by the complete development of the idea.[56]

54 *Ibid.*, p. 36.
55 The Aristotelian framework within which much of Hegel's thought in general is developed is well known. See W. T. Stace, *The Philosophy of Hegel* (London, Macmillan, 1924), Chapter 1, Section C, or, for a very strong statement of it, G. R. G. Mure, *An Introduction to Hegel* (Oxford, Clarendon Press, 1940), Chapters 1–6. Charles Taylor attaches perhaps less importance to it, but nevertheless acknowledges it at various points throughout his book. O'Brien, *Hegel on Reason and History*, Chapters 5 and 6, however, is particularly successful in showing how Hegel's conception of reason in history is developed within the framework of Aristotelian categories. Although I disagree with many aspects of his interpretation, I am much indebted to his clarification of this issue.
56 I shall discuss below both the concept of spirit and the reasons why Hegel takes freedom to be its substance. For the moment it will be sufficient to understand spirit as a rational force or will in the world, whose end is freedom.

In thinking of the final end, it is important to guard against an immediate possible misunderstanding. This is that of conflating the notion of the *actualisation* of the idea in a state with that of its *embodiment* in a state. It is certainly true that, when he talks of the actualisation of the idea, Hegel means, as part of this, that it should be concretely embodied in a state. But this can be understood in two different ways. The first is that the idea is never concretely embodied in the state until its actualisation. This is not what is meant. For there is a sense in which the final end is embodied in the state throughout the entire course of world history. To say, as Hegel frequently does, that the final end is the *actualisation* of the idea of freedom is not to imply that it has never existed concretely at any point prior to its becoming the governing principle of the Hegelian state. It is merely to imply that none of the prior embodiments of the idea are embodiments of the *fully developed* idea. They are always embodiments of it in its less developed stages. Thus the notion that the idea is the final end must not be thought to suggest that it is merely something towards the *embodiment* of which changes in history are moving. It is, on the contrary, something which is always embodied in the states which figure in world history. It is the embodiment of the *perfect idea* of freedom which is the final end of the embodiments of less perfect conceptions in prior stages of world history.

That this is so will become clearer shortly. But it might be helpful to approach the whole conception by developing first the suggestion that Hegel has grasped a point which eluded Hume and which was not, indeed, available to him within his overall conception of an empirical science of man: that ideas are partly constitutive of institutions. This may not be immediately obvious for, even if it is allowed that the final end of history is the actualisation of the idea of freedom, in the sense just explicated, this is still susceptible of two different interpretations. One is that the world contains a force, spirit, which works towards the actualisation of the final end, but which does not require, as part of the actualisation, that human beings should have a certain conception of themselves, i.e., should have a certain form of social consciousness. On this view, realisation of the idea of freedom would consist in a certain objective state of affairs in which, *whether they knew it or not*, men were in fact free, in Hegel's sense of the term.[57]

---

[57] Hegel uses the term 'free' in its positive sense, i.e., as describing a set of conditions in which men can realise their potentialities to the full, rather than in the negative sense of being free from coercion.

But, although it is true that Hegel insists that the idea of freedom should be the primary, constitutive principle in the organisation of the nation's life, he would not admit that any such state could obtain unless men were conscious of the idea and the form of the state was internally related to their consciousness of it. This is the reason why, in some of his alternative formulations of the actualisation of the final end, he describes it as a state in which spirit has achieved conscious-ness of its own freedom,[58] and the process leading up to it as 'the progress of the consciousness of freedom'.[59] Freedom, as a fully developed notion, requires man's consciousness of his freedom.

This can be made clearer by a brief glance at some features of Hegel's summary of the process of world history. Here it is necessary to refer only to his description of it in terms of a sequence from a state in which one alone is free, to a state in which some are free, culminating in one in which all are free. In commenting on the initial phase of this sequence, he remarks: 'The orientals do not know that spirit or man as such are free in themselves. And because they do not know this, they are not themselves free. They know only that One is free; but for this very reason, such freedom is mere arbitrariness ... This One is therefore merely a despot, not a free man and a human being'.[60] Later, alluding to the final stage of the sequence, he writes: 'The *Germanic* nations, with the rise of Christianity, were the first to realise that man is by nature free, and that freedom of the spirit is his very essence.'[61]

Here it is asserted that, because the orientals did not know that man as such is free, they were not themselves free. This implies that consciousness of a concept – in this case the concept of freedom – is a necessary condition of its appropriate objective state. The same point is, if anything, made even clearer when, having described the Germanic consciousness, Hegel goes on to assert that 'spirit's consciousness of its own freedom' is a 'precondition of the reality of this freedom'.[62]

Thus there is a conceptual relationship between the objective state of being free and the subjective state of being conscious of one's freedom: these are internally connected aspects of the single condition

---

[58] 'The spirit's consciousness of its own freedom (which is the precondition of the reality of this *freedom*) has been defined as ... the destiny of the spiritual world, and ... as the ultimate end of the world in general.' *Lectures*, p. 55.

[59] *Ibid.*, p. 54.   [60] *Ibid.*, p. 54.   [61] *Ibid.*, p. 54.

[62] See the quotation at n. 58 above.

which Hegel describes as the concrete application or embodiment of the concept of freedom. At the very least, therefore, he is implying that an objective state of social and political affairs presupposes the grasp and application of some concept which is partially constitutive of it.

This suggestion seems, however, to conflict with the earlier claim that for Hegel the idea of freedom is always embodied. For the orientals are here described as *not* having grasped the idea of freedom, despite the fact that they have an institutional life which is involved in the sequence which is made central to the understanding of human history. But this is the result of an ambiguity in Hegel's way of expressing himself, which can give rise to the wrong way of understanding his concept of the final end. He frequently says that the orientals had no concept of freedom, when he means not that they were wholly without it, but that they lacked it in its fully developed form. For it is clear from his own description that they had some, albeit imperfect, concept of freedom, since they at least believed that one – the despot – is free. It follows also, therefore, that he is not denying that objective states of social and political affairs presuppose the consciousness of concepts, since the oriental way of life is organised around consciousness of some concept of freedom.

In this case, however, it becomes necessary to consider a further ambiguity, which turns upon the nature of the relationship between the idea and consciousness. For the suggestion that a way of life, in this case that of the orientals, is organised around a limited or imperfect understanding of the idea of freedom can be interpreted in three irreconcilable ways, the difference between which is fundamental to the meaning of Hegel's theory.

The first possibility is that the concept is logically prior to consciousness of the concept. In this case, to say that the orientals had only an imperfect idea of freedom would be to say that their consciousness should be described as involving a failure to grasp a perfect idea, one that human beings could progressively come to grasp in history. On this interpretation, a history of the development of human consciousness would presuppose an independent account of the principles which determine the development of the concept in terms of which that history is to be described. It would then be incumbent on Hegel to offer an account of the principles appropriate to the development of the concept which was not grounded in an appeal to a developing consciousness of the concept but which could persuade us to accept the latter as partially constitutive of world history.

The second possibility would ascribe logical priority to consciousness. On this view, to say that the orientals had only an imperfect idea of freedom would be to say that the idea which they had was a reflection of an imperfect state of consciousness. But in this case, if consciousness were logically prior to the concept, we should require a grounding for the notions of an *imperfection of consciousness* and of a *development of consciousness* which was independent of any reference to the concept. Changes in the latter would be explained by, but could not themselves explain, changes in the former.

It might, however, be argued that both of these suggestions are alien to Hegel's intentions, on the grounds that it is part of his general position that consciousness and concepts cannot exist apart from each other. We must therefore accept a third possibility: that consciousness and concept form a logical unity. Thus consciousness and concept would require each other, and whatever principle were invoked to explain their development must apply equally to both. But if this were so, it would follow that any principle adduced to explain their mutual development would need to be both independent of them and yet more basic. We would seem, therefore, to be moving further from, rather than closer to, the claim that 'reason governs the world and that world history is therefore a rational process'.[63]

The argument for this third possibility is, however, fallacious. For although it is true that Hegel believes that consciousness and concepts require one another, this is a condition solely of their *existence*. But it is compatible with the principle that concepts cannot exist without consciousness or consciousness without concepts, that one should be logically prior to the other, in the sense that the development of their existential unity should be explained by a principle which pertains in the first place to one rather than the other. To take a simple example: although governing bodies cannot exist without subjects or subjects without governing bodies, this fact provides no reason to preclude the possibility that their mutual development may be explained by changes which go on in one rather than in the other.

To see where the priority lies, it is useful to return to Hegel's remark that the orientals are not free because they do not have the concept of

63 *Lectures*, p. 27.

freedom. Despite this, as we have seen, Hegel does not deny that their behaviour is governed by recognition of *some* concept, i.e., by recognition that one, the despot, is free. So, although he insists that this does not constitute the concept of freedom as such, for it lacks the universality which concepts must have when they are fully appropriate to their subject matter, it remains the case that it governs the structure of relationships which exist between the despot and his subjects.

In support of this point, it should further be noted that it is not open to Hegel to hold that the failure to implement the fully developed concept of freedom – that in which the *actualisation* of the idea consists – in the early phases of history derives from some shortcoming or lack of insight in man. For there is, in fact, at this stage, no fully developed concept into which he could have insight. The concept of freedom is, as Hegel sometimes says, an *ideal*.[64] Its progressive acquisition is, so to speak, identical with its progressive creation.[65] It is true, of course, that he maintains that this progressive creation requires a long period of painful experience on the part of man. But to say that the concept has to be created, and to be created with pain, is not to say that its development is nothing but the outcome of painful decisions taken by man. On the contrary, as we shall see, every phase in its development involves a necessity which stems not from the pain of human experience but from the structure of the idea itself. Human experience is painful not because man has an imperfect grasp of a fully developed concept which would be accessible to him if only his understanding were more developed, but because, at difference phases in its concrete development, the idea has inner contradictions in it, which give rise to the pain which men suffer.[66]

These considerations support the view that Hegel accepted the proposition that institutions presuppose concepts or, to put the point more generally, that human activity is structured by concepts which are logically prior to the activities themselves. He is therefore free of

---

[64] *Ibid.*, p. 66.

[65] 'The spirit is free; and the aim of the world spirit in world history is to realise its essence and to obtain the prerogative of freedom. Its activity is that of knowing and recognising itself, but it accomplishes this in gradual stages rather than in a single step.' *Ibid.*, p. 63.

'It might equally be said that the spirit produces its concept out of itself, objectivises it, and thus becomes the being of its own concept.' *Ibid.*, p. 64.

[66] For a more extended discussion of this important point, see below, pp. 108–14 and 117ff.

one of the difficulties which beset Hume: his inability to allow concepts the ontological status necessary for the existence of institutions and, hence, both for their development and a history of that development. Nevertheless, if this account is correct, Hegel has now set himself the task of showing how ideas in general, and the all-important idea of freedom in particular, develop. For, even if it is true that ideas cannot have an existence outside the sphere of human conduct and experience, he is committed to the logical priority of ideas, and of the principles of their development, over the activities and experiences which are structured by them. In addition, moreover, he is committed to justifying his claim that, from the point of view of a philosophical history of the world, the actualisation of the idea of freedom as the final end of history is an indispensable part of the 'valid perspective' which is required.

THE EFFICIENT CAUSE

It is possible now to turn to the second distinction mentioned earlier: the efficient cause, or the means, whereby the final end of history is to be realised. For this purpose, it is necessary to attend more directly to the Hegelian conception of mind or spirit and, in particular, to the distinction between the concrete idea of freedom, which forms its essence, and the will or volition by which the idea is to be developed to its fullest extent and, in this form, made to enter into the whole social and political life of a people or a community.

Hegel introduces the concept of will or volition because, he says, 'nothing whatsoever has been accomplished without the active interest of those concerned in it; and since interest can be described as passion (in so far as the whole individuality, to the exclusion of all other actual or possible interests and aims, applies itself to an object with every fibre of the will, and concentrates all its resources on attaining its end), we may say without qualification that *nothing great has been accomplished in the world without passion*'.[67] What he is talking of here may be called a governing or ruling interest, one which people are determined to satisfy. To put the matter in this way, however, is potentially misleading, in so far as it may suggest that the agent's volition is focused on some purely private interest. But this is not what Hegel means, for he dismisses from the field of world history

[67] *Lectures*, p. 73.

all actions which satisfy *purely* private interests. In doing so, however, he does not intend to deny that individuals have the right to be personally satisfied by the fulfilment of their interests. In fact, this is explicitly asserted as their right.[68] He is making the different point that the interests which are relevant, no matter why they are the interests of any specific individual, are those in which the individual may share *qua* member of the community and which can thus become the compelling force for communal deeds.[69] The interests thus involve public aims, in the furtherance of which individuals, *qua* members of communities, become wholly engrossed.

Hegel is thus insisting upon two points. The final end is fulfilled by means of the activities of individuals. The right of the individual to act in such a manner as to satisfy his desires is therefore preserved. At the same time, however, the means is limited to that sub-class of activities in which the individual, as a social agent, shares in ideas of a communal nature, i.e., ideas which have an internal reference to communal or social roles, rights, duties, obligations and powers. These are ideas in which, because of the social side of their nature, individuals can take a real interest, thus deriving personal satisfaction from them, and yet in virtue of which they have a supra-personal ontological status, i.e., are internally related parts of social wholes.

The means, therefore, are the activities of individuals in their public roles, in virtue of which they are involved in the realm of public debate. Whether, for example, a certain form of land-holding should be accepted in a given society will require discussion of general considerations relevant to the point or function of land-holding in general and of others more specific to the series of reciprocal relationships which will need to be observed, and to which behaviour will need to conform, if the change is made. These considerations are, moreover, objective or autonomous. They hold, that is to say, irrespective of the purely personal character of any individuals who may be involved in decisions to which they are relevant at a given historical time. This does not mean, of course, that they are invariant

[68] 'If I put something into practice and gave it a real existence, I must have some personal interest in doing so; I must be personally involved in it, and hope to obtain satisfaction through its accomplishment – in other words my own interest must be at stake.' *Ibid.*, p. 70.

[69] 'I shall therefore continue to use the word passion, by which I understand the determinate aspects of character and volition insofar as they do not have a purely private content, but are the effective motive force behind actions whose significance is universal.' *Ibid.*, p. 73.

as regards history.[70] On the contrary, they alter and develop in history. But at no given point do they depend upon the purely personal characteristics of those involved in the debate. They derive their force instead from defects in the system in which they inhere, a system which pervades and structures the life of man in his public practice and social consciousness, rather than in his purely private conduct and purely personal consciousness.

It follows that, while social conduct and ideas presuppose the *existence* of individuals, they are not reducible to individual conduct or ideas. It must be noted, however, that Hegel's insistence upon the logical priority and objectivity of concepts and upon their fundamental ontological status commits him to neither their metaphysical nor their phenomenal *independence*. The claim that considerations relevant to the desirability of a certain institution are internal to a whole institutional context entails neither that institutions could exist without people nor that they could exist without affecting, and being affected by, the *experience* of people. But what they are affected by are considerations which arise from the experience of people involved in the institutions, the character of which, in turn, depends upon the nature of the ideas which structure the institutions.[71]

The final end of history is, therefore, to be actualised via public activities, the character of which is explained by the system of ideas which is internal to the whole set of public institutions. At this point, however, it is necessary to take account of a further complicating factor. This is that, although the actualisation of freedom is the end to be realised by means of these activities, the ideas involved in the means often have little or no apparent connection with the idea of freedom. Hegel's position thus seems inconsistent. For although he wants to insist that institutions presuppose ideas, and that the development of systems of institutions in world history presupposes the successive phases of the development of the idea of freedom, the ideas which are presupposed by the means whereby the end is actualised comprise a totally different set of ideas. It looks, therefore, as though in describing the activities based upon these ideas as the means, indeed, the only possible means, for the actualisation of the idea of freedom, he is producing a means which is at best only externally or contingently related to the final end – if, indeed, it is related to it at all – and thus allowing that it is a matter of mere

[70] This is ruled out by Hegel's rejection of the constancy thesis.
[71] This point is developed further below, pp. 111–13.

chance whether the end has been, or will be, actualised. But if this were so he would be unable to maintain his claim that 'reason has ruled and continues to rule the world'.[72] For it would certainly not be in virtue of the development of the idea of freedom that its underlying pattern had arisen.

Hegel is well aware of the difficulty involved here. To see why he feels it necessary to introduce the claim which gives rise to it, and how he attempts to resolve it, it is necessary to examine a number of further concepts which he introduces, including those of the world-historical individual, the cunning of reason and the material cause of history.

To locate the source of the problem, it is useful to turn to Hegel's insistence upon the sacrifices involved in world history. 'Without rhetorical exaggeration', he writes, 'we need only compile an accurate account of the misfortunes which have overtaken the finest manifestations of national and political life, and of personal virtues or innocence, to see a most terrifying picture take shape before our eyes. Its effect is to intensify our feelings to an extreme pitch of hopeless sorrow with no redeeming circumstances to counterbalance it. We can only harden ourselves against it by telling ourselves that it was ordained by fate and could not have been otherwise ... But even as we look upon history as an altar upon which the happiness of nations, the wisdom of states, and the virtue of individuals are slaughtered, our thoughts inevitably impel us to ask: *to whom* or *to what ultimate end* have these monstrous sacrifices been made?' Nevertheless, he continues, from this beginning, 'we proceeded to define those same events which afford so sad a spectacle for gloomy sentiments and brooding reflection as no more than the *means* whereby what we have specified as the substantial destiny, the absolute and final end, or in other words, the true *result* of world history, is realised'.[73]

In considering this passage, it must be borne in mind that the agents who suffer are public agents. Hegel does not, of course, wish to deny that individuals can and do suffer in their private capacities. Nevertheless, he has expressly removed such individuals – and, hence, *a fortiori*, anything which pertains to them in their private capacities – from the field of world history.[74] The activities which are relevant to the means whereby the end of world history is actualised

---

[72] *Lectures*, p. 33.   [73] *Ibid.*, pp. 68–9.   [74] See above, pp. 92–3.

are public activities, and the suffering which is relevant to it is the suffering which these involve.

It must also be noted that, at the end of the passage, the activities of these agents are said to constitute only the means for the realisation of freedom. The reason for this restriction is that men do not, when engaging in them, know the final end as such. Their activities further the development of freedom without their knowing that the latter is the final end of history or that they are contributing to its realisation in the way in which they are.

This can be most easily seen if we turn to what Hegel says in the case of 'world-historical individuals', i.e., those great figures upon whose activities some of the most important developments in history depend.[75] For, despite the importance of their decisions and actions for the development of freedom, neither do they realise this importance nor are their decisions taken with knowledge of the idea of

[75] *Lectures*, p. 83. There is considerable disagreement over the degree of importance which should be attached to the activities of world-historical individuals. Hegel admired them greatly and levels some of his harshest criticism against those who fail to see, or try to belittle, the nature of their achievements: ' "No man is a hero to his valet de chambre" is a well known saying. I have added ... "not because the former is not a hero, but because the latter is a valet".' *Lectures*, pp. 87–8. The problem is not about his admiration for them but whether or not this may have led him to ascribe to them a status which his general theoretical framework does not require. O'Brien maintains that they are necessary, by arguing that, while passion is the means or efficient cause of the actualisation of the final end, world-historical beings are required to 'impress their passion ... onto a society'. *Hegel on Reason and History*, p. 125, but see also the prior discussion, pp. 116ff. But this appears to invert the order of dependence. For it is clear that world-historical individuals would never be able to achieve the things which they do do if what they try to do is not, obscurely, felt to be needed. Thus the developing content of the idea must already be internalised within the general consciousness of the society in which the hero operates. The success of the world-historical individual depends, therefore, upon the fact that he expresses what is already, as a matter of rational passion, understood to be needed rather than because he moulds that passion according to his own. The crucial point here is that the world-historical individual's actions can have an enduring effect only if there is a ground of support for them in the rational passion of other less gifted members of the community. Thus, world-historical individuals see the way forward, 'for they are the far-sighted ones ... And the others, as already remarked, flock to their standard, for it is they who express what the age requires ... The others feel that this is so and have to obey them.' *Ibid.*, pp. 83–4. If this were not so, Hegel would be unable to explain why some great men, such as Napoleon, contribute to the course of world history while others, apparently as gifted, such as Charlemagne, do not. If this is correct, there is no need for O'Brien to argue for the indispensability of world-historical individuals. Theoretically their parts could be played by a sub-community, a group of conspirators, or, at some points in world history, by the people itself. On the question of their 'ambivalent' place, see also Avineri, pp. 230–2.

freedom as such. For, Hegel writes, 'it is possible to distinguish between the insight of such individuals and the realisation that even such manifestations of the spirit as this are no more than moments within the universal idea. To understand this is the prerogative of philosophy. World-historical individuals have no need to do so. They know and will their own enterprise, because the time is ripe for it and it is inwardly present.'[76] Thus not even the activities of world-historical individuals are guided by knowledge of the idea of freedom or of the significance of what they are doing for the development of that idea. Their activities usually originate from some private aim and the passion with which this is sought. In fact, as Hegel points out, this is so obvious that it is all too easy to interpret the whole significance of what they do in such terms: 'It is indeed possible to interpret their lives in terms of passion, and to put the emphasis on moral judgements by declaring that it was their passions which motivated them'.[77] Since passion is required for anything great to be done this is hardly surprising. But it is also a mistake, for great men of this kind 'admittedly do seem to follow only the dictates of their passions and of their own free will, but the object of their will is universal, and it is this which constitutes their pathos ... In this respect the aim of passion and that of the Idea are one and the same; passion is the absolute unity of individual character and the universal. The way in which the spirit in its subjective individuality here coincides exactly with the Idea has an almost animal quality about it'.[78]

The significance of the actions of world-historical individuals lies, therefore, in the fact that the change which is the object of their passion is *identical* with a change which is necessary for the process whereby freedom is actualised. The world-historical individual does not know that this is so. He cannot, indeed, know it, for such knowledge is the product of philosophical history. What he needs to know is that the enterprise upon which he is engaged is both possible and necessary, for 'the time is ripe for it'. World-historical individuals are thus men of genius who both see what is wrong with the state and what can and must be done about it. But they have no idea that, in taking these steps, they are acting in a way required by the development of freedom.[79]

---

[76] *Lectures*, p. 83.   [77] *Ibid.*, p. 86.   [78] *Ibid.*, p. 86.

[79] There is considerable dispute also over the degree to which the world-historical individual is conscious of the idea which he is instrumental in realising. Avineri argues that Hegel holds at times that the world-historical individual is '(i) wholly

A certain species of public activity, guided by insight into what is institutionally possible, is thus the means for the concrete development of a principle of which the agents in question are not aware. In this case, however, the apparent incoherence in Hegel's position remains. The introduction of the activities of world-historical individuals has done nothing to remove it, for there is, so far, no explanation of the *identity* of the object of their will with what the actualisation of freedom requires. It is in this connection, however, that Hegel now introduces the concept of the cunning of reason:

> The particular interests of passion cannot therefore be separated from the realisation of the universal . . . Particular interests contend with one another, and some are destroyed in the process. But it is from this very conflict and destruction of particular things that the universal emerges, and it remains unscathed itself. For it is not the universal Idea which enters into opposition, conflict, and danger; it keeps itself in the background, untouched and unharmed, and sends forth the particular interests of passion to fight and wear themselves out in its stead. It is what we may call the *cunning of reason* that it sets the passions to work in its service, so that the agents by which it gives itself existence must pay the penalty and suffer the loss.[80]

The cunning of reason consists not in the fact that freedom develops through a process of public activity of which it is not the conscious object, although this is certainly something which Hegel believes. It consists in the further fact that the suffering and loss

conscious of the idea and its history, (ii) only instinctively conscious of it and (iii) totally unaware of it' and concludes that there is no adequate explanation for these contradictory statements, p. 253. Charles Taylor, on the other hand, taking a more sympathetic view, argues that Avineri makes insufficient allowance for careless wording in a text which was never prepared for publication. He concludes that 'world-historical individuals have a sense of the highest truth they serve, but, they see it through a glass darkly', p. 393, n. 1. If the point made earlier is correct, however, and the idea is meant to be something more like an ideal, which is created progressively in the course of world history, Taylor's claim cannot be correct, for there is no higher truth, in the sense of some formulation of the final end, into which to see darkly. These problems arise, I believe, from a failure to take into account the relationship between the efficient and material cause in Hegel's theory, as I shall try to explain below.

[80] *Lectures*, p. 89. Cf. *Hegel's Logic*, pp. 272–3: 'Reason is as cunning as it is powerful. Cunning may be said to lie in the intermediative action which, while it permits the objects to follow their own bent and to act upon one another until they waste away, and does not itself directly interfere in the process, is nevertheless only working out its own aims. With this explanation, Divine Providence may be said to stand to the world and its process in the capacity of absolute cunning. God lets men do as they please with their particular passions and interests; but the result is the accomplishment of – not their plans but his, and these differ decidedly from the ends primarily sought by those whom he employs.'

which must be incurred belong to the agents and aims involved in the means but not to the idea of freedom itself, even though the latter can exist only in these agents and aims.

This passage must not, of course, be understood literally, as though to imply that some *deus ex machina* were, in a wholly inexplicable manner, manipulating puppets for its own ends. Hegel himself indicates that this is not so by pointing out, at the end of the passage, that the agents by which reason achieves its ends are the very agents in virtue of whom it exists. Reason is something which exists in and through human activity, or, at least some part of it, not something which exists over and above it.

Indeed, it is by reference to a distinction between two parts of the *phenomenal* world, of which one is 'worthless' but the other of 'positive value', that Hegel proceeds to explain himself. The worthless part consists of the individual lives and aims which are sacrificed. Even Caesar comes into this category: he 'had to do what was necessary to overthrow the decaying freedom of Rome; he himself met his end in the struggle, but necessity triumphed.'[81] What is worthless here are Caesar's life, his aims and his passions. The part which is of positive value consists in three areas of spiritual life: ethics, morality and religiosity. These are among the 'spiritual determinants' which, as Hegel mentioned earlier,[82] must be taken into account and contained within the 'valid perspective' necessary for philosophical history. But these, he now proceeds to argue, are too important to be viewed as a means, even for the development of reason or freedom. The introduction of the spiritual determinants at this point is crucial for the explanation of the identity of the change which is the object of public passion with that which is required for the actualisation of freedom. For without them this identity would be left ungrounded, with disastrous consequences for the claim that reason rules the world. To see how the introduction of the spiritual determinants affects the situation, however, it is necessary to turn to Hegel's account of the material cause of world history.

THE MATERIAL CAUSE

The actualisation of the final end of history requires the development of a system of public life, the form and content of which is dependent upon man's conscious understanding of the idea of freedom as his

---

[81] *Lectures*, p. 89.   [82] See pp. 81 above and 100–1 below.

own real substance, i.e., his knowledge that he is at once both the creator and the creation of the state. In such circumstances the state will no longer seem, as it will at earlier periods in world history, something hostile and alien to the individual or, at best, a necessary evil. It will, on the contrary, be positively welcomed by the individual, for he will see that it provides the true conditions for the creation and expression of individuality as such.

It is clear that, given Hegel's insistence upon the satisfaction of self-interest as the legitimate right of every individual, such a state can be achieved only after a very considerable transformation of the individual, of his conception of individuality and of his understanding of his relationship to the state. It is for this transformation that the spiritual determinants, which Hegel says are too fundamental to be a means, are necessary. For these are the areas of the inner life of the nation in which the process of spirit's self-development occurs as it works itself towards its end:

We must now consider more closely the further determination of national spirit, its internal differentiation, and the essentially necessary phenomena in which the spirit appears as self-activating and self-determining: for these are the qualities which make it what it is. When we speak of a nation, we must analyse those powers in which the spirit particularises itself. These powers are religion, the constitution, the system of justice (including civil right), industry, trade, arts and science, and the military world, the world of valour, by which one nation is distinguished from the other ... All the features which stand out in the history of a nation are intimately connected with one another. The history of a nation consists solely of that process whereby the nation impresses on all the spheres of its activity the spirit's concept of its own nature. In other words, the state, religion, art, the system of justice, and the relation of the nation to other nations – all of these are aspects in which the spirit's concept of itself is realised, in which the spirit contrives to perceive itself and to know itself as an existent world, and to have itself as its own object.[83]

The reason why Hegel refuses to designate morality, religion, art, the constitution and so on, i.e., the 'spiritual determinants', as a mere means, then, is that these are the areas in which the transformations of consciousness and will, in which the concrete self-development of spirit consists, are actually taking place. It is here that man is an end in himself because it is in virtue of his involvement in these activities that he participates in the free self-determination of reason. In the

[83] *Lectures*, p. IOI.

activities proper to these spheres consciousness and will transform themselves.

The important point here is that, in a theory in which transformations of consciousness and will play such a central part, it is not sufficient to have an account of some means whereby transformations take place. We require also an account of something concrete which is both capable of being transformed and of providing the ongoing material for further transformations. Hegel's claim is that it is in the worlds of the spiritual determinants that the material of such transformation is to be found.

Before leaving this point, one further thing must be noted. Hegel tells us that it is in these areas of human activity that spirit's concept of itself is realised, that it contrives to perceive itself and to have itself as its own object. This means that the transformations of spirit which constitute the core of the developmental process which philosophical history traces take place primarily in these areas. But we must again be careful not to infer from this that reason is logically reducible to them. Reason can *exist* only as embodied in the activities of individuals within these areas of life. But, as noted earlier, it can nevertheless be logically prior to them in the sense that it is a principle which is proper to its development which determines how they develop and not one proper to them which determines how it develops. Hegel makes this very clear when giving his reason why the spiritual determinants cannot be mere means: 'man is an end in himself only by virtue of that divine principle within him which we have all along referred to as reason (or, in so far as it is internally active and self-determining, as freedom); and . . . we may nevertheless assert that religiosity, ethics etc., have their roots and source in this principle and are therefore essentially elevated above external necessity and chance'.[84] Thus, even if we take the spiritual determinants to be the forms of activity in which spirit is working out its own development, and their historical stages to be the stages of its development, we must still recognise that, in so far as they are *rooted* in it, reason is logically prior to them.

It is not possible to trace in detail how all this occurs in the various spheres of activity to which Hegel attaches particular importance. It might be helpful, however, to give just one example, that of religion, to show how the self-development which occurs in it is at the same

[84] *Ibid.*, p. 90.

time a self-development which is essential for spirit's final consciousness of its own freedom in a particular form of the state. Religion is
one of the most important areas in which spirit particularises itself.[85]
Hegel sees it as so closely connected with the determinate forms of
different states that he claims that the latter are 'founded on' and
have 'emerged from' different religions.[86] Religion, he asserts, is 'the
nations' consciousness of its own being and of the highest being ... A
nation conceives of God in the same way as it conceives of itself and of
its relationship to God, so that its religion is also its conception of
itself.'[87] On the other hand, the final end of history is spirit's
consciousness of its own freedom, a condition which requires that the
community of individuals wills the state because it affords the conditions of their own freedom, while recognising that it exists only in
virtue of their willing it.[88] It thus requires a certain understanding of
the relation of the objective to the subjective. But religion is concerned
with the various ways in which this can be understood through the
relation of the individual to God. It thus provides an understanding
which, in a rational world, must not only be worked out to its rational
conclusion, i.e., the identity of the individual and God, but which
includes, as a part of that conclusion, the application of the whole
conception to the relationship between the individual and the state.[89]

[85] *Ibid.*, p. 101.
[86] *Ibid.*, p. 108. Hegel adds: 'Thus the state and its constitution will correspond to the
religion which underlies them, ... so that the Athenian or Roman state, for
example, was possible only in conjunction with the specific form of paganism
practised by the nations in question, just as a Catholic state will have a different
spirit and constitution from a Protestant one.'
[87] *Ibid.*, p. 105.
[88] 'The living reality of the state within its individual members is what we call its
ethical life. The state and its laws and institutions belong to these individuals ... All
this is their property just as they are its property ...' *Ibid.*, pp. 102–3.
[89] 'In religion ... the national principle receives its simplest expression and it is on
religion that the nation's entire existence is based ... In this respect, religion is
intimately associated with the principle of the state ... Conscious freedom can only
exist when all individual things are recognised as having their positive existence
within the divine being and when subjectivity is related to the divine being itself.
Thus, the principle of the state, the universe on which its existence depends, is
recognised as an absolute, as a determination of the divine being itself.' *Ibid.*, p. 107.
In view of remarks like this, it is surprising that O'Brien should minimise the
importance of the notion of divinity in Hegel's philosophy of history. He does so
because, he argues, the crucial analytic distinction in Hegel's philosophy of history
is that between nature, which is not self-transforming, and spirit, which transforms
itself. Any attempt to identify God with spirit, he claims, must endanger this
distinction, since the traditional Christian God is creator both of nature and of spirit,
p. 106. Kaufmann similarly dismisses Hegel's references to God as 'mere frills'
occasioned by local circumstances, p. 165. Berry correctly opposes both of these

THE RELATIONSHIP BETWEEN THE FINAL,
EFFICIENT AND MATERIAL CAUSES

In the light of the foregoing discussion, Hegel's position may now be restated in the following way. The means for the realisation of the final end *are* certain public activities undertaken by men who are not conscious of that end as such. It is not correct, however, to say that they are wholly without any notion of it. For the ideas involved in ethics, religion, and so on – the areas in which spirit particularises itself and in which it is self-activating and self-determining[90] – form part of their being. These ideas are, however, internally related to the final end, since they have the idea as their ground and since the idea carries its end within itself. Hence, in taking part in activities which are grounded in reason's self-determination in these areas, men are, *mediately*, sharing in the process of reason's coming to be conscious of itself. It is true that the individuals involved and even some of the specific causes in which they engage are 'sacrificed' or lost, but the concrete development of the idea of freedom is not impeded by this because, since the whole process is grounded in reason, with its internal end, certain rational structures of consciousness and society grow and develop. The cunning of reason thus consists in the fact that, because reason is the *ground* of the public causes into which individuals put their effort, the changes which occur through them are necessary for the process of the actualisation of the final end.

The position as stated is still, however, not free from difficulties, both of interpretation and of philosophical coherence. One problem arises from the emphasis given to reason in the areas of activity which are *internally* connected to the final end and which ground public activity. For it is now difficult to see why any activities which arise under this influence should be described as merely the *means* whereby the end is actualised. Another concerns the apparently contradictory claim that, in precisely those areas, man is said not to

views and insists that the 'religious dimension in Hegel's philosophy cannot be over-emphasised', p. 181. Nevertheless, he also errs, in believing that Hegel's philosophy of history does not involve the secularisation or, at least, the socialisation, of the divine in the Hegelian notion of the state. For God and man, the infinite and the finite, the universal and the particular and so on always both require and are required by each other, and their final reconciliation is achieved when spirit, which exists only in and through man, becomes conscious of its own freedom, i.e., when a certain kind of state comes into being.

[90] *Lectures*, p. 101.

be a means after all but to be an *end in himself* and, as such, to constitute the *material* of history.

To take the latter point first, it has already been noted that the activities in question have been described formally as those motivated by passions with a public content.[91] It must be said, however, that Hegel is far from consistent on this point and often talks as though they include 'particular' interests of any kind.[92] In his more careful statements, however, he makes it clear that it is only those which have a public cause or issue as their content, no matter why this should be adopted in the case of any given historical agent, which are the means for the actualisation of the idea.[93] There need, however, be no real inconsistency in the two ways of talking, provided that it is accepted that, when he suggests that more or less any particular need, interest or subjective idea *may* be part of the means whereby spirit actualises the final end, this be understood as carrying the proviso that only such of these are relevant to world history as have public causes as their content. In other words, he is excluding from the means private interests with a private content, but including private interests with a public content. This amounts, in effect, to saying that the particular reason why an agent engages in an activity is irrelevant to the question whether it is a means according to Hegel's theory. All that matters is the content of the activity, that it be public rather than private.

It is true, as we have already seen, that Hegel's excessive admiration for world-historical individuals leads him to deny this in their case and to talk as if their particular interest is always the public cause itself.[94] But there is really no need for him to deny that gifted individuals can have great insight into what it is necessary to do, and be the first to give public formulation to what their fellows recognise implicitly,[95] while yet having unworthy motives for doing so. There is no need, for example, in asserting that Caesar's greatness lay in his having perceived that the republic was a lie, because the laws of *auctoritas* and *dignitas* had fallen into abeyance, and that this hollow structure must be replaced by one such as he – but also, eventually,

---

[91] See above, pp. 92–4.
[92] 'Thus, what we have called the subjective element – i.e., needs, impulses, passions, particular interests, and opinions or subjective ideas ... This vast conglomeration of volition, interests, and activities is the sum total of *instruments* and means which the world spirit employs to accomplish its end ... ', *Lectures*, p. 74.
[93] See above, n. 69.   [94] *Lectures*, pp. 87–8.   [95] *Ibid.*, p. 84.

others – saw to be necessary,[96] to maintain that he could not have been motivated by a desire for the personal glory which might come from achieving it. For unless this is at least *possible* in the case of world-historical individuals, it is difficult to see how it could be possible in the case of those who give them their support. But if the latter is not allowed, we should have to subscribe to the implausible doctrine that everybody who takes part, to a greater or lesser extent, in the momentous events of world history is *motivated* by a sense of the necessity of what he is doing.

The means, then, are certain public activities which take place within the areas of life designated as 'particularisations of spirit', in which man is an end in himself. When Hegel talks of a means–end relationship in history, however, he does not intend this to be understood in any ordinary sense, i.e., in the sense that the means is an external or contingent cause of that which it brings about. He has little sympathy in general with the idea that any means can lie in a purely external relationship to an end.[97] When it comes to the question of the means–end relationship in history, however, he wholly rejects such a conception: 'And the relationship of human beings to the end of reason is least of all that of a means in this purely external sense; for in fulfilling the end of reason, they not only simultaneously fulfil their own particular ends (whose content is quite different from that of the universal end), but also *participate* in the end of reason itself, and are therefore ends in their own right ... Individual human beings are ... *ends in themselves* by virtue of the content of the end which they serve. And under this category we must include all that we would exempt from the category of means, namely morality, ethics and religiosity. Man is an end in himself only by virtue of that divine principle within him which we have all along referred to as reason (or, in so far as it is internally active and self-determining, as freedom).'[98]

The key notion here is that of the *simultaneous fulfilment* of two things: man's own particular ends and the ends of reason, in virtue of which man is an end in himself. In the light of the foregoing exposition, the reference to man's particular ends must not be

[96] *Ibid.*, p. 89.
[97] A key might be thought of as the means for opening a lock. But even here, Hegel would argue, some reference to the idea of a lock is involved in that of a key, so that the means–end relationship is not purely external but involves reciprocally related notions.
[98] *Lectures*, p. 90.

thought of as a reference to a *purely* private end. It is a reference to a public end which he, as an individual, and for whatever *personal* reason, has made the object of his passion. He does not know that it is also reason's end but, in so far as it is also an expression of a necessity in one of the areas in which reason particularises itself, man here *participates* in reason's end. To see this we may revert to Hegel's example of Caesar's overthrow of the republic in the light of his knowledge of its 'hollow structure'. Here Caesar has his own particular reason for engaging in this activity. Let us assume again that this is a desire for self-glory. The activity is nevertheless a public activity, the necessity for which is felt, albeit obscurely, by others who support him, because it is grounded in one of the areas, that of the constitution, in which reason particularises itself. In perceiving or feeling this necessity, Caesar and his followers show an appreciation of the real or rational needs of the situation. But this is their own situation, and in acting thus they are expressing their rationality. The connection between their own particular ends and that of reason is therefore secured via the mediation of the grounding which the public cause which they support has in a particular area of reason.

They may thus be said to *participate* in reason's end, without this carrying any such implausible implication as that their actions involve some hazy perception of the fact that what they are doing is necessary in order for reason's end to be actualised. What their actions reveal is an appreciation of what reason *now* needs, in the area in which it has particularised itself, which is their special concern. Since reason can achieve its end only through the actions of finite individuals and finite communities, they can also be said to serve it or be its means. But they can be *its* means only because, mediately, they share in its end. The potentially disastrous externality of the means is overcome by the fact that man can only be reason's means in so far as, mediately, he also shares its end.

This should not be taken to imply that the hero does not have insight into a rational requirement of the situation. He realises what is wrong with it and why and how it must be changed. What he does not and *cannot* realise, however, for this is the prerogative of the philosophical historian, is the final end for the actualisation of which his action is necessary. He is taking a rational part in a rational process, but there is an aspect of that rationality, that what he is doing is necessary for the actualisation of the final end, which is hidden from him. Not merely is this hidden but it is necessarily hidden, since the conception of the final end which is made concrete when it is actualised does not yet exist. His action is, in fact, part of the process of the *self-formulation* of the final end. Hence it is correctly described as that of *participating* in reason's end.

It is possible now to rescue Hegel from the criticism that he is unable to show how individual actions can be the means to the fulfilment of reason's end. For, on the above account, the individual passions which are relevant are those which are grounded in certain aspects of reason. They may, indeed, be thought of as expressions of it or, better, as expressions through which it progressively becomes conscious of its own nature. They are not, therefore, merely causally connected to the final end. For they are means only in so far as they are also the mediate ends which are necessary to the self-formulation of the final end.[99]

DIALECTIC AND THE FINAL END

It is necessary now to address the further difficulty of understanding the sense in which history can be said to be that sequence of transformations of consciousness and ways of public life whereby reason actualises a final end which is *internal* to itself. For Hegel insists that reason is a principle *within* man, yet man has no consciousness of its final end as such, but only of certain other ends by which, on the above interpretation, because they are said to be grounded in reason, the final end can be said to be mediated. But matters cannot be left in this way. For unless Hegel can show how the *mediating* ends are internally related to the self-formulation of the final end, he will be unable to defend himself against the charge that what he calls the actualisation of the final end is simply that state of affairs, *whatever it be*, which *happens* to ensue from the activities described as the means of its realisation, rather than one on behalf of which they, and they alone, must occur. The question at issue,

[99] In Chapter 6 of his *Philosophy of History*, William Dray gives a sympathetic account of the operations of spirit as something immanent in history: 'It is nothing apart from the actions of individuals which unconsciously express its "activity" of self-development'. Nevertheless, he concludes that Hegel fails to offer a 'general account of the way individual actions come to "express" the purposive activity of the World Spirit', p. 81. This conclusion derives from his failure to see that the actions which are the means to the fulfilment of reason's end are grounded in the rational material of human consciousness, i.e., in the areas in which spirit particularises itself.

therefore, is how to make sense of the notion that the final end is internally related to the process whereby it develops. If this cannot be done, the idea that there is a final end on behalf of which certain things must occur in history will become vacuous or, at best, misleading.

To take the matter further, we must now consider some features of the transforming character of dialectical processes in history, which have so far been disregarded. This is a very large subject and the following remarks are, necessarily, highly selective. We may begin by recalling two of Hegel's claims. The first is that the final end of history is the realisation of a state in which reason is conscious of its own freedom. The second is that this is possible only via the development of a series of prior distinctions, at the level of both objective and subjective mind, within the spheres of the spiritual determinants. It is with this developmental process that the notion of dialectical trans-formation is history is concerned. To gain an initial idea of it, it is useful to turn to some explanatory remarks which Hegel makes when he gives his account of the first three main divisions of history, in the section entitled 'The Phases of World History' in the Appendix to the Introduction.[100]

History, he begins, can assume a developmental character only when, in implicit form, the principle of reason becomes active. It does so when it is recognised that at least one person, the despot or patriarch, is free. In this state, reason exists primarily as an aspect of the institutions of a country, forming a system of laws, duties and obligations concerned with the necessities of organised social life. From the subjective point of view, however, only one individual, the ruler, has any form of freedom, for recognition of his individual will is concretely established in the form of the system of institutions in question. Other individuals are not free, for the idea that the state should rest upon their wills is recognised neither in the form of the system of institutions nor in their own subjective consciousness. As against the state, therefore, they have no rights, nor need the laws of the state conform to their desires. Their attitude to the state, as a matter of subjective consciousness, is one of 'faith, trust and obedi-ence'.[101]

The most important point to notice here is that Hegel claims that, despite its primitive character, this situation contains 'all the determi-

---

[100] *Lectures*, pp. 196–209.   [101] *Ibid.*, p. 198.

nations of reason ... all that is contained within the Idea is essentially present and existent; but everything depends on the *manner* in which it is present, and whether its moments have been realised in their authentic form. And since subjectivity is an essential moment within the spirit, it must be present too.'[102] Objective freedom exists in so far as there is a public form of ordered life, which is autonomous in that the individual subject adopts 'an attitude of complete subservience' to it and does not think that it need accord to his will.[103] But although the individual does not know that he is free, he knows that somebody, the despot, is free, for he is thought of as embodying the will of the state, while other individuals 'have not yet attained true subjective freedom within themselves but appear as accidental properties within the underlying substance'.[104] In *some* form, then, both substantial or objective freedom and subjective freedom are present and 'the sole purpose of world history is to create a situation in which these two poles are absolutely united and truly reconciled'.[105] Thus all of the elements of spirit are present, although in a wholly unharmonised and only implicitly rational way, and the purpose of world history is to bring about their proper or rational reconciliation.

From these unharmonised elements, Hegel proceeds to trace the sequence which constitutes spirit's development. The guiding idea is the sequence of mutually connected transformations of concrete systems of institutional, national life and states of subjective consciousness by which a reconciliation is reached such that 'their free spirit is not submerged in the objective existence of the spirit, but is accorded its own independent rights; and at the same time the absolute spirit, the realm of pure objective unity, realises its absolute right'.[106] This sequence, as Hegel stresses, is dialectical in character.

A few points of reference may help to make this clearer. Although all the elements of spirit are present in the state of oriental despotism, this is a relatively static state: there is insufficient individual freedom in it for a genuine tension to develop between objective and subjective will. Only when, as in classical Greece, the state has sufficiently impressed its character on its members, in whom morality becomes an inner principle, can the state properly be said to have begun to

---

[102] *Ibid.*, p. 201.   [103] *Ibid.*, p. 197.   [104] *Ibid.*, p. 199.
[105] *Ibid.*, p. 198.
[106] *Ibid.*, p. 198.

develop its negation, i.e., the principle of subjective freedom,[107] from within itself, and a properly dialectical transformation can begin to occur. At this stage the distinction between objective and subjective freedom is realised, for the agents are aware of themselves as moral agents. But this is an *unreflective* ethical existence, 'for the individual will intuitively adopts the customs and habits laid down by justice and the laws. The individual is therefore unconsciously united with the universal end'.[108] Thus it must remain until the individual can become conscious of himself as an individual over against the state. This occurred, Hegel says, in the classical Roman period, where the will of the state became so detached from that of its citizens that it subjugated them to itself. In the course of surrendering themselves to the state, however, i.e., of giving up their rights to it, the individuals *necessarily* became aware of their own individuality.[109] In this process, however, unlike that of classical Greece, much pain and suffering were involved. For the Greek world was a world of unreflective harmony between the state and the individual: Greek ethical life was 'not reborn from the struggle through which subjective freedom is itself reborn'.[110] The Roman world, on the other hand, in which the interests of the state are detached from those of its individual citizens, 'is no longer a world of gladness and joy, but of hard and arduous toil'.[111] The individuality which the Roman citizen has forged is still, however, simply a matter of those rights which the state recognises as his in return for what he surrenders to it. The Roman lacks his own inner principle, hence his form of subjectivity, when fully developed, must lead to the triumph of an arbitrary will, alienating the citizens from one another and causing the state to assume autocratic powers over them. As the descent into this form of subjective individuality continues, indeed, the unity of the state can be maintained only by external compulsion, i.e., by a compulsion not grounded in a principle internal to the wills of the citizens themselves. In this phase, individuals still have rights, but this is a purely 'worldly' or 'godless' reconciliation and 'is accordingly counterbalanced by internal insurgency as the pains of despotism make themselves felt'.[112] In this state spirit abandons the godless world and

---

[107] 'The principle of individuality, of subjective freedom, has its origin here, although it is still embedded in the substantial unity.' *Ibid.*, p. 202.

[108] *Ibid.*, p. 202.   [109] *Ibid.*, p. 204.   [110] *Ibid.*, p. 203.

[111] *Ibid.*, p. 204.

[112] *Ibid.*, p. 205.

is driven inwards in an effort to know its own essential being, 'self-knowing subjectivity', a condition which requires it to know that it is its nature to create a world, the state, which is based upon recognition of individual freedom while providing the conditions for that freedom.[113]

Several points emerge from even this brief summary. First, it is clear that the sequence is thoroughly internal. At any point where a fundamental change in institutional conditions and individual being occurs, Hegel finds the reason for the change in something inherently or intrinsically dynamic in the situation. The Greek condition, for example, is inherently dynamic, in that, as a result of its very autonomy, the state cannot fail to impress its character upon its members, thus giving rise to those very beginnings of ethical freedom within the individual which will eventually give him a standing against itself. Yet the ethical life of the Greek is not stable, for it is not born of an inner struggle and, indeed, as Hegel points out in the body of the *Lectures* themselves, this is reflected in the fact that, lacking a real sense of their inner freedom, the Greeks look outwards, via the oracles, for an external guidance from the gods which they cannot provide for themselves from within.

Hegel does not describe these conditions, however, merely as inherently dynamic. He makes, instead, the stronger claim that they involve their own antithesis within themselves. But although he describes the course of these antithetical changes, he does not explain whether the antitheses involved are logical, metaphysical, or, *in some sense*, factual. Yet it is crucial to resolve this question, otherwise it will be impossible to understand the sense of 'govern' in which philosophical history is meant to demonstrate that 'reason governs the world and that world history is therefore a rational process'.[114]

The core of the problem lies in Hegel's insistence that what he is talking about all along is concrete rationality, i.e., a type of rationality which evinces itself in two areas, the institutional world of the state and the subjective consciousness of the citizen, between which there is an internal, yet often antithetical, relationship. If 'reason' were, for example, simply the *structure* inherent in these phenomena in different historical periods, it would be difficult to see how there could be any purely logical antithesis between them. In any ordinary sense of incompatibility, there is nothing odd about saying that the Romans, for example, lived in a world in which they felt that they

[113] *Ibid.*, pp. 207–8   [114] *Ibid.*, p. 27.

must dedicate themselves to the service of the state but that they found their individual lives arduous and unhappy as a result of this situation. In the face of this sort of consideration, one might be inclined to take Hegel's references to antithetical processes not as references to an *incompatibility* in the situation but to the presence in it of a certain dynamic tendency, which must be allowed for in, or presupposed by, the system of concepts through which world history is to be understood.

Attractive though such a view may be, I do not think that it can be sustained. It would be helpful, however, to develop one possible version of it, which I shall refer to as the 'dynamism of pain', to see why this is so. This can quickly be done if we return to the pain and suffering which, Hegel says, are necessarily involved in the actualisation of the idea of freedom.[115] Here it is useful to note his contrast between the Greeks and the Romans. Greek ethical life is unstable because it is an instinctive morality which men have acquired without having passed through the *struggle for subjective freedom*. When this struggle takes place in Rome, however, we move from 'a world of gladness and joy' to one of 'hard and arduous toil'.[116] Later, when the individual personality gains the ascendancy, the disintegration of the state can be prevented only by force, and this 'worldly' or 'external' reconciliation is 'counterbalanced by internal insurgency as the pains of despotism make themselves felt'.[117]

Pain, suffering and struggle are therefore necessary conditions of the transformations involved in the dialectic of history. But pain and suffering may be looked upon as psychological conditions which are factual or contingent in character. If this were Hegel's view, his references to antithesis and contradiction should be understood in terms neither of a logical principle proper to ideas as such nor of one proper to the idea of freedom itself. They should, on the contrary, be understood in terms of a series of psychological and institutional transformations which are factual rather than logical in character.

---

[115] 'From this beginning, we proceed to define those same events which afford so sad a spectacle for gloomy sentiments and brooding reflection as no more than the *means* whereby what we have specified as the substantial destiny, the absolute and final end, or in other words, the *true result* of world history, is realised.' *Ibid.*, p. 69. The reference to a 'true result' here must be understood in the light of Hegel's own conception of truth, i.e., the 'coincidence of the object with itself, that is with its notion'. *Hegel's Logic.*, p. 237. The 'true result' of world history is therefore the actualisation, in the technical sense, of the idea of freedom and not merely some result about which we can make a true statement.

[116] *Lectures*, p. 204.   [117] *Ibid.*, p. 205.

In this case the logic of history would be dependent upon certain contingent facts about the dynamic character of pain. Logic would therefore be subservient to fact rather than, as I argued earlier, fact being subservient to logic.[118]

This line of argument presupposes, of course, that pain and suffering are psychological states which have the character of unintelligible or brute fact. It is clear, however, that this is far from Hegel's view. In the foregoing examples, pain and suffering are treated neither as unintelligible brute phenomena, nor even as phenomena the explanation of which lies in merely external conditions. On the contrary, their character is explained by certain rational conditions, in the sense that the kind of pain which is felt depends upon an *internal* relation between features of the institutional context and those of human consciousness. Roman suffering, for example, is a condition which can obtain not just when individuals subjugate themselves to the will of the state, but when their subjugation is to the will of a state *which they conceive of, and can only conceive of, as alien to themselves,* and which, because they can only conceive of it as such, *is* alien to them. The pain which brings about the recoil from the 'godless' world to that of autonomous, self-determining consciousness is, again, a pain which requires consciousness of the 'godlessness' of the state as it exists, and as it must exist, in relation to the subjective will as it also is conceived. But these are internally related conceptions, and the pain which is felt by the individual is a function of their relationships.

The thesis of the dynamism of pain must therefore be rejected, if it implies that the pain in question is susceptible, at best, of an external or contingent explanation. For Hegel, the pain which men feel, without which history would lack its dynamic character, is a manifestation of the way in which they see their objective and subjective situations. The weakness of ascribing to him a factually orientated approach, such as the dynamism of pain, is that it fails to take into account his conception of the ideational or concept-structured nature of the contents of human consciousness. Hegel does not need to deny, of course, that there are kinds of pain for which no *rational* explanation, such as that above, can be offered – purely accidental pain or pain occasioned by external factors. But this kind of pain belongs to the area of purely personal experience which he

[118] See above, pp. 89–92.

has explicitly excluded from world history.[119] The pain which is of relevance to history is that which presupposes the concept in terms of which the individual lives in his society, the concept of freedom.

If this is correct, the pain which is involved in the series of dialectical transformations by which the final end is actualised must presuppose a logic which is inherent in the idea of freedom itself. The idea may well be concrete – that is to say, it can exist only in so far as it is the determinate object, albeit mediately, of people's will and only in so far as the latter is embedded in actual situations – but it must still have internal conceptual properties, which, even if not 'logical' in any non-Hegelian sense of the term, will enable one to discern their necessary connections and, in the light of this, trace a certain 'rational' process in history. Unless this is so, it is difficult to see how Hegel's descriptions of reason as *governing* the world and of world history as a *rational* process can be much other than a series of empty metaphors.

This suggests, however, that, in spite of his insistence that a philosophical approach to history must not involve the 'manipulation' of history by philosophical ideas, Hegel is open to the charge of being an *a priori* rationalist in history. It is true that he has constantly emphasised the need to consider the action of spirit concretely, i.e., as an informing principle of actual events – or at least of that sub-class of them which enters into his account of world history – but at every point it has turned out that the volition which is at the heart of the notion of spirit presupposes a grounding in an idea which, while it cannot *exist* independently of will, is nevertheless logically prior to it. If this is so, the history of human consciousness, in all of its concrete manifestations, must be determined by the logic or structure of the idea. Moreover, if the claim that spirit is self-determining is to be sustained, this can be done only if it can be shown that the idea which it presupposes is self-determining.

These are difficult claims to accept. The first implies that we cannot reach the truth in respect of the concrete manifestation of the spirit in history unless we can reach the truth of the idea which that presupposes. But this will then have to be done by the use of something other than historical methods.

The second requires not merely that we understand that spirit presupposes the idea, but that it presupposes an idea which freely

[119] See above, pp. 92–4.

determines its own phases or stages in the light of its own final end. Here it is irrelevant that the idea can exist only as embodied in the world of finite beings and communities. For if the latter presupposes the idea, we must make sense of the notion of the free self-determination of a logical or conceptual structure in accordance with its own final end. But the notion of self-determination, as Hegel's account makes clear, involves that of change, transformation and overcoming. If the meaning of these conceptions has to be pushed back from their quite intelligible application to the world of spirit as embodied in history to that of the logic of the idea which this presupposes, we have the much more difficult task of understanding the suggestion that conceptual structures *as such* can have such properties as being self-determining, of transforming themselves and of doing so in the light of their own final ends. For logical structures consist in a set of atemporal relationships, whereas properties such as change, transformation and self-transcendence are necessarily temporal. The suggestion that the idea itself can have properties which can be predicated intelligibly only of the logically posterior world in which it is embodied thus involves a serious category mistake.

In what follows, I shall say little about the second of these problems since from the point of view of the present study, it is necessary to discuss it more extensively only if a satisfactory solution to the first problem can be found. In considering what Hegel might say in reply to the first difficulty, I shall commence by considering one wholly unsatisfactory response, in order to bring out the nature of the problem more clearly. We have noted already that Hegel is rather careless in his remarks about the class of things which reason uses as its means, talking at times as though this includes the whole class of willed actions, arbitrary caprice, subjective fancy and the like – in short, everything which has occurred. In one sense, of course, this cannot be what he means, for the course which is designated as the historical self-realisation of spirit occurs only through developments in certain parts of the world. Hegel could hardly intend to deny, however, that willed action takes place in other parts of the world which he disregards. His position here must be that spirit is not evincing itself in these actions and reason is not using them as a means for its own end. But even if we disregard these parts of the world, and take the view that whatever kind of history can be written about them it cannot be a philosophical history, it could still be maintained that in the sphere where reason does rule the world, it rules *all* the world, i.e., that it uses, or *can* use, any or every occurrence to attain its own self-development.[120] In this case, however, it might be argued, no *a priori* insight into the logic of the idea is needed by the historian in order to trace the course of the self-development of reason. If we know or believe or are just prepared to entertain the hypothesis that reason has developed here, a careful empirical study of the facts, armed perhaps with the formal categories which Hegel has provided, will enable us to discern a convincing pattern in the concrete development of consciousness.

This view gives rise, however, to a number of problems. First, it would result in the assimilation of philosophical history and empirical history, when the whole point of Hegel's project is to distinguish the two by providing a higher, self-conscious viewpoint for philosophical history. In alluding to the difficulty about the relationship between history and philosophy, Hegel points out that even the 'ordinary run-of-the-mill historian who believes and professes that his attitude is entirely receptive, that he is dedicated to the facts, is by no means passive in his thinking; he brings his categories with him, and they influence his vision of the data he has before him.'[121] When he then goes on to recommend that whoever 'looks at the world rationally will find that it in turn assumes a rational aspect',[122] he cannot simply be recommending the use of categories, since the empirical historian is, apparently, already using them.

On the other hand, neither can he be merely advocating the use of the formal category of reason in place of whatever set of categories the empirical historian may be using, since this would assimilate his position, *mutatis mutandis*, to that which was ascribed to Anaxagoras and then rejected as inadequate. For to approach history knowing merely that reason was at work there, or that it was at work in the *manner* specified above, would be similar to approaching the natural world in the knowledge that it was law-governed but without any part of one's knowledge of its concrete content and inner connections deriving from this knowledge.[123] Knowledge of its concrete content and inner connections would have to come from elsewhere and

---

[120] The notion of a means, which I have used freely in this paragraph, must be understood in the light of the analysis offered earlier. It is convenient to use the expression, but I do not wish to imply that Hegel should be thought of as holding that a certain class, or sub-class, of occurrences is the external means whereby spirit actualises its idea.

[121] *Lectures*, p. 29.   [122] *Ibid.*, p. 29.

[123] This is explained more fully above, see pp. 83–6.

would thus be grounded in something other than one's knowledge
that it was a product of reason.

The suggestion that philosophical history requires no more than a
careful attention to the facts, armed with the conceptual apparatus
provided by the formal category of reason, must therefore be
rejected.[124] If, as Hegel insists, reason exists concretely in the world,
then to look at it rationally must involve looking at it from the point of
view of concrete reason, i.e., not merely knowing that reason has a
concrete or determinate content but knowing what that content is.

THE LOGICAL PRIORITY OF THE IDEA

We must return, therefore, to the difficult claim that to consider the
history of the world philosophically we must know, in advance, and
in its full specification, the idea, i.e., the concrete idea. The particular
difficulty here lies in the fact that while insisting upon our prior
knowledge of it, Hegel maintains that the idea exists nowhere else
than in the history of the world or, at least, in that of the rational
world. We must be careful, of course, not to interpret the first claim to
mean that we must know, in advance, the individuals, societies and
so on, who figure in world history, i.e., the empirical concretisation of
the idea. What we must know in advance is the internal structure
which Hegel purports to find in the movement of world history. But
the conjunction of the two propositions still gives rise to a contradiction. It cannot be the case that, in order to produce an account of the
history of the world, the historian needs antecedent knowledge of the
concrete principles which inform it and that these principles exist

[124] It is necessary to emphasise this point, since it is frequently denied by Hegel's
admirers, many of whom find the suggestion that he may be an *a priori* rationalist
uncongenial. Duncan Forbes, for example, takes W. H. Walsh to task for suggesting that the outline of history must be an *a priori* deduction. For Walsh's view, see
his *An Introduction to Philosophy of History*, p. 151. In denying this claim Forbes
argues that the task of the philosopher is 'to think experience concretely and to
describe the given', hence 'the philosophy of history cannot be an *a priori* scheme,
thought out prior to observation of the facts and the work of the historian as such'.
Indeed, he goes on to ask, is not Hegel's outline 'what is most obviously and
palpably given to observation? Men know and have and want freedom as they
once did not, just as they know and have and want electricity as they once did not.'
He concludes by warning that it is a mistake 'to think of the dialectic as a rigid
pattern of ultimate and unchangeable truth', p. xxiii. But on this view, it is difficult
to see how Hegel's philosophical historian can be more than an historical
equivalent of the Anaxagoras who disappointed both Socrates and Hegel by his
failure to be able to show that determinate rather than abstract reason was the
inner cause of things. *Lectures*, pp. 34–5.

only in virtue of their functioning in world history. The historian cannot both need an antecedent knowledge of the concrete principles of world history, in order to produce an account of world history, and also come to know what those principles are as a result of the history which he produces. The knowledge of the idea which the historian needs can either be *a priori* or *a posteriori*, but it cannot be both. Yet, despite his own remarks to the effect that the philosophical historian must not construct history *a priori*, the rest of Hegel's conception seems to imply that this is precisely what needs to be done.

An initial way of trying to remove the contradiction would be by drawing an explicit distinction between a philosophical history of the world, i.e., an actual account *informed* by a knowledge of the concrete idea, and a philosophical knowledge of the concrete idea which constitutes the world. But the advance here would be more apparent than real. Not only would this leave us with a question about the point of a philosophical history of the world, since what is important there would already have had to be specified in the concept of concrete reason,[125] but the problem about our mode of access to the latter would remain. For there seem to be only two possible modes: either through some *a priori* knowledge or through the actual history which this is supposed to make possible. Thus we would be faced again with the original difficulty.

It could be held, however, that these are not genuine difficulties for Hegel, because they fail to take account of the importance of the historian's, or the philosophical historian's, knowledge of the historical and rational nature of his own consciousness and of his recognition that this must be used as a basis for philosophical history. To see how such a suggestion might be developed, it is worth returning to two points at which Hegel drew upon the notion of spirit as being eternally present to itself. The first occurred in relation to the claim that, in moving from specialised history to philosophical history, one of our gains would be a general perspective which, unlike those of specialised histories, would not be 'abstractly general' but 'concrete and absolutely present; for it is the spirit which is eternally present to itself and for which there is no past'.[126] Taken by themselves, these remarks seem to imply some wholly ahistorical or,

---

[125] Hegel's complaint that the supposition of the uniformity of human nature made it irrelevant 'to refer to the great theatre of world history', see above, p. 70, might well be raised in connection with his own view.

[126] See above, p. 81.

at least, atemporal, standpoint upon which philosophical history is to rest. The second reference, however, shows that this is not what is intended. It occurs when, having described the oriental way of life, with all its difficulties and inharmonious, unresolved relationships, Hegel asserts nevertheless that all 'that is contained within the Idea is essentially present and existent', after which he goes on to say that everything depends upon the *manner* in which it is present and whether its moments have been realised in their authentic form, adding that 'since subjectivity is an essential moment within spirit, it must necessarily be present too'.[127]

The suggestion is, therefore, that all aspects of spirit must always co-exist and be mutually implicated as it develops throughout its career. For unless this were so, the development of reason would not be a process of *self*-development and, hence, neither would it be free. When Hegel traces the course of the self-development of reason, this must therefore involve nothing but a series of transformations of elements which are always present as necessary aspects of reason and which mutually require one another. Once they are present in spirit, one might say, they must always be present and, conversely, if they are now present in spirit, they must always have been present. This does not mean, however, that they must always have been known to have been present *as partial manifestations of their final form* for, as we have seen, the agents through whom reason manifests itself in the world can only be said to have *mediate* knowledge of the final end. The philosophical historian, on the other hand, *can* have knowledge of the final end because it has actualised itself in his world. The claim would thus be that the philosophical historian can use his knowledge of the actualisation of the final end to reconstruct the course of rational transformations through which reason has developed its substantial content.

These considerations help to explain Hegel's insistence, stated most explicitly in the Owl of Minerva passage in the *Philosophy of Right*,[128]

---

[127] See above, pp. 108–9.
[128] 'One more word about giving instruction as to what the world ought to be. Philosophy in any case always comes on the scene too late to give it. As the thought of the world, it appears only when actuality is already there cut and dried after its process of formation has been completed. The teaching of the concept, which is also history's inescapable lesson, is that it is only when actuality is mature that the ideal first appears over against the real and that the ideal apprehends the same real world in its substance and builds it up for itself into the shape of an intellectual realm. When philosophy paints its grey in grey, then has a shape of life grown old. By philosophy's grey in grey it cannot be rejuvenated but

that philosophy comes on the scene only after the event, i.e., that it is necessarily, but not trivially, backward-looking. His point is not that philosophical history is, as a matter of definition, knowledge of the past. It is that philosophical history requires a standpoint in which an understanding of actualised reason gives us access to materials, transformed but always carried forward in the process of its self-development, by which *retrospectively* to trace the course of its self-development. Thus, we could say, philosophical history becomes possible only at the point of convergence between *rational* being and knowledge, a point reached only with spirit's consciousness of its own freedom, which constitutes the actualisation of the final end.[129] For, even if all the aspects of spirit are present throughout its career, this *convergence* never obtains in any prior phase, since in none of them do the agents through whom spirit develops itself know that their rational being consists in their participation in this process.

Although there are difficulties in this suggestion, I shall begin by trying to defend it against one possible criticism. As already noted, Hegel's account of the viewpoint of the philosophical historian seems to involve a dilemma: either the categories with which he approaches history include that of concrete or determinate reason, in which case he requires an *a priori* knowledge of the fundamental outline of the history which he seeks to recover; or, alternatively, he has some more abstract or formal knowledge, in the light of which he interprets the historical past, in which case he would need to ground knowledge of the concrete content of history in something other than the idea of reason.

One might try to circumvent this difficulty, however, in the following way. Although philosophical history becomes possible only at the point of convergence between rational being and knowledge, it

only understood. The owl of Minerva spreads its wings only with the falling of the dusk.' *Hegel's Philosophy of Right*, translated by T.M. Knox (Oxford, Oxford University Press, 1967; reprinted 1973), pp. 12–13. These comments must, however, be treated with some caution, since it is known that Hegel inserted them at a late stage in the preparation of the manuscript and it is possible that he may have done so to comply with the restrictive Carlsbad Decrees. See K.-H. Ilting, 'Hegel's Concept of the State and Marx's Early Critique', in *The State and Civil Society: Studies in Hegel's Political Philosophy*, ed. Z. A. Pelczynski (Cambridge, Cambridge University Press, 1984).

[129] Historical knowledge, on this view, would be made possible by such a convergence in a manner somewhat analogous to that in which Hume thought that it was made possible by a convergence of the evidential and the existential in some present premise known to be true.

is not necessary for the philosophical historian to know all that this involves, which would amount to a complete knowledge of the principles which determine the concrete self-development of reason, *prior* to his attempt to write such an history. A philosophical history would be his *aim*, but he would not need to know the convergence in its complete determinacy before setting out to fulfil that aim. Instead, he should be prepared to alter his determinate understanding of the present convergence as he tries to write an history in which it was the final end and, vice versa, to alter his determinate understanding of the past as he tries to see it as the expression of a rational will or spirit of which this convergence was the final aim. The point was made, when discussing Hegel's comments on the pragmatic historian,[130] that one's conceptions of the past and the present must stand in a reciprocal relation to each other, so that an alteration in either must require an alteration in the other. Hegel himself asserted this quite explicitly, so there is no reason why he could not use it in his defence against the present difficulty.

But the defence is only partially successful. It rescues Hegel from the difficulty of grounding historical knowledge upon some determinate but, as yet, itself ungrounded knowledge of the present, by arguing that knowledge of the present and of the past are mutually implicated. But in so doing it introduces the further problem of the basis of this knowledge of the mutually implicated present and past. For wholly false accounts of a mutually implicated present and past can be produced just as easily as can wholly false accounts of the past which presuppose wholly false accounts of the present. This, again, was a point which Hegel himself made in his criticism of some aspects of pragmatic history, and which was carried forward in his demand that the viewpoint of the specialised historian should be transcended by the introduction of a *valid* perspective, such as only philosophical history can provide.

We remain faced, therefore, with the problem of the grounding of the concept of concrete reason. 'Grounding' is, perhaps, not the right word here, if that is taken to imply an appeal to some other concept, by its derivation from which that of reason can be justified, for reason is Hegel's basic category. What is required, rather, is some way of grasping the *self-justifying* nature of the concrete concept. A further possibility, which has not yet been explored, is that it is justified by the

---

[130] *Lectures*, p. 20.

fact that the actualisation of spirit's end is the rational resolution of a paradox central to the concept of human nature. For it is, surely, the resolution of a considerable paradox to realise that one's nature as an individual is neither to be a part whose properties determine those of the state, nor one whose properties are determined by the state, but one which can fulfil itself only through its conscious willing of a form of the state which, it knows, can exist only in and through this willing. The paradoxical problem of the relationship of the individual to the state is resolved by people's knowledge that it is in their nature to share consciously in the creation of the conditions of their mutual individuality and this means, of course, to come to a certain understanding of the concept of individuality. Thus, the suggestion might be, the idea of reason is self-justifying because its actualisation resolves a central paradox about human nature from which we cannot otherwise escape.

But there is a difficulty in this line of argument. For the paradox is a philosophical one, revolving around the problem of reconciling the concept of individuality with that of being, in some sense, a part of a social whole. Even if, for the sake of argument, we grant that Hegel has resolved this paradox, or that he has shown that it has been resolved in the history of human consciousness, this would do nothing to justify the claim that the final end of history must be the resolution of this paradox, i.e., that history must take the course which it has in order that the paradox be resolved. Thus the teleological notion which is central to Hegel's concept of reason and his account of history is given no support by this suggestion. This is not to deny, of course, that we could understand such an account. We can see how it could make perfectly good sense to write a history of the world, or some part of it, on the assumption that those changes in institutions and consciousness which are central to all others are explained by dissatisfaction or pain which is experienced or felt because life has been organised round unsatisfactory concepts of individuality, or of the relation between the individual and the state, and by the growing development of insight into what would be more satisfying. There would, at the very least, be nothing logically unacceptable about a history of this sort. What has not been established, however, is that history must be of this sort or that a history of this sort, merely in virtue of being of this sort, is logically prior to any other kind which we might produce.

The proposal could be strengthened, however, by relating it to

Hegel's further claim that the superior standing of philosophical history depends upon its access to a perspective which 'is not abstractly general, but concrete and absolutely present: for it is the spirit which is eternally present to itself and for which there is no past'.[131] As we have seen, the point which Hegel is making here is an extension of one which he made in connection with the pragmatic historian, i.e., that we must understand the past, if it is to be our past, in the light of some relationship in which it stands to the present. In philosophical history this becomes the claim that we must understand the spirit of the past only in the light of some internal relationship in which it stands to that of the present, for it is one and the same spirit. This involves the notion of a dialectical transformation of spirit, in which its modified contents are retained and carried forward in the material of history, i.e., in man in so far as he participates in his own end. What we might call the 'real' or 'rational' past is always *present* in spirit, because spirit contains within itself the materials which it has developed along with the continuing formulation of its own end. The past with which the philosophical historian is concerned is thus not merely spirit's *past* – although, of course, it is spirit's past, since it occurred – but a past the elements of which remain within present spirit and which can therefore provide the basis for philosophical history. Thus, to take a simple example, the Greek world represented a reconciliation of the individual and the state. This reconciliation was not satisfactory, for in it the individual unreflectively adopted the will of the state as his own. Nevertheless, the concept of the will of the individual being at one with that of the state is a necessary part of the final end and so is carried forward and progressively modified as spirit transforms itself in history. The philosophical historian therefore knows that the elements involved in the final resolution of the paradox, arose, were transformed and carried forward to their final and proper relationship in the course of the self-development of spirit.

This modified suggestion is, however, susceptible of a number of possible interpretations with different outcomes. The first is just that the philosophical historian knows that his task is to write the history of the world in the light of his knowledge that it is an historical or dialectical creation. This must certainly be regarded as too weak on the grounds that it is purely formal. It would give the philosophical historian no idea of the present content of spirit in the light of which its past is to be written and by which it is to be explained. In the absence of a 'valid perspective' with a concrete content, we should simply end up with a number of competing histories, dialectical in form but different in content, between which we would have no grounds for exercising a rational preference.

A second interpretation would be that the philosophical historian both understands the nature of the reconciliation and knows *that* it has been achieved historically. But this would still be too weak, since it would fail to take into account the requirement that there be an internal connection between the different phases of spirit's career. For, if the understanding of the nature of the reconciliation is logically distinct from an understanding of how it has come about, there would still be no grounds for the elimination of all sorts of different historical accounts of the latter.[132]

A third possibility is that a knowledge of how the reconciliation has been achieved is part of spirit's own understanding of the reconciliation, i.e., of its own nature. But this is now too strong. For such a knowledge would provide the concrete principles of a philosophical history of the world, and if that knowledge were part of spirit's *self*-understanding, there would be no scope for the distinction between a philosophical and an empirical historian. Such an understanding of the content of concrete reason would now be available to everybody, simply in virtue of living in the period of the actualisation of spirit's end, which must, of course, express one aspect of itself in the consciousness of individuals. The ordinary empirical historian would thus possess whatever concrete categories were necessary for a philosophical history of the world as part of his ordinary *unreflective* consciousness. In short, this suggestion would reduce the philosophical historian to the state of the original historian by eliminating the need for the work which the philosophical historian is supposed to do.

A final possibility is that the knowledge is implicit rather than explicit within spirit's self-understanding and that it can be made explicit by means of some sort of philosophical reasoning about, or reflection upon, the latter. This would at least preserve the distinction between the philosophical and the empirical historian. But it would

---

[132] In fact, this simply reintroduces the difficulty urged against Duncan Forbes in n. 123 above. Even if we now know that we are free – and many would, in any case, dispute this, because of the contestability of the concept of freedom – that knowledge is compatible with many different ways of explaining historically how we have come to be free.

do little more than that, since it would simply reintroduce one of the suggestions examined and rejected earlier. For even if, as seems possible, we could produce a fully coherent account of some such conception, this would commit us to a wholly *a priori* knowledge of the fundamental principles which govern the content of world history. But Hegel has, of course, denied the need for, or the desirability of, such *a priori* knowledge.[133]

It thus transpires that none of these interpretations is satisfactory. With the exception of the claim that the history of the world is determined *a priori* by the logic of the idea, none of them suffices to ground the view that the most fundamental feature in world history, to which all others must be subordinate, must be that which has been necessary for the resolution of the paradox. Moreover, with regard to the *a priori* interpretation, it has been argued that, if this involves the grasp of a merely formal or abstract idea, it will be impossible to show how the concrete content of history has been determined by reason; while, if it involves a grasp of the concrete idea, we would need some independent access to those very principles which are supposed to evince themselves only through their development in rational history.

It is noticeable that most of the difficulties encountered here arise from Hegel's emphasis on a combination of two points: that reason is a concrete self-developing force in the world, and that, since it is self-developing or free, it must also be self-justifying or self-grounding. The claim that reason is self-justifying is, if not unarguable, at least fairly familiar, in the sense that it is a standard objection to sceptics that they must presuppose rational standards of argument in order to reach their sceptical conclusions. But a reference to rational standards alone is not what Hegel means by the concept of concrete reason, and it is this difference which gives rise to the difficulties which he faces.

Hegel is thus unable to give a convincing account of the history of human nature or consciousness. This is not because he has made it dependent upon the *development* of human consciousness, but because he has made the latter dependent upon the developing structure of an idea, or ideal, which, since it must be wholly self-determining, must have the status of metaphysical necessity and access to which must, accordingly, be *a priori*.

[133] See above, p. 82.

In the light of this conclusion it is possible now to see that, whereas Hume made it impossible for the historian to allow for any changes in human nature of consciousness, Hegel has done precisely the reverse, i.e., made it impossible for him to allow for any large-scale constancies in human nature or consciousness. For if it is a presupposition of philosophical history that the fundamental forms of consciousness must have developed in accordance with the self-development of an idea, the content of which can only be known *a priori*, any assertions or discoveries by historians to the contrary must be false. Thus, different though they may be, the constraints which Hegel's theory impose upon the historian are just as severe as those which emanate from Hume's theory.

FIRST-ORDER AND SECOND-ORDER HISTORY

Despite this, it must be acknowledged that many commentators have found Hegel's account of the development of human consciousness highly persuasive, and this fact alone may be held to be an argument against the analysis which leads to the above conclusion. I shall conclude this chapter, therefore, by considering this objection, but will do so indirectly, by connecting it to another point, which is of importance to Hegel, but which has, as yet, received no direct discussion.

One may feel particularly reluctant to accept the view that Hegel is an *a priori* rationalist in history when one recalls his assertion that the philosophical historian must not be open to the charge of constructing history *a priori*, or according to preconceived notions, or of manipulating the facts. For, as was noted earlier, not only is he conscious of this danger, but he explicitly claims that the contradiction between fact and necessity, which might seem to be involved in the idea of philosophical history, must be overcome.

It seems clear, nevertheless, that he has not resolved this contradiction in a satisfactory way, because his thought has moved at two different levels. For to show that reason governs the world or that world history is a rational process, he would need to show that the facts of history should themselves be reinterpreted so as to be seen to have reason as their inner constitutive principle. When we turn to the account which he offers in the rest of the *Lectures*, however, no such first-order reinterpretation is provided. What we find, instead, is what might be called a higher- or second-order interpretation, utilising the categories discussed in the Introduction, of facts which have been independently established by ordinary, empirical historians. Although Hegel is prepared to reject some putative facts as *a priori* fictions, those which are involved in his own detailed historical account are at no point supported by an examination of evidence. They appear to consist of such facts as were considered authentic by the community of scholars of his time, i.e., to be products of empirical research. But the categories which the empirical historian brings to bear upon his materials are, as Hegel makes clear, quite different from those of the philosophical historian. It follows that philosophical history is primarily concerned with relations between facts rather than with the constitution of facts. But if the relations between facts with which philosophical history is concerned presuppose facts which have an independent set of constitutive principles, Hegel has failed to show that reason is the inner cause of the determinate, concrete facts of history.

If this is correct, it could be said that Hegel has resolved the apparent contradiction between history and philosophy, but only by abandoning his own claims about philosophical history. For it is impossible to see how reason can produce, from its own resources, the world with which the philosophical historian is concerned, if it turns out that the latter presupposes a world of fact constituted by the principles of the empirical historian, which have no internal connection with those of the philosophical historian. The conclusion to be drawn here should surely be that the whole world of the empirical historian, and not just some part of it, is a world of *a priori* fancy, which ought to be replaced by a world of philosophically informed fact. But that is certainly not the conclusion which Hegel draws. The reason why Hegel's account of the development of human consciousness has seemed so appealing to some commentators, it might therefore be said, is just that it is an attractive example, with a good factual basis, of the more theoretical kinds of accounts that such histories tend to be, but not that it provides a demonstration of the rational nature of the forces at work in that development.

This line of argument depends upon two assumptions, both of which may be thought questionable: that everything that is involved in the idea that reason is active in the world must be accessible to the philosophical historian, with his internally related set of categories; and that the latter cannot involve those of the empirical historian. The first, that the operations of reason in the world should be wholly accessible to the philosophical historian, seems, perhaps, less questionable. Hegel, who frequently identifies God with spirit or reason, insists that the only proper attitude to take towards Him is that His activities are wholly knowable: 'God does not wish to have narrow-minded and empty-headed children. On the contrary he demands that we should know him; he wishes his children to be poor in spirit but rich in knowledge of him and to set the highest value on acquiring knowledge of God. History is the unfolding of God's nature in a particular, determinate element, so that only a determinate form of knowledge is appropriate to it.'[134] Thus God demands that we should know Him and this knowledge must take the form of a determinate knowledge of the self-development of spirit in history.

The position may seem somewhat less obvious with regard to the claim that the categories of the philosophical historian cannot involve those of the empirical historian. For, it might be argued, even if the latter does not know that what he is dealing with is, in a sense, part of the subject matter of philosophical history, it nevertheless is, and the philosophical historian, who does know this, is therefore entitled to put the material to his own use.

The point can, however, be established by two connected considerations. First, it should be noted that the methodology employed by the empirical historian is indifferent as between those facts which are included in, and those which are excluded from, philosophical history. The empirical historian proceeds in precisely the same way when establishing such facts as those about pre-Roman Britain, for example, which have no place in the self-development of reason, and when establishing others, such as those about the Reformation, which are of crucial importance to it. The class of events relevant to a philosophical history of the world is therefore a sub-class of the class of events with which the empirical historian deals. The empirical historian nevertheless approaches both in precisely the same way. His treatment of the sub-class is neither informed, nor affected, by knowledge that it constitutes the class which is of concern to the philosophical historian. But if it is allowed that the empirical historian constitutes a world of fact in the same way both for the class and the sub-class, and that the class is only externally related to the self-development of reason, it follows that the sub-class also can only be externally related to it. There is thus nothing in the empirical

---

[134] *Lectures*, p. 42. The whole section, from pp. 36–43, is concerned to show that God, or spirit, is intellectually, i.e., demonstrably, knowable.

historian's procedure which can lend support to the suggestion that, since he deals with some facts which are of importance to the self-development of reason, the philosophical historian can simply take over his account of these, without giving them a wholly new constitution through their grounding, as facts, in the categories appropriate to spirit.

We arrive at the same result if we pursue the objection from the opposite, but related, side, i.e., from what history is about rather than from one's way of establishing it. 'Whoever looks at the world rationally', Hegel asserts, 'will find that it in turn assumes a rational aspect; the two exist in a reciprocal relationship'.[135] The empirical historian, unfortunately, does not look at the world 'rationally', in Hegel's sense. But the relationship between thought and what thought is about remains reciprocal. It follows that that about which the empirical historian and the philosophical historian think cannot be identical. There can therefore be no question of reason evincing itself in the content of both: if it does in the one, it cannot in the other. But in this case the categories of philosophical history cannot simply presuppose those of empirical history. Rather, they must replace them to produce an entirely new kind of historical fact, one in which reason really is the sole governing factor.

From these considerations several consequences follow. First, it is clear that if philosophical history is to live up to its pretensions, it ought to be a different kind of first-order history, the constitutive principles of which are provided by the idea of reason, rather than be a second-order history based on principles which are external to those of the first-order histories which it presupposes. In a sense, this is something with which Hegel would have agreed. For, although he presents philosophical history as an advance upon the various forms of reflective history and, in particular, upon specialised history, it is superior only in that it can do that to which they aspire but cannot achieve. But the sorts of history to which Hegel refers as specialised histories, such as constitutional histories, are first-order histories, in so far as they provide accounts of what occurred, based upon an assessment of evidence. Philosophical history can be a successful way of doing that which specialised history ought to do, only if it also provides accounts of what occurred, but within a more satisfactory conceptual framework.

---

[135] *Ibid.* p. 29.

If this is so, it follows also that the concept of the self-development of reason, as explicated by Hegel, cannot be, as he claimed, an alternative to that of the uniformity of human nature or of human consciousness, which he explicitly rejected. For the uniformity of human nature was advanced as a presupposition of first-order history, whereas, as we have seen, Hegel has developed the concept of philosophical history in such a way that it presupposes the latter. But a concept cannot be incompatible with one which it presupposes. Alleged weaknesses in the latter cannot therefore be rejected upon the strength of alleged merits of the former. In the last chapter arguments were advanced against the uniformity of nature thesis. It is clear, however, that, since these were directed against it as a presupposition of first-order history, they neither support, nor are supported by, Hegel's second-order account of the role of reason in history. It is evident, in fact, that Hegel was mistaken in his belief that an incompatibility with the concept of reason justified his rejection of the uniformity thesis since, in so far as there is any incompatibility, it must be removed by making the second-order concept conform to the conditions of the first-order concept which it presupposes. Hegel's rejection of the uniformity thesis, therefore, cannot be justified by his claims about the idea of reason as he has developed them.

CONCLUSION

It may be useful now to summarise some of the results of the foregoing discussion. Despite the difficulties into which he ultimately runs, Hegel makes an impressive case for two fundamental points: the importance of the internal connections between consciousness of ideas and institutional practice and, as a consequence of this, the importance of the concept of social consciousness for human history. The difficulties which have been encountered, on the other hand, arise from a thesis which is entailed by neither of these points, the motivation for which comes from an entirely different direction. The thesis is, of course, that of spirit as a determinate self-developing force in the world. This led first to the logical priority of ideas over consciousness and, thence, to the priority of the self-development of the idea of freedom over the most fundamental developments in human consciousness and, hence, in human history. But these claims gave rise to a number of difficulties. The first of these concerns the notion of the *self*-development of reason. It was pointed out that there appears to be no difficulty in the idea that reason can be embodied and can direct changes in the medium in which it is embodied. The problem is entirely concerned with the idea that the reason which is embodied can be both logically prior to that in which it is embodied and also be responsible for its own development, in the sense of giving rise to its own antithetical phases. For this meant ascribing to the idea, as a system of conceptual relationships, predicates which can be coherently applied only to the existential or historical world of change and transformation, which is supposed to be determined by the idea. Hence the category mistake.

The second difficulty concerns the form of knowledge which the philosophical historian is supposed to have and his reason for accepting it. For, if the self-development of reason as a determinate principle is identical with the history of the world, the categories required to write the latter must be identical with the concretisation of those categories in the history which they are to make possible. In this case, if a regress is to be avoided, the philosophical historian would need an *a priori* knowledge of determinate reason, i.e., of reason as a set of concrete categories which must be embodied in the history of the world, in order to write such a history. This is plainly unacceptable. Even were a convincing deduction of the phases of the self-development of concrete reason available, it would have the consequence of imposing on the historian the requirement that consciousness must necessarily develop, and that, in certain areas at least, no constancy could be admitted, with as much severity as Hume imposed upon him exactly the opposite requirement. On the other hand, the suggestion that the philosophical historian might be able to operate with any less determinate knowledge comes up against Hegel's own objections to the use of merely formal categories, from which the real content of history could not be deduced. Finally, it was noted that, when Hegel himself came to give a determinate account of the content of world history, he presupposed, and made use of, a content derived from a completely different source, the contingent world, and arrived at by completely different methods, those of the empirical historian, the incompatibility of which with the idea of reason posed a greater threat to it than it did to them.

Nothing has been said about the motivation which drove Hegel to these lengths. Historically, there is little doubt that it lay in the appeal which the theological notion of God as immanent in a world of His own creation had for him. Philosophically, however, it is not difficult to see, in the light of the earlier discussion, that it lay in a conviction that it must be in the nature of reality that it should be knowable in its full determinacy and that this could be so only if determinate knowledge of itself were *part* of its nature. Hence, knowledge that its history is the necessary process whereby it becomes conscious of its own self-developing nature becomes, as the actualisation of the final end, a constitutive principle of spirit. But this, I have argued, gives rise to irresolvable problems.

Apart from the specific difficulties in relation to history to which it leads, it is worth noting that the line of reasoning which Hegel adopted involves a general philosophical mistake. Many thinkers would agree that reality must be knowable and, in principle at least, knowable to whatever degree of determinacy it possesses. But it does not follow from this, as Hegel's view implies, that it is necessary that it be known to this degree, so that the latter proposition becomes part of the definition of reality. The notion of a reality which cannot, by its nature, be known is difficult to accept. No such difficulty, however, attends that of a reality, some parts of which, for purely contingent reasons, may not be known. If it is a contingent matter that we do not know some parts, it will be contingent that we know others, though not that we know any at all. It is compatible with holding that it is contingent *which* parts we know that it is necessary that we know *some* parts. But this is something which Hegel could not accept, given the conjunction of his beliefs in the holistic nature of reality and in the necessity that it be known. For it follows from this conjunction that we cannot know some parts of reality unless we know it as a whole. But, if scepticism is self-defeating, reality must be known, in part or in whole, and, if it cannot be known in part, then, necessarily, it must be known as a whole. Hence, in any rational conception of reality of Hegel's type, it must be a constitutive property that it should give rise to knowledge of itself and, accordingly, that spirit must give rise to knowledge of itself. If, to use Hegel's more theological language, God is ultimate and all-powerful, and if He demands that we should know Him, then, necessarily, we must come to know Him. But all this follows only from a particular conception of the relation between reality and knowledge to which there are many alternatives.

3

VICO: THE IDEAL ETERNAL HISTORY

VICO AND HEGEL

There exist between Vico and Hegel certain similarities which are sufficiently strong to have given rise to a well-supported, if also much-disputed, tradition of interpretation in which Vico's thought is regarded in a very Hegelian light.[1] I believe that this is an incorrect way to look at it, because of certain fundamental differences which I hope to establish by the end of this chapter.[2] It is useful, nevertheless,

---

[1] The most influential and powerful version of this interpretation is Benedetto Croce's *La filosofia di G. B. Vico* (Bari, Laterza, 1911), frequently reprinted, the English translation of which, by R. G. Collingwood, was published under the title *The Philosophy of Giambattista Vico* (London, Howard Latimer, 1913). Among many affinities which Croce noted were those between Vico's attempt to relate philosophy to philology and Hegel's identification of thought and being; Vico's recognition of the limited nature of mathematics and the exact sciences and Hegel's repudiation of the reality of the fruits of the abstract intellect; Vico's theory of the poetic mind and Hegel's view of art as one of the forms of absolute mind; their joint repudiation of the possibility of any form of society which lacked religion; and, finally, the identity of Vico's concept of providence and Hegel's cunning of reason. For a summary of these and other points, see Chapter 20 of Croce's book. There is no doubt that many of the similarities to which Croce drew attention exist. Equally, however, he neglected certain fundamental differences between the thought of the two thinkers, as I hope will become apparent in the course of this chapter, because his reading of both was mediated by the development of his own philosophy of spirit. For a useful commentary on the Hegelian interpretation of Vico, together with a criticism of it, which is very different from that which I shall advance, see Pietro Piovani, 'Vico without Hegel', in *Vico: An International Symposium*, ed. Giorgio Tagliacozzo and Hayden V. White (Baltimore, the Johns Hopkins University Press, 1969), pp. 103–23.

[2] Croce's pioneering study has stimulated a vast amount of research on Vico in this century, much of which has issued in views quite contrary to Croce's own. These can be very generally classified as follows. First, there is a naturalistic interpretation, in which Vico views man as part of the physical world and is concerned to extend the

to take advantage of some of these similarities in commencing this account of Vico's view of the relationship between human nature and history and how he thought the historian should address the problems to which this gave rise. To those who deny the importance of the similarities, to proceed in this manner may seem to run the danger of assimilating Vico's thought to that of a later age and thus to fail to do justice to it in its own terms. Such a danger certainly exists, but it is not inescapable nor, indeed, would it justify paying no attention to the similarities, some of which are quite striking. Both thinkers were very well read in the history of their subjects and it would be a mistake to assume *a priori* that they might not have seen their work, in part at least, as a response to certain similar problems. It is plausible, for example, to see much of Hegel's work as an attempt to overcome the stultifying dichotomy between the phenomenal and the noumenal which Kant forced upon himself by his excessive

methods of the natural sciences, in which he was undoubtedly interested, to the study of human history. This view is most fully developed in Nicola Badaloni's *Introduzione a G. B. Vico* (Milan, Feltrinelli, 1961). It has been stated differently by Frederick Vaughan, in *The Political Philosophy of Giambattista Vico* (The Hague, Martinus Nijhoff, 1972), who uses it to explain the long-standing idea that Vico deliberately obscured some of his views in order not to run into trouble with the Catholic censors. For an extremely detailed development and refinement of this view, in a work which, unfortunately, has been published too late for me to take specific account of here, see Gino Bedani, *Vico Revisited: Orthodoxy, Naturalism and Science in the 'Scienza Nuova'* (Oxford, Berg, 1989). Secondly, there is a series of interpretations which centre round the idea that Vico was concerned with the differences between man as a social and historical being and the natural world in which he lived, and which offer alternative accounts of the methodology by which he thought we could come to knowledge of human history. Central studies here are Isaiah Berlin's *Vico and Herder: Two Studies in the History of Ideas* (London, Hogarth Press, 1976), in which great emphasis is laid upon the imagination as an indispensable requirement of knowledge of history; B. A. Haddock's *Vico's Political Thought* (Swansea, Mortlake Press, 1986), and his *An Introduction to Historical Thought*, in which Vico is presented as sharing the interest of his humanist predecessors in the interpretation of documents and artefacts in general and as being primarily concerned to produce a canon for their interpretation which allowed for their specificity within unique historical cultures; and, finally, Donald Phillip Verene's *Vico's Science of Imagination* (Ithaca, Cornell University Press, 1981), in which the imagination in its primary mode is made central to Vico's account of the ontology of the historical world and, in its secondary mode, as the recollective imagination, is fundamental to his account of knowledge of that world. In my own previous work, I have been nearer to the second group than the first, while not accepting their account of the role of imagination in Vico's methodology, which, I have argued, is meant to be scientific in a rather unusual way. My reasons for not accepting their account of the role of the imagination are to be found in my *Vico: A Study of the 'New Science'*, 2nd edn (Cambridge, Cambridge University Press, 1990), Chapter 18.

admiration for the natural sciences and which led him to relegate some of the most important features of man – freedom, morality and rational self-determination – to the unknowable world of the noumenal. Much of Hegel's work can be seen as an attempt to make these 'noumenal' features constitutive principles within the world of human experience. Vico, similarly, was distressed by the arid dualism to which the Cartesian search for certainty had led, which separated man's essence from the social and historical context in which his capacities are nurtured and developed and in which many of them receive their historical content. Much of his thought can be seen as an attempt to overcome this dualism by stressing the conditioning effect of the social and historical context upon human nature, as had been argued in the educational, social, political and jurisprudential writings of his Renaissance predecessors. In addition, just as Kant's dualism followed from an epistemological position which had to be overcome if Hegel were to view man's historical development as a teleological, self-determining process, so Descartes's followed from an epistemological position which had to be overcome if Vico were to pay due regard to the way in which man had developed historically. For if, as Descartes claimed, the certain knowledge of mind which we possessed was possible only if mind had an ahistorical and asocial essence, it was impossible to see how many of the assumptions involved in education, politics, jurisprudence, and so on, which presupposed the necessity for a social, cultural and historical context, could be sustained.

As it is no part of my present task to explain the origins of either Vico's or Hegel's thoughts on history, these few remarks must suffice to justify the claim that it is possible, at least, to begin an account of Vico's position by concentrating on certain features in which it resembles Hegel's, without necessarily being guilty of conceptual anachronism. This will provide a basis for investigating certain radical differences in their approach to what, I shall argue, is essentially the same problem.

The first point to be noted is that Vico shares with both Hegel and Hume the desire to put forward what the latter called a 'compleat system of the sciences'. As we have seen, Hume's admiration for the success of the natural sciences led him to believe that this required showing how a methodology derived from the natural sciences could be made appropriate for understanding all forms of knowledge whatsoever, including, therefore, historical knowledge. On the other hand, Hegel's emphasis upon the concrete, internally related nature of reality led him to view natural science as a partial and abstract way of regarding the world, so that the task of philosophy became that of proposing a system of thought whereby we could go beyond science, with its external and abstract view of the world, and see reality in its concrete individuality. With regard to this difference between them, Vico is very much nearer to Hegel than to Hume. For it is a central point in his later philosophy that he thinks that the natural world can never be made fully comprehensible whereas, for reasons to be discussed below, the world of human history and of the history of human thought can be. There is, of course, an obvious difference between the claims that natural science should be superseded because it is too abstract and that it should be disregarded because it is, at best, only relatively intelligible. But at least Hegel and Vico are at one in thinking that the world of history has a higher epistemological status than that of the natural sciences, whereas Hume's view is that, although historical knowledge is in practice more difficult to secure than that of the physical world, because of our inability to set up the experimental conditions to establish the relevant uniformities, it is in principle of the same standing.

A second point of resemblance is that Vico took, as did Hegel, a holistic view of the character of an historical society. In Hegel's case, as we have seen, this was largely confined to those societies through which reason had developed itself, and it was exploited mainly in terms of the way in which the idea of freedom, at any specific phase in its career, grounded the governing conceptions in any of the main areas in which it particularised itself. A single example of this is given in the claim that different determinate forms of the state are 'founded on' and have 'emerged from' the different determinate forms of religion which are themselves expressions of different conceptions of the relation of the particular and the universal.[3]

Vico holds a similar holistic view, which he stresses through the claim that the history of each nation will, in certain circumstances,[4]

---

[3] See above, pp. 101–2.

[4] Since the circumstance is the highly unlikely one that the nation should have developed in complete or relatively complete isolation from other nations, this requires some explanation. There is no doubt that, historically, Vico's account of the main features which he associates with the history of each nation was inspired by an intensive study of Roman history, in the course of making sense of which he had to draw on a number of principles. One particular problem which arose was that of explaining a number of striking similarities between Roman culture and institutional life and that of other earlier nations. Vico rejected the fashionable view that these

reveal three characteristic phases, the unity of each of which is based upon a certain kind of human nature which expresses itself in the whole cultural and institutional life of the nation at that stage. Vico puts the point in the following passage which, although over-schematic, brings it out with sufficient clarity to merit quoting at length. Having mentioned the division of the history of each nation into three ages, he writes:

For, in accordance with this [division], the nations will be seen to have been guided by a constant and uninterrupted order of causes and effects, ever operative within them, through three kinds of nature; from these three natures came three kinds of custom, from which, [in turn], three kinds of the natural law of the gentes were observed and in consequence of which three kinds of civil states or governments were ordered. For the communication of the foregoing three most important kinds of thing among men who had come to human society, three kinds of language and of characters were formed; and for their justification, three kinds of jurisprudence, supported by three kinds of reason [embodied] in as many kinds of judgement, these kinds of jurisprudence being practised in the three sects of times which the nations profess in the whole course of their lives. These special triadic unities, with many others which follow from them, fall under one general unity, that of the worship of a provident divinity, which is the unity of spirit which informs and gives life to this world of nations.[5]

should be explained by transmission from some original nation, largely on the grounds that, as we shall see, the culture and institutions of a people must conform to their internal characteristics. Accordingly, he proposed that these similarities should be viewed as evidence of a single pattern of development which was intrinsic to a nation as such. For later periods of history, where he accepted that there was much international communication, he proposed, but did not develop, further principles to explain the way in which the interaction between nations at different stages of development would affect one another. Thus his claim does not depend upon the fact that nations rarely develop in isolation and is therefore not open to refutation by it.

[5] *Principles of a New Science Concerning the Common Nature of Nations*, paragraph 915. This is the third edition of the *New Science*, being a new version of the second edition of 1730, upon which Vico was working when he died in 1744. It differs completely in presentation, and to some extent also in substance, from the first edition of 1725. For convenience I shall hereafter refer to the three editions as the *First*, *Second* and *Third New Science*, and, in footnotes, as *N.S.*[1], *N.S.*[2] and *N.S.*[3] respectively. I shall also use the system of numbered paragraphs, not Vico's own, adopted by Fausto Nicolini in his editions of the various works in the *Scrittori d'Italia* series, Vols. III and IV (Bari, Laterza, 1931, 1928), which has gained widespread currency. This will enable the reader to use either the complete translation of the *Third New Science*, by Thomas Goddard Bergin and Max Harold Fisch, revised edition (Ithaca, Cornell University Press, 1968), or my own *Vico: Selected Writings* (Cambridge, Cambridge University Press, 1982), which contains parts of the *First* and *Third New Science*. I

Here, we are told, each nation will, as a result of the operation of a constant and uninterrupted order of causes, be guided through three consecutive kinds of nature. Each of these provides the basis for three different, but connected, sets of institutions. The first runs from the customs of the nation to its natural law and, thence, to its form of government. For each such set, and for the purpose of communicating its contents, there arises an appropriate form of language and of writing. And for the justification of the content of each set there arises an appropriate form of jurisprudence, of reason or right, and of judgement.

At first sight it might look as though this is an hierarchical rather than holistic view of society, for the nature of the nation at any one stage appears to determine its customs and these, in turn, to determine its natural law and so on. But to see that it is holistic one must note that, although the nature of some kinds of institutions is determined by that of others, the nature of the nation, upon which everything rests, is not itself an institution.

To show this it is worth turning to Vico's account of the first nature, that of the most primitive sort of man. This nature is said to be 'poetic or creative or, as we may even call it, divine' because, in the absence of any very recognisably rational faculties, its primary mode of operation consists in the creation of imaginary entities by the imaginative projection of its own properties upon the world. Since Vico holds that man with this nature, 'poetic' man, is also wild, cruel, and self-regarding in the most unenlightened sense, this means that he projects these particular properties on to the world. The latter is thus conceived of in the most anthropomorphic way.[6] The world *is* a cruel and vindictive being, who demands that others be at his service just as poetic man would like to use them for his own means. Hence poetic man tries to satisfy Him by sacrifices and offerings and tries to find out what He wants by developing the art of divination and the taking of the auspices.[7] Moreover, this theological conception of the world affects every aspect of life. The law, for example, which Vico thinks is necessary to any remotely social form of life, is conceived of as the penalties and retributions which this cruel and vindictive being demands of man for his misdemeanours and sins.[8] Since the only form of authority which poetic man recognises is that of this divine

shall use the expression 'the New Science' when referring to doctrines which are common to all versions of the work.

[6] *N.S.*³, 374–7, 916.   [7] *Ibid.*, 379.   [8] *Ibid.*, 922.

being, this must mediate all other authority. Political power must therefore have divine approbation, with the consequence that in early societies the office of king and of priest are united.[9]

Here, it is clear, a primary aspect of the nature of 'poetic' man consists in a fundamental mode of mental activity – imagining – which explains the unified character of the whole set of institutions. It would be a mistake, however, to suggest that this mode of mental activity determines the institutions, for Vico does not limit the human nature of a nation to its mode of thought. Rather it consists in the three attributes of knowledge, will and ability,[10] the development of which, although logically prior to that of the institutions and customs of a society, occurs in and through them. Institutions, one might say, exist for a purpose and must conform to certain capacities but, in the end, knowledge is the foremost of the attributes of human nature because it governs the conceptions, be they true or false, by which the objects of will are characterised.

A third similarity to Hegel is to be found in Vico's rejection of anything like the uniformity of nature or consciousness theses. This point can be most easily demonstrated if we turn first to Vico's account of the differences between the three kinds of natures which develop in the course of the history of a nation. In the first kind of nature imagination, unconstrained by truth, is the primary characteristic of mind. It is a nature by which man creates a world through a failure of understanding.[11] In the second kind of nature, which is a development of the first, a certain kind of rationality has been acquired. It is the sort of rationality which puts a high premium upon the undeviating observation of rules. Vico illustrates it best in relation to the law, in which sphere it consists in ensuring the rigid application of the formulae in which the laws are expressed, which are still thought of as having had a divine origin. Thus, as he puts it, 'whoever drops a comma loses the case'.[12] But this is not full rationality, for here there is too much reliance on a non-human authority, to the extent that it is more important to apply the law

---

[9] 'Assuming that all nations originated in the cult of some divinity, in the state of the families the fathers must have been the sages in the divinity of auspices, the priests who made sacrifices to procure them, that is, to understand them properly, and the kings who brought divine laws to their families.' *N.S.*[3], 250.

[10] *Il Diritto Universale*, Liber Uno, Caput X.

[11] 'This imaginative metaphysics shows that *homo non intelligendo fit omnia.*' *N.S.*[3], 405.

[12] '*Qui cadit virgula, caussa cadit.*' *N.S.*[3], 965.

than to understand its purpose. In the third age, the age of 'fully developed reason', men have a grasp of the nature of things and use them in accordance with that nature. Hence in law, again, they understand the rational principle of equity and frame and change laws in accordance with that principle.

Thus, on Vico's view, in the course of the development of human nature, there is a change in the primary mode of mental functioning from one which is almost wholly imaginative, to one which involves an inflexible and blind acceptance of authority, to one in which man can discern the truth. And this development affects, and is expressed in, every area of human practice and activity.[13]

Another respect in which Vico's denial of any uniformity in human nature reveals itself is in his incessant attacks on the natural law theorists and, in particular, on Grotius. The error of which he constantly accuses them is that of having believed 'that natural equity, in its most complete conception, has been understood by the gentile nations from their very beginnings, without reflecting that some two thousand years were needed in order that philosophers should arise in them.'[14] The criticism here is not against the concept of natural law as such, for Vico thinks of himself as, in some sense, a natural law theorist,[15] but against the assumption that the natural law of one age can be the same as that of another, and a failure to see that the human mind develops so that what it can grasp in a later age could not have been grasped in an earlier one.

A fourth resemblance, which follows almost directly from that

---

[13] In *Vico's Science of Imagination*, Donald Verene denies that Vico sees this sequence as progressive. Since, on Verene's account, the imagination is always the primary mode of mental functioning, he sees any displacement from the robust character of the early era towards the abstract thinking of the third era as regressive and in need of redress. Addressing the implications of this view for the notion of truth, Verene concludes that perhaps Vico never thought that truth, in any conceptual sense, could be reached. To grasp the truth which the New Science contains, he suggests, is to perform the imaginative operations required to recollect its content. On this point, see also Verene's 'Vico's Philosophy of Imagination' and Isaiah Berlin's 'Comment on Professor Verene's Paper', both in *Vico and Contemporary Thought*, ed. Giorgio Tagliacozzo, Michael Mooney and Donald Phillip Verene (London, Macmillan Press, 1980), pp. 20–39, and my own 'Imagination in Vico', in *Vico: Past and Present*, Giorgio Tagliacozzo (Atlantic Highlands, N.J., Humanities Press, 1981), pp. 162–70.

[14] *N.S.*[3], 329.

[15] *N.S.*[1], 14, 48–56, where he offers an account of the 'natural' order in which our ideas of a universal and eternal justice arise. The sense of 'natural' involved here is that discussed below, pp. 148–52 and 179–82. For a quite different alternative, however, see Gino Bedani's *Vico Revisited*, pp. 245–74 *passim*.

above, is that Vico shares Hegel's view that a straightforwardly empirical approach to human history will not suffice. Hegel made the point that there was an important difference between the impulses and inclinations which operated in a restricted sphere and those which operated in the conflict of interests in world history, and that we had to move from empirical to philosophical history to take account of the latter. Vico similarly thinks that we cannot simply take over the concepts and understanding appropriate to our own age and apply them to history at large. To do so is to run the risk of wholesale conceptual anachronism as has occurred, he claims, in the attempt to find something akin to present philosophical wisdom in the great poems and myths of the past.[16] The answer to this difficulty is not, however, to apply more detailed and careful empirical research, for when he turns to the philologists, who have done precisely that, Vico finds that their failure to work in accordance with a knowledge of universal principles has left them totally at variance with one another over many – indeed, most – of the important issues of interpretation in history. Thus he condemns the philologists for having failed to correct their work with the reasoning of the philosophers and the philosophers for similarly having disregarded the work of the philologists. The answer, he asserts, is to find a way of bringing the two into a fruitful collaboration.[17] The nature of this collaboration will be discussed later, but it is not difficult to see, in these remarks, a rejection both of a purely *a priori* and of a purely empirical approach which was echoed, if not achieved in practice, by Hegel in his insistence that while a philosophical viewpoint was required, philosophical history must not be guilty of *a priori* manipulation of the facts. On the very lowest estimate, then, we can say that Vico concurs with Hegel in holding that, while history must not be a product of *a priori* philosophy, neither can it dispense with something rather more systematic and reflective than the approach of the empirical historian.[18]

---

[16] Vico refers to this tendency as the *boria*, i.e., vanity or conceit, of the scholars. See *N.S.*³, 127–8. That he was concerned to show how to avoid conceptual anachronism is common ground to almost all Vico scholars, though they differ in their accounts of his recommendations as to how to do so. See the works by Berlin, Haddock, Verene and myself, referred to in n. 2 above.

[17] *N.S.*³, 138–40.

[18] It should perhaps be noted that while Hegel thinks that the empirical historian uses some categories, Vico rather harshly appears to credit them with none and complains constantly about their failure to try to set their source materials in a context which will lend their interpretations of them some credibility. *N.S.*¹, 23.

From the foregoing points we can conclude that Vico shares with Hegel the aim of providing a *scientia scientiarum* at the basis of which will be a theory of the development of human nature as such, thus giving its history a significance which we may describe as philosophical, in so far as it will provide a framework for understanding the whole range of human activities and phenomena and the different bodies of knowledge which have been produced. Similarly, he shares with Hegel the view that when it comes to a theory of the development of human nature, the categories appropriate to an understanding of contemporary history are inadequate and some other set of categories must be adduced. Although much more could be said, both in detail about these similarities and about many others, enough has already been done to justify the claim that Vico and Hegel are at one when it comes to the importance of history as a mode of knowledge. It is not, as Hume would have it, one of the subaltern sciences, but a science fundamental to any proper understanding of ourselves in the world in which we live. Properly conceived, history must combine with philosophy to form a united discipline – what Hegel called 'philosophical history'. Vico does not use this term, referring to his work as 'a new science concerning the common nature of nations', but he is quite clear about its combined character.[19]

THE NON-RATIONAL ORIGINS OF HUMANITY

It would not be profitable, I think, to proceed to develop an account of the way in which Vico tried to fulfil his aims by a lengthy discussion of the many points of dissimilarity between him and Hegel. It would, however, be helpful to start with two such dissimilarities which go more or less to the heart of the differences between the two thinkers.

It was noted, in the discussion in the last chapter, that Hegel himself was very insistent on the need for a commitment to a

[19] In the *First New Science*, he explains why his Science has not yet been discovered as follows: 'The unfortunate reason for this lack is that we have not yet possessed a science which constituted both a history and philosophy of humanity together. For the philosophers have meditated upon a human nature already civilised by the religions and laws in which, and only in which, philosophers originated and not upon the human nature which gave rise to the religions and laws in which philosophers originated; while ... the philologists have handed down vulgar traditions which are so disfigured, mutilated and displaced that, unless their proper appearance is restored to them, their fragments are pieced together and they are returned to their [proper] places, no serious thinker can believe them to have been created thus.' *N.S.*[1], 23.

substantial theory of rationality. This means not merely that philosophical history should ignore all those parts of the historical world in which reason had not developed itself, but that original history, which provides the philosophical historian with his materials, must exclude all legends, folksongs and poems, for these are the products of nations whose consciousness is still obscure and as such they cannot be 'the object of the philosophical history of the world, whose aim is to attain knowledge of the Idea in history'.[20] For although the original historian cannot have the reflective knowledge which philosophical history provides, he still 'participates in', or is in immediate contact with, the spirit of his age and, therefore, with the rational. Thus the *philosophical* notion of the object of philosophical history determines what is to be admitted as original history and this excludes legends, folksongs and so on, which are the products of nations of obscure consciousness, i.e., nations in which reason has not manifested itself.

When we turn to Vico there could be no more striking contrast. Not only does he not disregard the consciousness of obscure nations, as it expresses itself in legend, myth, traditional tales and so on, but, he tells us, we shall never come to a proper understanding of the development of human nature if we do not come to see how it has developed necessarily from such beginnings. The beginning to which he is prepared to go back is, in fact, far more obscure than those which Hegel is forced to reject. He describes it as the 'first human thought born into the gentile world'[21] and asserts, though with considerable exaggeration, that it has cost 'a good twenty years of research'[22] to discover it.

The account which he gives of this first form of 'thought' is, indeed, an astonishing one. Its primary feature is that of conjuring into existence, naturally and imaginatively, the theological conceptions mentioned earlier, by spreading man's conception of himself over the world.[23] Vico attributes to poetic man the thought of himself as a

---

[20] See above, pp. 73–4.   [21] *N.S.*[3], 338.

[22] *Ibid.*, 338. This must be an exaggeration, for the thought in question, that the world *is* a god, was first formulated by Vico in *Il Diritto Universale*, which was published between 1720 and 1722. Vico's previous philosophical works, from the *First Inaugural Oration* of 1699 to *De antiquissima Italorum sapientia* of 1709, show no concern with this problem nor, given their conceptual orientation, is it easy to see how Vico could then have been thinking of it. In the *First New Science* of 1725, he says that its discovery had involved twenty-five years' work. *N.S.*[1], 261.

[23] For Vico's most dramatic depiction of this process, see *N.S.*[3], 374–84 and 400–3. For an account which puts Vico's theory of the primitive mind in the context of

living body, so that by proceeding in this way he *naturally* sees the physical world as a very large body, and thunder and lightning as the very loud grunts of this being, identical to those through which poetic man sought to express himself. This being is the Jove in which all gentile religions originated.[24] And, in the same way, as man begins to discriminate more features of his world and, later, certain qualities of character, and certain social needs and utilities, he takes these to be a series of other gods, the children of Jove, so that a theogony of gods is naturally born in the minds of the first people *in terms of which they think*.[25] This first human thinking is very different from our present thinking, for poetic man had no capacity whatsoever to see things as instances of abstract universals – a capacity which Vico attributes to man only in the third age. His 'thinking' has more of the character of our experiencing, for everything is seen as particular and the best that he can do is to take different particulars – those which we would identify as instances of universals – as parts of a whole, which is itself a divine being.[26]

other eighteenth-century thinkers, see Frank Manuel's *The Eighteenth Century Confronts the Gods* (Cambridge, Mass., Harvard University Press, 1959).

[24] It should be noted that Vico's account is almost wholly confined to the gentile nations. The history of the Jews, he claimed, took a different course because, as God's chosen people, they received divine help. Whether he believed this or whether he claimed it solely to avoid investigation by the officers of the Inquisition, is an unresolved issue, although it is beyond doubt that his doctrines were held in suspicion during his own lifetime. On this point, see Frederick Vaughan's '*La Scienza Nuova*: Orthodoxy and the Art of Writing', *Forum Italicum*, Vol. 2, No. 4 (1968), his *The Political Philosophy of Giambattista Vico*, and Gino Bedani's *Vico Revisited*. Irrespective of the sincerity of his claims about Jewish history, it is clear that almost the whole of Vico's account of the course which the histories of nations must take is about that of the gentile nations and is explicitly said by him to be so. Nevertheless, it is difficult to see how, if his account of the 'ideal eternal history' is as I shall suggest, he could fail to have applied it to Jewish history as well, thus, effectively, depriving it of the unique status which Christian thought attributed to it. Thus it is not necessary to subscribe to the naturalistic interpretations of Vico offered by Badaloni, Vaughan and Bedani in order to see why he may have felt a certain reluctance to make some of the implications of his thought too explicit.

[25] The influence of Lucretius' *De rerum natura* upon Vico has long been known. See Badaloni, Bedani, and Vaughan, *The Political Philosophy of Giambattista Vico*. Vico's account of the nature of this primitive thinking, however, goes well beyond that of Lucretius. For two of the most thorough interpretations of it, see Verene's *Vico's Science of Imagination*, and Gianfranco Cantelli, *Mente corpo linguaggio* (Florence, G. C. Sansoni Editore Nuova, 1986).

[26] 'Thus, for example, they understood Jove, Cybele or Berecynthia, and Neptune and, first by mute pointing, interpreted them as those substances of the sky, earth and sea which they imagined to be animate divinities, and therefore, in accordance with truths delivered by their senses, believed them to be gods. Through these three divinities ... they interpreted everything pertaining to the sky, the earth and the

Thus, unlike Hegel, Vico is prepared to take the world of myth seriously, as an expression of human consciousness, albeit in an admittedly primitive area. But what, it may be asked, is the significance of this difference? Hegel has dismissed this sort of consciousness from philosophical history, on the ground that it is not even implicitly rational. Vico, on the other hand, has insisted on the necessity to take it into consideration, even although, as the foregoing remarks suggest, it is so primitive and irrational in character that it is difficult to see what, apart from sheer comprehensiveness, would be lost in terms of the comprehensibility of the rest, if it were to be omitted. What, to put the question the other way round, is Hegel losing by the fact that his rationalism forces him to dismiss the obscure – Vico's 'poetic' – from philosophical history?

The short answer to this, from Vico's point of view, is that Hegel cannot have a correct conception of the second necessary stage in historical development, the 'heroic' age. It is difficult to put exact limits upon the notion of the heroic age, a difficulty which arises from the fact that Vico himself seemed to change his mind over the boundary which distinguished it from the poetic age. Its central features are, however, clear enough. It arises in a period when, according to Vico, after the poetic and theological way of life has arisen, and its benefits have become apparent, strangers from outside appeal for asylum to the communities, or 'families', which have grown up around the theological world view, and are taken in on the basis of something akin to a very low level feudal arrangement. They have, for example, almost no rights in law, because law is the preserve of the king – usually the 'father' of the family – and through him, at best, of the rest of the family. They have no rights of possession, no rights to marriage, hence no legitimate offspring to whom to transfer their possessions and thus strengthen their access to possession as such. This whole mode of life finds its justification not in the actual strength of the rulers and their family proper but in their claims to be descended from unions of the gods and ordinary mortals. It is their semi-divine status which ensures that they, and nobody else, should have the mediate right to possession of the land, its produce and its workers, which belongs ultimately to the gods. The period of heroism is also, according to Vico, the start of the period of

sea; and, in the same way, with the other kinds of divinities they symbolised the other kinds of things which pertain to each god, such as all flowers to Flora and all fruits to Pomona.' *N.S.*[3], 402. See also *N.S.*[3], 399.

the class war. The situation in which the newcomers to society find themselves is one of considerable hardship. It is a situation in which they can have none of the solaces of religion, of the comforts and companionship of marriage, of children who can be a legitimate extension of themselves and to whom they can leave a heritage and so on. It thus becomes a period of class war in which, step by step, these virtual slaves – the 'plebs' in Rome – win the legal right to equality in these economic, social and human spheres of life. But the barrier all along is the myth of the semi-divine status of the nobles, which, although used by them to their own advantage in the war, is nevertheless one which they also believe.[27] Thus the rationale of the institutional structure at the start of the heroic period is to be found in a set of wholly false beliefs, and no change in the institutional structure can take place without being accompanied by, and eventually being grounded in, a change in that set of beliefs.

The principle of heroism is treated by Vico so seriously that he is prepared to put down a large part of the defects in other histories to a failure to identify it:

Heroic nature, which lay halfway between the divine and human things of nations, has been largely unknown until now, because we have either relied on memory alone or imagined it other than it was. It has thus concealed from us the divine things of nations, from which it originated, while leaving us without a science of human things, all of which were born of divine things. Thus the material for working out not merely the systems of the natural law of the gentes but the whole science of human learning, divine and gentile, has come down to us in a distorted and despoiled form.[28]

What would be lost, then, according to Vico, by a failure to go back to the very origins of human history, would be an ability to appreciate how what we take to be human nature is a development from a nature part of which consists in a wholly mythical consciousness and to appreciate how these origins have had their effect upon the whole

[27] 'The second nature was heroic, which the heroes themselves took to be of divine origin, for since they believed that the gods created everything, they took themselves, as those generated under Jove's auspices, to be his children; and being of the human species, they located in this heroism, and did so with justice, the natural nobility by which they were the princes of the human race. This natural nobility they vaunted over those who repaired to their asylums to save themselves from the perils of their infamous bestial communion in which, coming without gods, they were taken to be beasts ...' N.S.[3], 917. See also N.S.[3], 1101, where Vico makes it clear that the plebs have to overcome this vanity of the heroes, and recognise that they themselves share the same human nature.

[28] N.S.[1], 89.

way in which, over the course of history, a more rational human nature has been forged. Hegel's presupposition of an implicit but concrete rationality, as part of what it is to be 'historical', Vico would say, forced him to take far too rational a view of its origins, and to start far too late in the real process by which it arose, to be able to do anything to correct his mistake.[29]

FIRST-ORDER HISTORY AND EMERGENT RATIONALITY

It is possible now to deal, rather more briefly, with the second dissimilarity from Hegel. The point was made, in the last chapter, that although Hegel's intention was to show that reason governs the world, i.e., to make it a determinate constitutive principle, he was unable to do so because he failed to see that what such an enterprise required was a reconstitution of the historical facts themselves and not merely a higher-order interpretation put upon facts drawn from other sources. What he should have produced was a philosophically enlightened first-order history and not, as he did, some sort of second-order history presupposing facts of a different sort.

It will be apparent, from what has already been said, and even more from the most cursory glance at any of the versions of the New Science, that what Vico is offering is, in one aspect, a new first-order history, one which, as he puts it, is 'both a history and philosophy of humanity together'.[30] His account of the poetic age, for example, in which he goes back beyond the existence of written evidence, is heavily dependent upon an interpretation of the Homeric poems which he puts forward, which commits him to the view that, irrespective of whether or not a single Homer ever existed, the contents of the poems must be compilations of beliefs and customs drawn from two very different peoples living in places far apart,[31] that the poems had been created in the poetic age, corrupted in the heroic age and received thus in the Homeric age,[32] and that at no point had they disguised an esoteric and lofty philosophical wisdom such as many writers, from Plato onwards, had contrived to find in them.[33] What

---

[29] The view that doctrines 'must begin with the times in which their subject matter begins' is fundamental to the New Science. See *N.S.*[3], 314.

[30] *N.S.*[1], 23. See also *N.S.*[1], 248.   [31] *N.S.*[3], 880.   [32] *Ibid.*, 905.

[33] *Ibid.*, 780. For an interesting analysis of Vico's work on Homer as an example of his applied methodology, see B. A. Haddock, 'Vico's *Discovery of the True Homer*: A Case Study in Historical Reconstruction', *Journal of the History of Ideas*, 40 (1979). As

they are, when properly interpreted, is an expression of the way in which an original poetic age saw its own civil history. Similarly, Vico engages in a sustained polemic against the widely accepted view that the Law of the Twelve Tables was first produced by Solon for the Athenians and later transferred to Rome, thus concealing, what Vico takes to be true, that they were a compilation of the natural law of the gentes of Latium in their heroic period, and can therefore throw light both upon a particular section of history and upon the nature of heroic law in general.[34]

In this connection it remains only to point out that this is a part of what Vico explicitly asserts that such a science as his must contain. In Section II of Book II of the *Third New Science*, he lists seven principal aspects of his science. These include a history of human ideas and the principles of universal history. Vico does not, it is true, claim to have provided a universal history and, indeed, he frequently asserts that this would involve more learning than he himself possesses. Nevertheless, he does preface the *Second* and *Third New Science* with a list of some of the most important facts in the histories of seven ancient nations, including, of course, those of Greece and Rome, constituted according to the principles involved in his science, while in Book V he attempts to extend this to include parts of European history after the Dark Ages.

But although the New Science is, amongst other things, a history, it is not just a history. It was mentioned above that Vico himself claims that it must involve a relationship between philology and philosophy and that its product must be 'both a history and philosophy of humanity together'. Moreover, another of the principal aspects of the science, to which he makes constant, if rather unhelpful, reference, is that of an 'ideal eternal history traversed in time by the histories of all nations'.[35] This is an important, but problematic, notion which is nevertheless integral to the idea of something which is both an history and a philosophy together. Thus, in the *First New Science*, Vico writes:

By means of the foregoing properties we have established the eternity and universality of the natural law of the gentes. Since this law emerged with the common customs of peoples, which are themselves the invariable creations of nations, and since human customs are practices or usages of human nature,

will be evident, Haddock's account of the relevant methodology differs from that which I ascribed to Vico in my earlier writings and to which I shall adhere below.
[34] *N.S.*[1], 21, 41, 50, 66, 81–7 *passim*, *N.S.*[3], 154, 902.   [35] *N.S.*[3], 393.

which does not all change at once but always retains an impression of some former habit or custom, this Science must provide, at one and the same time, both a philosophy and history of human customs, which together provide the kind of jurisprudence with which we are concerned, i.e., the jurisprudence of mankind. It must provide these, moreover, in such a fashion, that the first part unfolds a linked series of reasons [or rights] while the second narrates a continuous or uninterrupted sequence of the facts of humanity in accordance with these reasons, [rather] as causes produce effects which resemble them. In this way the certain origins and the uninterrupted progress of the whole of the universe of nations should be discovered. And in conformity with the present order of things laid down by providence, this science comes to be an ideal eternal history traversed in time by the history of all nations.[36]

Two claims emerge fairly clearly from this passage. First, that with regard to jurisprudence, which is Vico's special concern here, a linked series of reasons or rights must be unfolded in one part of his science, while a second part must narrate the actual facts of the history of jurisprudence in such nations in accordance with this series. Second, and as a result, what is revealed is some kind of eternal pattern – an ideal eternal history – which is exemplified by the history of all nations.

To see how this works out it would be useful to glance briefly at Vico's account of the first two agrarian laws which, though he develops it in connection with Roman history, is meant to be a feature of all histories. This can be picked up at the point where, according to Vico, all ownership belongs immediately to God and mediately to the 'fathers' of the families in whom are united the roles of sage, priest and king. The father's dominion extends over his family proper, who share with him the right to religion, marriage, children with certainty of descent and so on, and the *famuli*, i.e., those who have come to the family for protection and whose status is that of serf or slave. As a result of a prolonged period of war between these two classes the fathers are forced first to unite into aristocratic states under a yet higher king, to whom they make over some of their powers, and to grant bonitary ownership of the fields to the workers who, in return, accept the burden of the census and free service to the fathers in time of war. This law, the 'first agrarian law', was granted in Rome, according to Vico, at the time of Servius Tullius,[37] and he says of it that 'nothing could be more restricted by nature',[38] for it allowed the

---

[36] *N.S.*[1], 90.   [37] *N.S.*[3], 107.   [38] *Ibid.*, 265.

famuli only to do their own cultivating, but denied them the right to bring civil actions when their ownership was breached, or even to defend it by force. This meant that their ownership was entirely at the mercy of the will of their lords or those members of the family from whom they held the land. To rectify this unstable condition, the *famuli* therefore struggled to obtain quiritary, i.e., military or defensible, ownership of their lands, which constitutes the 'second agrarian law', and, in the case of Rome, Vico asserts that this is what was involved in the struggle for the Law of the Twelve Tables. But quiritary ownership is also an inherently unstable form of ownership, for the plebs, as they now were, could neither leave their possessions intestate to their family heirs, since, lacking the right to marriage, they had no heirs recognised in law, nor leave them by testament, for they were not citizens. Hence, their lands simply reverted to the lords upon their deaths. To rectify this they therefore proceeded to demand the right of *connubium* or solemnised marriage[39] and, since this required access to the religions of the nobles, the right to the latter as well. Thus, by a series of steps involving a demand for an improvement in their legal rights, the plebs gained such an equality of status with the nobles – the heroes – as, in the end, to require a change in the form of the state from the aristocratic state, whose governing principle was the protection of the heroes' great private interests, to the free popular state. Vico claims that this is what was involved in the enactment of the Publilian Law in Rome.

This example may help to clarify some aspects of the claim that the New Science must provide both a philosophy and history of human customs, in this case of jurisprudence, by providing a 'linked series of rights' and a 'continuous or uninterrupted series of facts' in accordance with the series. For, first and most obviously, it shows that the series of rights provides a principle which bears upon the constitution of the facts. It explains, that is, what people were trying to do and what it was that occurred in the major changes in Roman legal and constitutional history. In this sense, then, the series of rights can be thought of as contributing to the constitution of the facts themselves and thus as providing that inner connection for which Hegel unsuccessfully searched. It would be incorrect, however, to claim that it did more than contribute to their constitution since, as mentioned earlier,

---

[39] *Ibid.*, 598.

Vico finds the most fundamental principles involved in the nature of the nation itself.[40]

Second, it throws some light on the nature of the links in the series of rights which Vico traces. The important point here is that, once the *famuli* have embarked on the quest for even the most minimal form of ownership conceivable, nothing can guarantee them in their possession of it short of full civil status in a state, the form of which is determined by that end. Thus the impossibility of guaranteeing even the notion of bonitary ownership, because of the inherent instability of a situation in which such a demand can arise, generates a sequence of demands for rights which can come to rest only when there is a change in the basis of the state.

A further point to be noted in this connection, although it is not made in the above example, is that Vico views this sequence as rational because it finds its culmination only in a state in which an intelligent human nature exists and evinces itself. For, the third kind of law, that in which the sequence comes to rest, is 'the human law which fully developed human reason dictates',[41] while the third kind of governments, the form of which alone can guarantee this kind of law, 'are the human governments in which, through that equality of intelligent nature which is the nature proper to man, all are equal in law'.[42] But Vico is insistent that this is the sort of state which is proper to man only when his nature is fully developed, for the third kind of nature is 'human, an intelligent and therefore modest, benign and reasonable nature, which recognises conscience, reason and duty as laws'.[43]

---

[40] This is made clear in the following passage: 'when facts are problematic they should be taken in accordance with laws, while when laws are problematic they should be interpreted in accordance with nature, whence we must accept such problematic laws and facts as create neither absurdity nor impropriety, much less impossibility'. *N.S.*[1], 92.

[41] *N.S.*[3], 924.

[42] *Ibid.*, 927. Vico is not consistent on this point, since, in the same paragraph, he explains that either all are born free in such states or, if such states are monarchies, the monarchs make all their subjects equal in law by retaining for themselves the force of arms. But the second possibility is hardly compatible with the notion of a state which rests on 'an equality of intelligent nature which is the nature proper to man'. To be consistent he ought to have admitted only the first alternative.

[43] *N.S.*[3], 918. See also *N.S.*[1], 254, where Vico says that this 'intelligent' substance is 'the human substance proper to us'. At *N.S.*[1], 54, he also describes it as a state in which 'men should no longer judge themselves to possess a nature different from, and superior to, that of others because of [differences in] strength, but should recognise that all are equal in respect of their rational nature, which is the proper and eternal human nature'.

This suggests that the governing notion in the principle which Vico adduces to explain the constitution of the facts is that of an emergent rationality, or capacity to understand, which enables men to see what is defective about inherently defective situations. This emergent rationality will not, however, consist in just the capacity to see what is defective or unstable in the situation, for the presuppositions which justified the situation must also be seen in their true light. Thus, the superior status of the nobility in law can only be overcome when the plebs realise that the divine origin of the nobles is a myth and that all share the same intelligent and reasonable nature.[44]

The notion of an emergent rationality is so important in Vico, although it has often been denied by many commentators, that it is worth quoting one further passage from the *First New Science*:

It will be one of the continuous tasks of the Science to show in detail how, with the development of human ideas, laws and rights emerged first from the scrupulousness of superstitions, then from the solemnity of legitimate acts and the limitations of words, and finally from any of the physical aspects which were believed at first to constitute the very substance of the matter; and how they must be led to their pure and true principle, their proper substance, which is human substance: our will determined by our mind through the power of truth, which is what we call 'conscience'.[45]

Here, as human ideas develop, so laws and rights change. But they do not change only in their content. For at the start their very substance is thought to be physical, whereas, by the end, they are understood to be nothing but expressions of will – the public will – informed by knowledge of the truth, i.e., knowledge of the equality of our human nature.

EMERGENT RATIONALITY AND THE 'IDEAL ETERNAL HISTORY'

It is possible now to turn to the second point involved in the conception of a science which is 'both a history and philosophy of humanity together', the proposal that one of its aspects will therefore

---

[44] 'But as, with the passing of the years and the further unfolding of the human mind, the plebs of the peoples finally saw this vanity of heroism for what it was, and understood themselves to share the same human nature as the nobles, they desired equal access to the civil orders of the cities.' *N.S.*[3], 1101.

[45] *N.S.*[1], 51. As mentioned earlier, in *Vico's Science of Imagination*, Verene denies that there is any such progress and sees Vico's third age as involving a collapse into an arid, over-intellectualised and over-technologised form of life. There is some

be an 'ideal eternal history traversed in time by the histories of all nations'. In the *First New Science* this is introduced in connection with the claim that what is required is 'a linked series of reasons' and 'a continuous or uninterrupted sequence of the facts of humanity in conformity with these reasons [rather] as causes produce effects which resemble them'.[46] This might suggest that the 'ideal eternal history' just is the series of linked reasons which, as is argued above, is at least partially constitutive of the facts in that continuous and uninterrupted sequence. For, as we have seen, the links in the series are necessary links, in so far as the stages in the series arise from the fact that, because of its inherently defective nature, the aim of the first right can be fulfilled in any satisfactory or stable manner only after a transformation of the total situation, achieved via the mediation of other unsatisfactory concepts of rights. Thus the 'philosophy of humanity' would consist in this account of the necessary development of human consciousness which, while it laid down the phases of that development, laid down also the principles which partially determine the facts of the history of each nation.

In a sense this is, I think, correct. But certain qualifications must be made. First, it was noted above that the links, though necessary, are not conceptually necessary. Each stage follows from its predecessor only when people become sufficiently rational to recognise not merely that the earlier stage is deficient, but to see through the false or unfounded claims which justified it. Until the plebs can come to see the 'vanity' or emptiness of the nobles' claims to divine origin, nothing can be done to alter their unsatisfactory situation.

Secondly, when we turn to the *Second New Science*, in which Vico tries to set out the basis of his system in axiomatic form, it is clear from the propositions devoted to the 'ideal eternal history' that the latter includes much more than just the series of rights which determine, or partially determine, the facts of the history of law. Here, all the axioms from LXVI to XCVI are said to be 'principles of the ideal eternal history', and their scope is very extended indeed. There are axioms stating principles of a necessary sequence of the springs of action in men,[47] of a sequence of kinds of human nature,[48] of kinds of governments,[49] and of the natures and properties of the different

evidence for this, in so far as the third age is supposed to end in the 'barbarism of reflection' which, in turn, leads to the recurrence of the whole life-cycle of the nation. This is a standard difficulty of interpretation in Vico, which I shall discuss below, pp. 164–7.

[46] *N.S.*¹, 90.   [47] *N.S.*³, 241.   [48] *Ibid.*, 242.   [49] *Ibid.*, 243–64.

forms of state.[50] It is true that many of these 'axioms' have a somewhat mixed nature, since Vico ascribes their historical source to some historic figure, or to vulgar tradition, before proceeding to endorse them as elements in his science. It is true also that there are others which could hardly be fundamental to any science whatsoever. Nevertheless, when allowance has been made for Vico's notorious incapacity to set out systematically what he explicitly claims is a systematically related body of propositions,[51] if one accepts that these principles stand to the facts of political and constitutional history as did the 'linked series of rights' to the facts of legal history, it will be evident that the 'ideal eternal history' is a body of principles which is partly constitutive of all of these areas of history as well. They are, in other words, principles purporting to lay down the necessary sequence of stages through which human nature, in the various areas of human life in which it expresses itself, develops the final rationality which is always potential within it.[52]

A third, and last, qualification must now be noted. It can be introduced most easily by returning to the passage in the *First New Science* in which Vico drew the distinction between the linked series of rights and a history of the facts of humanity which would be in conformity with this series, thus leading to the idea of an 'ideal eternal history traversed in time by the history of the nations'.[53] I

[50] *Ibid.*, 267–94.
[51] The most explicit statement of this claim is at *ibid.*, 330, where he asserts of his basic propositions, surely wrongly, that 'each is compatible with all'. Nevertheless, there can be no doubt that he portrays himself as aiming to produce a systematic account of the development of man's humanity. See also, *N.S.*[1], 44, and *N.S.*[3], 345. Some commentators claim that this is so unlike what he actually produced that it is difficult to take the claim as being seriously meant, and they consequently disregard it as a piece of window-dressing. My own interpretation is based upon accepting it as a serious intention.
[52] The claim that Vico holds such a view of human nature has been denied by many, who see him as a philosopher who elevated the powers of the imagination over those of the intellect. But although it is true that he lays enormous stress upon the original imaginative modes of experience in which man's ascent to humanity originated, it seems clear to me, for reasons already given, that he sees these as the corporeal origin from which a truly spiritual and rational nature can develop. For works which, in different ways, deny that Vico sees history as a movement towards rationality, see Berlin, *Vico and Herder: Two Studies in the History of Ideas*; Haddock, *An Introduction to Historical Thought*; Verene, *Vico's Science of Imagination*; and Hayden White, 'The Tropics of History: The Deep Structure of the *New Science*', in *Giambattista Vico's Science of Humanity*, ed. Giorgio Tagliacozzo and Donald Phillip Verene (Baltimore, the Johns Hopkins University Press, 1976), pp. 65–85.
[53] *N.S.*[1], 90.

have interpreted this to mean that the facts are partially constituted by this series, but it is necessary now to consider why this qualification must be made and how it will affect Vico's theory.

In his *Autobiography*, when mentioning two of the four philosophers by whom he has been most influenced, Vico writes:

Up to this time Vico had admired two only above all other learned men: Plato and Tacitus; for with an incomparable metaphysical mind Tacitus contemplates man as he is, Plato as he should be. And as Plato with his universal knowledge explores the parts of nobility which constitute the man of intellectual wisdom, so Tacitus descends into all the counsels of utility whereby, among the infinite irregular chances of malice and fortune, the man of practical wisdom brings things to good issue. Now Vico's admiration of these two great authors from this point of view was a foreshadowing of that plan on which he later worked out an ideal eternal history to be traversed by the universal history of all times, carrying out on it, by certain eternal properties of civil affairs, the development, acme and decay of all nations. From this it follows that the wise man should be formed both of esoteric wisdom such as Plato's and of common wisdom such as that of Tacitus.[54]

The interesting point here is the connection of the notions of 'man as he is' and 'man as he should be', grasped by Tacitus and Plato respectively, as foreshadowing the notion of an 'ideal eternal history'. In addition, one should note also the reference to Tacitus' capacity to 'descend' into the counsels of utility, which is closely connected to his insight into 'man as he is'.

A broad reading of the passage would suggest that, at the least, the 'ideal eternal history' must involve both of the notions which Vico recognised in the writings of Tacitus and Plato. This suggestion is, indeed, carried forward in Vico's other writings. In the *Third New Science*, for example, we are told that 'philosophy must raise and support fallen and weak man, not distort his nature nor abandon him in his corruption'. But this claim is advanced along with a criticism of Plato, who is rebuked for having failed to consider man with all his faults,[55] together with some laudatory remarks about the way in

---

[54] *The Autobiography of Giambattista Vico*, translated by Max Harold Fisch and Thomas Goddard Bergin, Great Seal Books (New York, Cornell University Press, 1963), pp. 138–9.

[55] 'Philosophy considers man as he ought to be, and thus can profit only the very few who wish to live in the Republic of Plato and not wallow in the filth of Romulus.' *N.S.*[3], 131.

which legislation does consider man as he is and, indeed, puts his vices to good, social use.[56]

The conclusion to be drawn here is that we cannot ascribe to Vico the view that man is as he ought to be. The historical facts which trace the development of humanity must be in conformity with the 'linked series of reasons' with its necessary culmination in an ultimate ideal, but cannot be wholly constituted by them. And in this case, neither can the 'ideal eternal history', even if it is temporarily thought of as no more than a pattern which is exemplified in all national histories, be identified with this linked series.

To proceed beyond this it is necessary to turn to a further claim which Vico advances, still, fortunately, in connection with the development of law. If we consider the linked series involved in the first and second agrarian laws, as described earlier, it might seem that Vico is saying that the various changes which occur in the legal history of each nation are caused by a desire, on the part of the legally underprivileged, for an equal share in the necessities and utilities of life which society can provide. For, as we have seen, Vico certainly holds that such a struggle, amounting to a class struggle, goes on. Nevertheless, while maintaining this, he constantly denies that a desire for these necessities and utilities is the cause of the legal outcome at any particular stage, which he calls 'the just'.[57] On the contrary, the drive for the utilities of social life is described as the *occasion* but not the cause of the just, the latter being said to be 'eternal reason which, in immutable geometric and mathematical proportions, distributes the variable utilities upon the occasion of different human needs'.[58]

When Vico says that the cause of the just is eternal reason, he certainly does not mean to refer to that notion of reason which, as used by Grotius and the other natural law philosophers, he constantly criticises. What he is talking about, rather, is a developing notion of reason, i.e., the linked series of rights. This is made clear in the following passage:

The natural law of the gentes is an eternal law which traverses time. But just as within us lie a few eternal seeds of truth, which are cultivated gradually from childhood until, with age and through [various] studies, they develop

[56] 'Legislation considers man as he is, in order to create of him good practices in society: as, from violence, avarice and ambition, which are the three vices prevalent throughout the whole of mankind, it creates the army, commerce and the court, and thus the strength, wealth and wisdom of states.' *N.S.*[3], 132.

[57] *Ibid.*, 341.   [58] *N.S.*[1], 41.

into the fully clarified notions which belong to the sciences, so, as a result of [human] sin, within mankind were buried the eternal seeds of justice which, as the human mind develops gradually according to its true nature from the childhood of the world, develop into demonstrated maxims of justice.[59]

The suggestion, then, is that while a desire for access to the necessities and utilities of social life is the occasion of legal change, the reason for the change which occurs is the developing concept of justice or equity. In a famous passage Vico makes it quite clear that the desire which is the occasion of the change springs from that aspect of man into which Tacitus could 'descend', the world of the 'irregular chances of malice and fortune':

But because their nature is corrupt men are tyrannised by self-love, whence they pursue first and foremost only what is useful for themselves; so that, desiring all that is useful for themselves and nothing for their fellows, they are unable to bring their passions under conatus in order to direct them towards justice. Whence we establish: that in the bestial state man desires only his own well-being; having taken wife and fathered children, he desires his own well-being together with that of the families; having come to civil life, he desires his own well-being together with that of the cities; when the powers of the cities are extended over several peoples, he desires his well-being together with that of the nations; when the nations are united by wars, peace, alliances and commerce, he desires his well-being together with that of the whole of mankind; [but] in all these circumstances man desires, first and foremost, what is useful to himself. Therefore by divine providence alone is he constrained to remain within these orders to celebrate in justice [the practices of] the family society, civil society and, finally, human society; for though man is unable to achieve all that he desires, he may at least expect to achieve all those utilities which he needs, and this is called "just". Hence, that which regulates the whole of human justice is divine justice, which is administered by divine providence for the preservation of human society.[60]

Disregarding the reference to divine providence, to which I shall return later, several points stand out in this passage. First, Vico is adamant that, because of his corrupt nature, man seeks only what he takes to be for his own advantage. Second, however, the content of this changes as, in new institutional roles – father of the family, citizen, and so on – the concept of self alters and expands so as to include an identity of interest with others. Hence, when the individual demands 'his' rights, this will take the form of demanding the rights of his 'family' or of a certain class in society and so on. There is thus a movement from 'his' rights, understood as those of the particular individual he is, to those of the citizen or, even, to those of man as such. These demands provide the occasion of the changes, referred to earlier. They are not, however, the cause of the changes. The latter is a yet wider concept described in the above passage as 'all those utilities which he needs'. This involves the notion of the distribution of utilities according to the needs of different situations. Thus, to take an example given already, when the first family societies have established themselves, others appeal to them for asylum, thus constituting, in effect, a class of serfs, the *famuli*. When they, in turn, seek the first minimal share of the rights of the family proper, i.e., bonitary ownership of the fields which they work, and succeed in winning it, they do so because it is recognised, on both sides, that it is right or equitable in the circumstances that, in return for this right, the *famuli* should be subject to the census and provide service for the family proper in times of war. This is part of the 'linked series of rights' which arises from a sense of what is just in the circumstances, but which cannot be adequate to any situation until it culminates in a sense of what is equitable for man as such. Thus the notion of what is just or equitable in the circumstances has itself an historical career, the phases of which provide the cause, i.e., the rational ground, of the arrangements arrived at by the nation at different points of its career. The *occasion*, we may say, is what is desired by man as his social being changes and develops, but the cause is an ideal which develops progressively in the light of its proven incapacity, in its earlier phases, to satisfy its aim.

If this is correct, the linked series of reasons cannot wholly determine the constitution of the facts, for the latter requires also an account of the part played by human desire. It follows also that the 'ideal eternal history' cannot be identical with the 'linked series' because the 'ideal eternal history' is an account of a path to be traversed by all nations, and, as argued above, such an account must include both occasions and causes. The 'ideal eternal history' must therefore be an account of the necessary sequence of both occasions and causes and of the relationship in which they stand to each other. When Vico says, therefore, that a history of the 'facts of humanity' must be in accordance with the 'linked series of reasons', this must be understood to mean that the latter is partially, but not wholly, constitutive of the former.

Putting this more generally, Vico's insistence that a science of the development of man's humanity should take into account both man as he is and man as he ought to be can be interpreted as involving an inherently dynamic relationship. 'Man as he is' is never man with a fixed and constant nature. It is always man at some stage in the historical development of his social being. This will involve the implementation, both in his consciousness and in his institutions, of certain earlier ideals, affecting his sense of self-interest. 'Man as he ought to be', on the other hand, will be a related series of conceptions of an ideal, which changes progressively when, as each earlier conception is applied in the world, it proves unable to fulfil its aim. The latter governs the direction, but not the occurrence, of the changes which take place in history. An account which is both an history and philosophy of the development of humanity must show, therefore, that the underlying reason why man has come to be what he is lies in the necessity to apply ideals which, because of his own undeveloped nature, cannot fail to be inadequate but which, when embodied in his consciousness and way of life, provide a basis for more adequate ideals.

PROVIDENCE

This account suggests a further similarity between Vico and Hegel, in so far as for both the development of some kind of reason is a governing principle in a 'philosophical' history.[61] For Hegel, however, that development is determined transcendently, in virtue of the logical priority of the phases of the idea, whereas, for Vico, it develops internally and incrementally, so to speak, starting from a wholly imaginative basis, via the operation of the factors identified above. Nevertheless, in both conceptions there is a teleological aspect and it is important to see whether or not and, if so, to what extent, this overrides the above difference in their views about the role of reason in history.

In Hegel's case there is no doubt about the teleological character of the theory. Spirit, he repeatedly says, carries its end within itself and everything which happens in world history happens on behalf of that end. It is this, of course, which enables him to claim that what he is presenting is a theodicy, a justification of God's ways to man: for the

---

[61] Vico does not actually use this term, preferring to refer to his work as a science of humanity. Nevertheless, as mentioned above, he does conceive it as involving both an history and philosophy of the development of humanity at once.

pain and suffering involved in history are asserted to be the only way in which man's divine nature, his freedom, can be actualised and, hence, to be justified by that fact.

At first sight there seems nothing so strongly teleological in Vico's theory. In the account developed above, the interplay between the occasion and the cause or reason does not require that anything should occur on behalf of some further end. 'Man as he is' and 'man as he ought to be' are two elements, one of desire, the other of a slowly developing rationality or intelligence to which desire becomes subject, which are involved in the explanation of the occurrence and direction of historical change. But here it is necessary only that reason develop to the extent of our being able to see that a new ideal must be created and implemented if a previous ideal is to be fulfilled. There need be no suggestion, as in Hegel, that some unseen but higher purpose or end is actualising itself through this process. The growth of man's humanity can therefore be the outcome, even the necessary outcome, of this process, without the implication that the process occurs on behalf of that outcome.

The account is nevertheless insufficient as it stands, for Vico talks of the process in two different ways. On the one hand, in a way which is quite consistent with the account as it has been developed so far, he talks as though history is the story of man's gradually developing intelligence, as he slowly frees himself from a life based on imagination, belief in the false, the superstitious and so on, until he is able to understand the true nature of things and govern his desire by that understanding.[62] On the other hand, even as he talks in these terms, Vico continually reverts to the operations of another mind, that of providence, whose aims not merely differ from those of man but are fulfilled in place of them:

For, though men have themselves made this world of nations – and this became the first indisputable principle of this Science, since we despaired of discovering a science among the philosophers and philologists – it has without doubt been born of a mind often unlike, at times quite contrary to

---

[62] 'Men first [have a] sense [of things] without [conscious] consideration, then they consider [them] with a perturbed and agitated spirit, finally they reflect [upon them] with a pure mind.

  This axiom constitutes the principle of poetic judgements, which are formed by a sense of passion and feeling, in contrast to philosophical judgements, which are formed by reflection involving reasoning, whence the latter draw nearer to the true the more they ascend to the universal, while the former become more certain the more they are appropriate to particulars.' *N.S.*[3], 218–19.

and ever superior to, the particular ends these men had set themselves, which narrow ends, made means to serve wider ends, it has always used to preserve the human race on this earth. Thus men would indulge their bestial lust and forsake their children, but they create the purity of marriage, whence arise the families; the fathers would exercise their paternal powers over the clients without moderation, but they subject them to the civil powers, whence arise the cities ... Yet that which did all this was mind, for men did it with intelligence; it was not fate, for they did it by choice; nor was it chance, for, to the end of time, by their ever acting thus, the same things are born.[63]

Here there is a strange mixture of claims. We are told simultaneously both that the world is the product of man and that it is the product of a superhuman mind, which uses man's particular ends to secure its own wider ends, including the preservation of man. The argument for this depends entirely upon the unintended, but salutary, consequences of the actions undertaken on behalf of man's particular ends – the creation of the family proper, of the city and so on. On the other hand, the defence of the assertion that the world is a product of mind lies wholly in the claim that 'men did it with intelligence'. For Vico denies that it is the work of fate, on the grounds that men did it by choice, or that it was the work of chance, because men always do the same things at the corresponding points in the histories of nations, from which the same things arise. Thus, on the one hand, we are told that the world is not a product of man, on the grounds that through the unintended consequences of his actions new institutions arise. And on the other hand, we are told that it is a product of mind because men create it by intelligence, by choice, and by making uniform intelligent choices on the same occasions.

Faced with these apparently different claims, it is not surprising that there exists a wide range of interpretations of Vico's concept of providence. Vaughan[64] views it as a deliberate attempt by Vico to obscure a strongly naturalistic tendency in his thought, which would explain the reason why he felt it necessary to guard himself against potential accusations of heresy. Verene identifies it with the 'ideal eternal history', which he sees as an eternal but tragic pattern, in virtue of which man's activities engender their opposites and what seems like progress is, ultimately and necessarily, movement towards dissolution and recurrence.[65] Croce again, as mentioned earlier,

[63] *Ibid.*, 1108.   [64] *The Political Philosophy of Giambattista Vico.*
[65] *Vico's Science of Imagination.*

assimilated it to Hegel's concept of the cunning of reason.[66] These are very different interpretations from that which I shall offer below. It is not possible, in the space available, however, to offer a detailed defence of my reasons for not accepting them. In general, however, I hope that in what follows my reasons for dissenting from the assimilation of providence with the cunning of reason will become evident in the light of what I have already said about the latter concept. In the case of the naturalistic reading of providence, in which it is seen as a kind of natural, and naturally recurrent, pattern arising from man's nature as part of the natural world, I shall try to show that this is incompatible with Vico's notion of the nature of historical development. For the moment, therefore, I shall proceed by considering what sense can be made of the doctrine within the framework of the foregoing exposition of Vico's general approach.

It becomes evident, in fact, that a considerable part of Vico's claims about providence can be made intelligible in the light of the distinction between the occasion and the cause of historical change.[67] In the passage quoted above, for example, it is clear that it is man's particular ends which provide the occasion for the change, and providence's wider aim which is the cause, or ground, òf the result, for the fathers' abuse of their powers over their clients is the occasion of a change, the unintended result of which – the formation of the cities – is presented as the fulfilment of a higher aim.

The first point to be decided here is the relation of the two aims. If Vico's claim were that the individual's particular aim was the occasion of a change to which somehow, and in a quite incomprehensible manner, providence gave a certain rational structure, the position would be indefensible. This would be to view providence as the action of a *deus ex machina* and, as with all such beings, if their operation is wholly inexplicable, their introduction merely serves to mask a failure of explanation in the theory which requires us to appeal to them.

The distinction, developed earlier, between occasion and cause points, however, to a quite different conception. The occasion was the

---

[66] *La filosofia di G.B. Vico.*

[67] I do not intend to suggest that what I shall offer will suffice to explain the many very different kinds of contexts in which Vico refers to the action of providence such as, for example, implanting in poetic man a confused idea of divinity, or causing him to classify things before explaining them. These may well have to be dealt with in other ways. My concern here is with the one general claim that providence achieves its aims through those of man.

aims of individuals in their various social capacities – the fathers, for example, abusing their legitimate paternal power over their clients – but the cause was a wider conception, the rational force of which was felt by all concerned. Hence in the case of the first agrarian law, the necessity to submit to the census and to fight for their lords was seen by the members of the *famuli* as just if they were to have bonitary possession of the fields. And the reason why this is so is, as we have seen, that the occasion is related to, and reveals faults and inadequacies in, an earlier phase of the development of a rational ideal. The fathers do not, of course, abuse their clients in order to reveal this deficiency. Their action springs from that self-love to which Vico drew attention earlier.[68] But in so far as it is abuse of their clients, it reveals the unsatisfactory nature of the institutional system and thus serves to occasion further thought about how to secure the ideal which it is failing to secure. Viewed in this way, the cause is the new conception which arises from progressively more rational reflection upon faults in the principle revealed by the breakdown which occasions the reflection. 'Providence' thus becomes the name for a higher wisdom, an understanding of more adequate concepts, which develops in nations in the course of their historical experience. It is a wisdom which can develop only in the context of a nation, for it is concerned with the moral and legal relationships between classes in a community. Hence it is something in which an individual can share only as a member of an historical community or nation and, for that reason, it can be termed 'superhuman'.[69] Here the term 'superhuman' serves to describe an historically developing collective wisdom as the nation works its way through a series of intermediate but necessarily connected concepts to a grasp of those concepts which reveal the nature of things.[70] There is thus no need to think of the owner of this wisdom as anything other than the nation as such and, therefore, no need to think of it as a *deus ex machina*.

This suggestion needs to be modified in the light of certain possible criticisms before it can be accepted. First, it might be argued that it lays altogether too much stress on an implicit rationality in man as the directive force in history, thus drawing Vico, with his accen-

[68] See above, p. 157.
[69] 'And must we not consider this the plan of a superhuman wisdom, regulating and leading [things] in a divine manner, not by the force of laws ... but by utilising those very wisdoms of men whose practice is as free from force as is man's celebration of his own nature?' *N.S.*[3], 1107.
[70] *Ibid.*, 326.

tuation of the importance of the obscure and the irrational primitive eras, implausibly close to Hegel. In reply to this, it could be pointed out that Vico does take the history of a nation to be the history of the emergence of a rational humanity from an irrational barbarism and that, at some point, recognisably rational elements must start to play a role. Or, again, it might be noted that self-love and human corruption are still indispensable to the process. But these replies would not fully meet the point, for the objection would be to the suggestion that Vico thinks that historical change is grounded in an appreciation of the rationality of the change, whereas corrupt beings, such as men, can see that something is rational but still fail to do it for reasons of self-interest.

What is required, therefore, is some explanation why corrupt, self-loving beings should accept what is rational. To understand this we must turn again to providence and to Vico's claim that it uses man's narrow ends to preserve the human race upon earth. For, if providence is interpreted as a growing communal wisdom, the recognition that certain things must be done, if society is to be preserved, becomes part of that wisdom. The explanation why people who are individually self-centred and vicious will accept an institutional arrangement grounded upon a rational ideal will then be that they see that, if they do not, they will perish along with the nation. Thus a form of individual self-interest is situated at the centre of historical change. This still leaves intact, however, the claim that it is the nation's developing rational insight into certain ideals which explains the direction of historical change, without requiring that the individual acts only under the inspiration of that developing ideal. For it is his sense of self-interest, *in whatever that consists*, which eventually forces him to do so.

The second, and perhaps more important, objection which can be raised against the foregoing interpretation is that it cannot explain Vico's claim that at a certain point, a nation's development ceases, and that a state of sophisticated corruption and vice, the 'barbarism of reflection',[71] prevails, from which the only salvation – providence, Vico says, 'avails itself' of this remedy[72] – is a return to the original barbaric era and a recurrence of the complete civilising process.[73] This is a serious objection, which must be met if the present interpretation is to be at all acceptable.

Vico's general explanation for the recurrence of the course of

[71] *Ibid.*, 1106.   [72] *Ibid.*, 1106.   [73] *Ibid.*, 1106.

national history is that the advent of the 'fully human age' brings with it finally an arrogance of the intellect which coincides with, and is responsible for, a decline in religious belief which, he maintains, is the only force capable of holding man's vicious nature at bay, through its hold on his emotions. He is thus committed to the indispensability of religious belief for any recognisable form of human society.[74] This is clearly incompatible with the foregoing interpretation, according to which there is a general development of human rationality, which ought to lead to an improvement rather than a deterioration in our capacity to resolve any problems of social and political structure which may confront us.

The answer which I shall suggest to this problem is that Vico's belief that religion was indispensable for any form of social life is incompatible with the theoretical foundations of his account of the progressive socialisation of human nature. To see that this is so, it is necessary to recall two claims which are maintained throughout the New Science: that man is by nature 'weak and fallen'; and that a major part of his historical development consists in the way in which he is freed from the potentially disastrous consequences of his naturally vicious proclivities by his progressive socialisation. Given these two claims, the question at issue is whether it is open to Vico to argue that, when the state of complete rationality is reached, human nature can relapse into its state of original bestiality, as though the intervening process of socialisation had never occurred and had never had any internal effect upon his human nature.

To resolve this point, it is useful to return briefly to his account of the way in which the progressive socialisation of human nature takes place. As we have seen, Vico insists that human beings always act in the light of what they take to be their self-interest. The social progress which occurs in the course of human history, however, depends largely upon changes in what they take that self-interest to consist in. According to the sequence which is offered, original brutish man conceives of his interests without any social constraint and as solely those of the particular individual he is; the more socialised father conceives of his interests as an individual as identical with those of his family; later the nobles conceive of their particular interests as

---

[74] Vico himself believed the thesis so strongly that he was prepared to reject Bayle's claim that non-theistic societies can exist (*N.S.*[1], 8, *N.S.*[3], 334, *N.S.*[3], 1110) and to castigate travellers who told of such societies as 'seeking a sale for their books with their outrageous reports,' (*N.S.*[3], 334).

identical with those of semi-divine genesis; and later again the citizens and the members of the nation conceive of them within similarly altered conceptions. Throughout this process, as Vico insists, man acts only in what he takes to be his own interests. What is occurring, however, is that his conception of these interests is changing in accordance with an increasingly socialised sense of the self. Consequently, what counts as *his* interests is changing, as increasingly he thinks of himself as basically identical in nature with some or other legally and socially structured section of the total nation. As the notion of equity develops, moreover, the movement is from conceiving of himself as identical in nature to some sub-section of the total nation, to conceiving of himself as identical in nature with the whole nation, a nation in which everyone is equal under the law. This does not mean, of course, that he does not have interests which are proper to himself as the particular individual he is. But it does mean that he conceives of himself in such a way that his right to pursue these interests is conditional upon the extent to which the pursuit of these interests is compatible with his conception of himself as a member of the nation. The latter conception is, ontologically, prior to the former.

If this is so, however, and if the developing sense of the self and of where its legitimate interests lie is fundamental to the progressive socialisation of man, it is not open to Vico to suggest that, in the fully human age, people could – or *must*, as he claims – lose this progressively socialised nature and revert to a kind of nature which is proper only to man in his original brutish and unsocialised state. The fact that, in the third age, the individual's interests are subservient to those of the nation as a whole, rather than to some sub-section which is at war with some other sub-section within it, does not mean that they are sub-servient to nothing at all, as in the case of original man. For, were this to be possible, Vico would have had to alter his general theory of the progressive socialisation of human nature in such a way as to allow that in one part of his nature man always retained his original brutish capacities and instincts and yet to show how, despite that, progressive socialisation could take place. The requirement would, in fact, be stronger than this, since his claim is not merely that this socialisation can and does take place but that it takes place because it must take place. But if, as is implied by the theory of the collapse of social man in the third age and the re-emergence of original man in his full horror, it is always possible for original man to reassert himself, no matter what degree of socialisation has taken place, this must, logically, be possible at any prior stage. It would consequently be impossible for Vico to maintain, as he does, that the sequence through the three kinds of natures is both necessary and fundamental to the constitution of human nature itself. We are thus faced with two incompatible alternatives: either primitive man is transformed in his progressive socialisation in history in such a way as to entail that he cannot arise, full-born, in the third age, in which case Vico's accounts of the collapse of civilisation in the 'barbarism of reflection' and of the recurrence of the pattern must be rejected; or he is not thus transformed and can arise both then and at any prior stage in the progressive socialisation of man, in which case Vico's claim that this process is necessary must be rejected.

It follows that Vico's theory of the recurrence of the developmental pattern is incompatible with his account of the factors which make the pattern necessary in the first place and stems from a failure on his part to think through the full implications of his theory of human nature. From this, in turn, it follows that he has no good grounds for maintaining that, in the third age, 'fully developed reason' cannot resolve whatever social and political problems may arise or that it cannot, should it be necessary, replace the social bond which religion supplies by some other conception. I do not wish to deny, of course, that Vico himself believed that religion was a necessary social bond. The point which I am concerned to make is only that, since this belief is incompatible with his general theory of social development, the fact that the foregoing account of his theory cannot explain why he held this belief is not, after all, an obstacle to accepting it as a plausible account of his general theory.

If this account is correct, it has two consequences. The first concerns the naturalistic interpretation of Vico. According to this, Vico's theory of the providential pattern and its necessary recurrence in history is explained by the fact that he views man as part of the natural world and, consequently, sees no reason why the pattern of birth, growth, decline, decay and rebirth, which is found throughout the organic world, should not also be a property of the life of the nation. On this view, therefore, his account of the necessity for the pattern and its recurrence can only be a consequence of his treating the life of a nation as though it were another organic pattern in nature. But in this case it is almost impossible to make sense of the distinction between the occasion and the cause of the developments which constitute the life of the nation. This distinction is intelligible only within a conceptual framework within which human nature is regarded as necessarily social and in which ontological primacy is accorded to social consciousness. But this, as we saw in Hume's case, is impossible on a purely causal view of human nature or of human consciousness. A naturalistic view of human nature can never explain the development of new institutions, since the ideas upon which these depend must be ontologically dependent upon institutions themselves. Hence, either the naturalistic account must be false or some way must be found of dispensing with what Vico says about the way in which new ideals are engendered, at the social level, as former ideals are seen to be inadequate to their task. In asserting this, it is not my intention to deny that Vico's view of the life, death and rebirth of the nation, as a cultural and social entity, may not have been affected by an analogy between this process as it happens in nature and in individuals. This will be investigated later. My present point is solely that, if Vico's philosophy were as completely naturalistic as has been maintained, his attempt to explain the development of new ideals and new modes of institutional life based upon them, in the way outlined above, would be incomprehensible and could only indicate a quite irredeemable conceptual confusion on his part.[75]

Secondly, despite Vico's use of teleological language, primarily as expressed in his statements about providence and the way in which its aims relate to those of the agents in human history, there is no appeal to any transcendent teleology in his conception of the historical development of man's humanity. Nothing that happens earlier does so on behalf of the attainment of some hidden end, even though what comes about does so necessarily. There is thus nothing remotely akin to Hegel's notion of spirit creating the conditions necessary for the actualisation of an end which is internal to itself. The ends which are important in Vico's theory are transpersonal or communal ends, formalised, albeit not willingly, by the insight which a developing social mentality can have into the real deficiencies in the concepts, moral, social and political, in terms of which it structures its life. The 'superhuman' mind, whose ends transcend those of individuals and classes, is just the collective wisdom of the nation as, upon the occasion of self-interested individual and class conflict, it

---

[75] See below, pp. 180–2, for the sense of 'necessity' which is involved in one, at least, of Vico's uses of the idea of what is natural.

re-examines the rationality of its own procedures in the light of its knowledge of their historical development.

But if Vico is free of some of the difficulties which faced Hegel, particularly those which arose from the notion of spirit actualising an end which it contains within itself, his theory has difficulties of its own, to which attention must now be paid.

THE LOGICAL STATUS OF THE 'IDEAL ETERNAL HISTORY'

The 'ideal eternal history' turns out, on the above interpretation, to be a theory about a sequence of stages of the development of both consciousness and institutions which must be exemplified, in certain circumstances, by the actual history of all nations.[76] A first question which might be put to Vico concerns the question why the history of all particular nations must follow this sequence. Could there not be a set of individuals, for example, who are so self-centred and vicious, so blind to what is in their best interest, that they act in ways wholly contrary to the sequence set out in the 'ideal eternal history'?

Put in these terms the objection would have little force. Vico would, of course, have to admit that there could be such a set of individuals. But, he could legitimately ask, what could make us think of them as a set of human beings? It is true that they are described in terms which he himself adopts – 'vicious', 'self-interested' and so on – but to make the suggestion coherent they would have to be ascribed one extra feature: a total disregard for their own self-preservation and a total refusal to accede to whatever, in particular situations, they see that this requires. We can, of course, think of single individuals like this, but we cannot think of any sort of a community composed of such individuals since, according to the theory set out, such a regard for self-preservation is one of the cohesive elements of a society. Thus, if we think of such a set of individuals, they can neither be members of a society, nor can they have any of those properties which, necessarily, only members of a society can have. They can, at best, be a set of pre-social atoms, lacking nearly all the elements which go to make up the notion of a human being. And even if we accept the possibility

---

[76] For an interesting discussion of the 'ideal eternal history', see 'The Logical Status of Vico's Ideal Eternal History', by W. H. Walsh, in *Giambattista Vico's Science of Humanity*, ed. Giorgio Tagliacozzo and Donald Phillip Verene (Baltimore, the Johns Hopkins University Press, 1976), pp. 141–53.

of such a set of individuals, this would in no way conflict with the claim that the history of all recognisably social communities must go through the phases of the 'ideal eternal history'.

A much more serious point is raised by the question why any actual history should exemplify the stages of the 'ideal eternal history'. For this brings to the fore the question of the logical status of the 'ideal eternal history' itself. In one sense, of course, the answer to this question is simple: any actual history must exemplify the stages of the 'ideal eternal history' because the latter represents the nature of the nation. Something which failed to do so would therefore lack the nature of a nation and thus not be a nation.

But this answer is unhelpful. It might amount to the, probably false, claim that we call 'nations' only such communities as have gone through the proposed sequence, or to the ungrounded proposal that we ought so to call only those which have gone through it. In either case, however, it would offer a purely nominal answer to what is a question of serious philosophical import.

At this point it might be profitable to divide the question itself into two component questions. Instead of asking why any nation should go through the specific phases of the 'ideal eternal history', we should ask, first, why any nation should have a nature *of a kind* such as is exemplified by the 'ideal eternal history' and second, why, if it should have such a nature, the latter should be that which is explicated in the 'ideal eternal history'. This will have the advantage of enabling us to distinguish the formal from the substantive claims involved in the 'ideal eternal history'.

The point of the question why any nation should have a nature *of a kind* such as is exemplified by the 'ideal eternal history' is to ask whether the most general philosophical presuppositions involved in it are acceptable. For it is a fundamental feature of the 'ideal eternal history' that it is composed entirely of social entities and kinds and not of individuals as such. It contains, for example, an account of the three kinds of natures, religions, customs, natural law, jurisprudence, languages, and so on, in the development of which the development of the nation is said to consist. Even if, for the moment, we disregard Vico's claims about the substantial content of all this, it is clear that in offering this kind of account he is committed to the claim that it is a necessary feature of the conception of the nature of a nation that it should have related forms of institutions which together undergo a necessary process of development. As with Hegel, Vico's theory does not imply that in the actual world social entities can exist without individuals. Nevertheless, the fact that he offers an account of the way in which institutions are mutually related and maintains that the nature of nations is such as to require developments in them which occur without reference to the contribution of individuals as such – there is, of course, reference to kinds of individuals – shows that he accords priority to the social type over the individual. This means, of course, that the connections traced in an ideal eternal history must be necessary. For the 'ideal eternal history' mentions no individuals at all. When it is exemplified in actual histories, therefore, the pattern which is revealed cannot be affected by such contingencies as which actual individuals were kings or which were jurists or politicians and the like. In actual histories, of course, some individuals must be kings, others jurists and so on. But the point is that nothing will hinge on their particular character as individuals. What will count in the explanation of the development of an actual history is only what social kinds they are, for it is this alone which is mentioned in the 'ideal eternal history', and this is necessarily connected with all the other institutional and social developments which are essential to the nature of the nation.

It turns out, therefore, that it is a presupposition of the particular account of the 'ideal eternal history' which Vico offers that one must conceive of a nation as consisting, at least in part, of certain sets of institutions so related that changes in one cannot occur without correlative changes in the others. The most basic form of explanation in any actual history which involved this presupposition would consist in tracing these necessarily linked changes.[77]

Some of this might now seem relatively uncontroversial. It is true that historians are prone to issue stern warnings about the ineliminability of the role of the contingent or accidental in history. But few would go so far as to say that it was contingent what form, for example, a given institution took in the society of which it formed a part. The way in which such a claim would be denied would be by showing how the form of an institution related to other aspects of society at the time. Thus the form of government, say, would be related to such things as the basis of the belief upon which its authority rested, the class or classes from whom its members might

[77] 'Governments must conform to the nature of the men governed.
This axiom establishes that the public school of princes is, by the nature of human, civil things, the morality of the peoples.' N.S.[3], 246–7.

be drawn or to whom it was responsible and so on. In this way it would be shown that it cannot be contingent that, within a given society, its government takes a form which will differ from that which it will take in later periods. To take Vico's own example, governments of the form of the aristocratic commonwealths can exist only when there exists belief in the natural nobility of a certain class, the members of which are both the mediate possessors of all property and the only people eligible for membership of the sovereign body. For then the form of government is determined by the right of the nobility to protect their great private interests. The possibility that in such a context a government could be democratic in form is ruled out by one's conception of the relationship between the nature of a government, and its relation to the law of the nation and the level of its self-understanding.

But if this minimal claim seems plausible, things seem very different when we turn to the other thesis which presupposes this: that there is a necessary pattern to the development of the human nature upon which the historical development of the nation depends. One might agree, for example, that it is necessary that governments in agricultural societies should differ in form from those in industrial societies, without accepting that it is necessary that agricultural societies must develop into industrial societies or, to put it more generally, that any one kind of human nature, as expressed in the institutions of a society, must be followed by some particular specifiable successor.

A first question which might be raised here is not whether Vico is correct in his own account of the substantial content of this necessary sequence but whether he is correct in thinking that there must be any necessary sequence at all. Why should it not be the case, it might be asked, that while some countries advance from, say, a slave economy to a free economy, via the intermediary stage of a feudal economy, others should make the change without the intermediate stage as, for example, happened in America in the nineteenth century? And, indeed, is a counter-example such as this not sufficient to show that there need not be one necessary sequence?

Vico's claim is, of course, about a necessary pattern in the 'ideal eternal history', while the counter-example is drawn from an actual history. Nevertheless, since Vico's claim about the 'ideal eternal history' implies a proposition – that there is one necessary sequence in the development of all nations – to which American history offers a counter-example, the objection must be met.

There are a number of ways in which Vico might try to do so, although it is far from clear that he would have availed himself of them. He was, for example, aware of the fact that a number of actual histories did not satisfy the specifications of the 'ideal eternal history'. To mention just one, he tells us that philosophy arose in Greece in its barbaric period, although according to the claims of the 'ideal eternal history' it should arise only in the 'human' era of a nation's history, when the mind has developed the capacity to grasp abstract universals.[78] But he offers no explanation how this could be possible if his general case were correct, and one wonders whether he realised quite how damaging it was to admit the existence of such a counter-example.

In the case of Greek philosophy, indeed, it seems clear that he should either have reconsidered his account of the history of Greece, in order to show that the conditions under which, according to his account of the 'ideal eternal history', philosophy was possible, actually obtained, or have rethought his account of these conditions. In the case of the abolition of slavery in America a different option would be available: to deny that America was, in the appropriate sense, a nation. The ideas which inspired the abolition of slavery, he could maintain, would have a history in some other nation or, perhaps, in a number of them. And given the degree of migration from such countries, where the stage of feudalism had been experienced, it would then be quite natural that that experience, and the consciousness developed through it, should bring about a more abrupt change in America than that which, according to the 'ideal eternal history', would have occurred had America been an independent, self-sufficient nation, not affected by a huge intake of European immigrants.

This seems to be a plausible reply, although it involves the admission that pure exemplifications of a single historical or developmental pattern involved in an ideal eternal history might be rarer than Vico supposed. This would not, however, be a very damaging admission, since it could be pointed out that pure exemplifications of the connections involved in, say, the fundamental laws of physics are even rarer. It might, however, with justification, be held that an answer to the case of the abolition of slavery in America of the above sort could be advanced by Vico only if he were prepared to extend the notion of an ideal eternal history to give an account of the principles

[78] *Ibid.*, 158.

which determine what occurs when nations at different stages of development came into contact. For, if it is in the nature of a nation that certain necessary principles, to do with the development of mind, are at work in it, these could not cease to function simply by being brought together as components in a new 'nation', although they might be affected by such an occurrence. But this, in fact, is something which Vico himself accepted in principle. For although he did not progress very far with it, he envisaged the idea of an etymologicon for words of foreign origin, which would provide the principles by which to explain their changing history,[79] just as the idea of an etymologicon for words common to all native languages, which is a proper part of his own 'ideal eternal history', is meant to give the principles which explain their development within the nation.[80] Thus the suggestion that the idea of necessary principles of development, which is involved in the notion of an ideal eternal history, would commit Vico to a further account of the operation of these principles in different circumstances, turns out not to be an objection of any serious weight and, indeed, to involve something which, in one aspect of his science, he explicitly endorsed.

Nothing has been adduced so far to discredit the thesis that there must be a necessary sequence of phases involved in the development of the substantial content of the nature of a nation, where this occurs in conditions which can be specified, and a different, but related, sequence where this occurs in different, specific conditions. Moreover, the discussion of the objections to it has shown that the notion of an ideal eternal history is Vico's way of making the point, with which Hegel would certainly have agreed, that the development of a rational consciousness embodied in the life and institutions of a people is a matter neither of contingency nor chance but of a certain kind of necessity. But, of course, the kind of necessity which is involved is very different in the case of the two thinkers, since for Hegel it is grounded in the logic of the concept, whereas for Vico it resides in the capacity of the people of a community to improve upon the inadequacy of certain concepts and to accept rational improvements because it conflicts with their understanding of their self-interest not to do so.[81]

It may be, however, that the viability of this conception must still be reconsidered, particularly in the light of Vico's account of how we

[79] *N.S.*[1], 383–4.   [80] *Ibid.*, 381–2; *N.S.*[3], 145.
[81] See above, pp. 165–6.

can come to know of the substantial content of the sequence of necessary phases. And, since this aspect of his theory has not yet been discussed, I shall now turn to it.

PHILOSOPHY AND PHILOLOGY

It was noted earlier that Vico had criticised both philosophers and philologists for the way in which they had pursued their studies, claiming that each had, in effect, erred by failing to take the other into account.[82] The answer which he proposed, and which is funda-mental to the New Science, is to bring the two into a mutually supportive relationship.[83]

At first sight it is difficult to see why either should have anything to do with the other. Philology, Vico says, is concerned with the authority of human will, i.e., that of which the will is author or creator, and this is the particular. Philosophy, on the other hand, 'contemplates reason, whence comes knowledge of the true'.[84] Why, then, should philologists, who are concerned with the particular products of human will – what peoples have done or made – need the support of those truths which philosophy discovers by contemplating reason? And how can the truths which philosophy discovers by the use of reason be affected by knowledge of the particular things which men have done or made in the past?

Some assistance in understanding this can, however, be derived from our earlier discussion of Vico's account of the development of law.[85] The helpful point here is his claim that what is required is both an history and a philosophy of law at once, involving the notion of a continuous and uninterrupted history of the facts written in conform-ity with a linked series of reasons or rights. Nevertheless, as we saw, the latter does not wholly determine the former, since Vico is insistent that we should take into account both 'man as he ought to be', i.e., man as an emergently rational being, and 'man as he is', i.e., man as a being who will always put his own self-interest first. In the end, therefore, what is produced is a philosophy of the development of man, i.e., a substantive theory of the principles of human develop-ment, which shows how human will, dominated ultimately by self-interest, can create an increasingly rational world by man's capacity to see that the implementation of new and improved

[82] See above, pp. 141, 148.   [83] *N.S.*[3], 140.   [84] *Ibid.*, 138.
[85] See above, pp. 148–52.

procedures is the only way of securing his own self-preservation, with whatever he takes that to involve. In all this, the task of philosophy, at least, is not difficult to discern: it is to produce a substantive theory of the way in which will and thought interact in the development of a human nature which is necessarily both social and historical. Nor, indeed, is the task of the philologist too obscure. In all the versions of the New Science, Vico stresses that one of its main tasks consists in providing the philologist with the principles for a new art of criticism which will enable him to interpret historical evidence and, through that, to produce a 'continuous and uninterrupted' history of the facts whereby man's humanity has emerged.[86] It is true that Vico, who was most interested in the obscure or poetic era, himself devotes the major part of his energies to the interpretation of evidence relating, largely indirectly, to that period. But he nevertheless points out that his principles of interpretation apply also to 'recent facts',[87] and Book V of the *Second* and *Third New Science*, indeed, consists in an attempt to interpret the period from the Dark Ages up to his own day by the use of the same principles.

From this point, moreover, it is not too difficult to see what is gained by the mutual collaboration of philosophy and philology. Vico has continuously made two complaints. In the first place he has criticised the philosophers – Plato, Grotius, Pufendorf and Selden in the New Science, but Descartes also in earlier works – for having given an unacceptable, over-rational account of human nature. The source of this mistake he locates largely in their having mistakenly taken the rationality which obtains, necessarily, in the third period of historical development, to be an essence which belongs to human nature throughout its career. This has led both to completely false accounts of human history and to completely false expectations about the future since, if Vico's whole account were accepted, this would involve a relapse into barbarism.[88] Nevertheless, if philosophy can provide philology with a theory of the development of human nature which will enable philology to overcome its defects, it will, in so doing, gain support for its theory.

---

[86] *N.S.*[1], 91–3, *N.S.*[3], 348, *N.S.*[1], 94–116 give a series of particular principles of interpretation which presuppose the substantial philosophical theory Vico produces, as do *N.S.*[3], 351–9. *N.S.*[3], 392 and 359 are particularly helpful on this point.

[87] *N.S.*[1] 93.

[88] See above, pp. 164–5. In addition it should be noted that in the *First New Science* Vico offers, as one justification for his theory, that it will enable us to recognise 'the indubitable signs of the state of the nations'. *N.S.*[1], 391.

The philologists, on the other hand, have been criticised for having no systematic theory of the development of human nature by which to guide their interpretations of the evidence. Having no conception of the poetic and heroic mentalities, their interpretations of evidence relating to these mentalities have been arbitrary, confused and, often, anachronistic, leading to histories which have the same character. What philology has to gain, therefore, is a set of principles which will make possible a systematic interpretation of the evidence, capable therefore of maintaining itself in the face of critical examination, and of leading to histories of nations which will be 'continuous and uninterrupted'. The introduction of this systematic set of principles will, in effect, reduce philology 'to the form of a science'.[89]

It is evident, however, that something more than what has so far been offered is required if these claims are to be maintained. It is true, for example, that if historical evidence is interpreted according to a systematic set of principles its results will themselves have a certain consistent character. But it does not follow that they must be true. As was pointed out earlier in the case of the man suffering from a persecution complex, his interpretations of various events may be consistent with one another, but it does not follow that they are true. Consistency is only a necessary and not a sufficient condition of truth. The claims of the New Science about the development of human nature could not be maintained, therefore, if the only argument in favour of them were that they offered a consistent interpretation of the history of human nature, made possible by the application of a systematic theory of its development. It is necessary therefore to consider the further arguments which Vico offers for his theory.

It is noticeable that although, when describing in general terms the need to relate philosophy to philology, Vico talks as though they will be equal partners in the resultant relationship, when talking about them in more detail he lays greater emphasis on the role of phil-

---

[89] N.S.[3], 7. In *An Introduction to Historical Thought*, p. 71, B. A. Haddock suggests that on Vico's view the function of philosophy is to produce a model of human nature which will assist in the systematic interpretation of human artefacts. Thus 'Vico's three ages of gods, heroes and men function as historical paradigms to describe the parameters of historical meaning which can be attributed to the artefacts of a particular epoch.' It will be evident from what follows that this view can hardly be strong enough to explain why Vico believes that he can reach historical truth, since all that it appears to guarantee is the coherence of historical interpretation. There must, in addition, be some answer to the question why we should accept this particular set of paradigms as those relevant to truth, since many other sets of paradigms could produce interpretations of equal coherence.

osophy. He draws a distinction, for example, between the philosophical and philological proofs for his science and asserts that, of these,
the former are 'absolutely necessary to attain it' and that the
philological proofs must therefore 'take last place'.[90] Moreover, the
philological proofs are described as serving 'to allow us to see in fact
the things pertaining to this world of nations which were meditated
in idea, according to Verulam's method of philosophising, which is
cogitare videre [think and see] ...', although he then goes on to assert
that each kind of proof is confirmed by the other.[91] There is thus a
definite suggestion of the priority of philosophy, although this might
be only a methodological matter rather than an epistemological one.

To see that there is more to it than this we must turn briefly to the
kinds of proof themselves. Vico mentions seven kinds of philological
proof. These vary considerably in character but include the following
claims. First, that his historical interpretations are consistent with
things 'meditated in idea'.[92] Second, that they offer 'natural, direct
and simple' interpretations of myth[93] and appropriate interpretations
of the phrases of the heroic era.[94] Third, that the etymologies of
languages are 'in accordance with the order of ideas (which ... is the
basis upon which the history of languages must proceed)'.[95] Fourth,
that they enable Vico to develop a universal mental language, i.e.,
ideas of social entities which are part of the history of all nations.[96]
Fifth, that they enable him to strip the great traditions, and the great
literary fragments, of the distorted interpretations which they have
acquired over the centuries.[97] And, finally, they allow him to explain
'the effects related by certain history'.[98]

It is clear that there is considerable repetition in this list of proofs.
With the exception of the last one, they amount to the two general
claims that Vico's interpretations of myth, literary remains and
language are plausible and convincing in themselves and that they
are consistent with 'things meditated in idea' in the work in general.
Moreover it seems that these are hardly proofs at all, in any rigorous
sense of the word. It is, for example, simply an assertion – although
not necessarily a false one – that Vico's interpretations of myth,
language and so on are correct or true, while the claim that they are
consistent with 'things meditated in idea' carries no probative force at
all, if we have no prior reason for believing the things meditated. In

---

90 *N.S.*[3], 351.   91 *Ibid.*, 359.   92 *Ibid.*, 352, 359.   93 *Ibid.*, 352.
94 *Ibid.*, 353.   95 *Ibid.*, 354.   96 *Ibid.*, 355.   97 *Ibid.*, 356–7.
98 *Ibid.*, 358.

effect, then, his philological proofs come down to the assertion that actual evidence can be interpreted according to the principles which he has offered. But unless they gain epistemologically in virtue of this fact, they can hardly be proofs. Taken independently of their connection with the philosophical proofs, their probative power is fairly low. But, of course, they are not meant to be taken independently of the latter, since they involve extensive reference to them. And Vico seems to think that they acquire considerable probative power from their connection with – and, indeed, dependence upon – the philosophical proofs, thus implying the epistemological, rather than merely methodological, priority of philosophy.

When we turn to the philosophical proofs there is, again, a number of them. One is that it is not possible that 'in the series of possibilities which we are allowed to understand ... we can think of more, less or different causes than these [which we have proposed] from which arise the effects of this civil world'.[99] Without the initial qualification this would seem very weak indeed, for Vico's opponents alone, on his own admission, had shown themselves capable of offering a series of interpretations of history different from those which he has produced. But, if the qualification is taken into account, the claim becomes not that we cannot offer different interpretations but that they exceed 'the possibilities which we are allowed to understand'. It is clear that Vico is implying that there is something in his account which gives it a superiority in intelligibility over those of others.

A second, and most important form of proof, is that by going back to the circumstances in which things are created or arise, we discover both their nature and their ineliminable contribution to the subsequent character of the development of the nation.[100] The reference here to the discovery of the nature of the thing through its mode of birth is not difficult to understand since, as discussed earlier, this consists in the conjunction of an occasion, which is human will, and a cause, which is an emergent, rational ideal. The reference to the effect of this upon the later properties of the nation is, however, very interesting, for it shows that, for Vico, institutions always retain some of their original character in the course of their development. Thus, as

[99] *Ibid.*, 345.
[100] '[By going back to the starting points] we explain the particular mode of ... [the] birth or, as it is called, "nature", [of each kind of thing] which is the most characteristic feature of science; and, finally, we confirm the theological proofs by the eternal properties which [things] retain, which cannot have arisen other than from such births.' *Ibid.*, 346.

we saw earlier, the whole organisation of the heroic way of life depends upon the fact that an idea born in the poetic age – that God is the owner of all – is carried forward in human consciousness and continues to play its part. Ideas have a history in the course of which they change, but they retain certain characteristics which can be identified and traced only by a knowledge of the circumstances of their birth. The importance of this point resides in the fact that it expresses Vico's belief that the historical process must be thought of as having sufficient continuity – such as this principle provides – for accounts to be rejected on the grounds of lack of this continuity, of which he frequently accuses his opponents. Putting this slightly differently, and in a way in which Vico does not, we can say that history could not be a form of knowledge if we were to allow that anything could follow anything – that Einsteinian physics, let us say, could immediately follow Aristotelian physics – and not utilise a principle to preclude this possibility. And this, surely, is an indispensable requirement if any rational choice is to be made between different competing historical accounts. Thus, if it is true that actual histories written according to the principles of the 'ideal eternal history' have more continuity than those written according to other principles, this will provide us with greater reason for accepting the former.

Nevertheless, this is merely a formal requirement, whereas the 'ideal eternal history' contains a substantive theory. We are therefore faced with the question of the nature of the continuity which the substantive theory of the 'ideal eternal history' contains, and which should therefore devolve upon actual histories written in accordance with it and not in accordance with others.

From our earlier discussion, it might seem that the answer lies in the capacity of the 'ideal eternal history' to show how, by taking into account both 'man as he is' and 'man as he should be', a series of necessary phases of development of the same institutions can be engendered. But this cannot be the answer to the present question for, although true, it is also a purely formal answer. What is now required is some explanation why we should find the particular substantial sequence involved in the 'ideal eternal history' compelling. Or, to put it rather differently: why do we find the series of phases necessary rather than contingent?

To answer this question, some attention must first be given to the sense of 'necessity' involved. It seems plain that the connection between the phases is neither logically not conceptually necessary. It is evident, for example, that the earlier phases are not unintelligible except in connection with their successive phases. Nor, similarly, are later phases unintelligible except in their connection with earlier phases. It is the sense in which we think that it is necessary for one phase to develop into another that is at issue, and this cannot be a matter of conceptual necessity, since the question cannot be posed without an adequate distinction between the two phases.

On the other hand, neither can it be a straightforward causal connection, of the Humean kind, since it is clear that man's capacity reflectively to alter his concepts, in the light of his perception of their inadequacy to his situation, is a fundamental feature of the situation. Any straightforward causal connection would have to allow that the new ideals involved might not be improvements upon, or even connected with, a perception of the inadequacy of current conceptions, since Humean causation is, from the point of view of reason, blind.

Some of Vico's remarks on the subject might seem to favour the suggestion that a blind Humean causation is at work here, in so far as he describes the various sequences of ideas as 'natural'. In the *First New Science*, for example, there are chapters devoted to 'the natural order of human ideas of an eternal justice',[101] 'the natural order of human ideas of a universal justice',[102] and 'the natural order of gentile human ideas of God'.[103] But this form of expression does not, in fact, support a Humean interpretation. For in the first case, for example, he goes on to claim that the natural law of the gentes is an 'eternal law which traverses time' and explains this in terms of a few eternal seeds of justice implanted in man, which 'as the human mind develops gradually according to its true nature from the childhood of the world, develop into demonstrated maxims of justice'.[104] This is not, however, an error on Vico's part, for what he means by a 'natural order' is an order which belongs to man 'by nature' rather than 'by convention'.[105] Thus, if an order is natural, there must be some sense in which its phases are necessary.

The most plausible suggestion is that Vico is thinking of a kind of rational necessity, i.e., a necessity which rests upon the capacity of human beings to reflect upon the inadequacy of their concepts and, on the basis of this, to alter them in a direction which enables them

---

[101] *N.S.*[1], 48–54.   [102] *Ibid.*, 55–6.   [103] *Ibid.*, 57–60.   [104] *Ibid.*, 49.
[105] *N.S.*[3], 135, 309.

progressively to meet the real needs of the situation, although always under the stimulus of their sense of self-preservation. It follows from this, of course, that there must be 'real needs of the situation'. But this need not constitute a difficulty. For the latter are not independent ideals which inadequate concepts fail to satisfy. They are, on the contrary, needs which follow from the inadequacy of the concepts themselves and they should disappear when 'man recognises that all are equal in respect of their rational nature, which is the proper and eternal human nature . . .'[106]

PHILOSOPHY OF THE SELF AND SOCIETY AS A SELF

The necessity, then, is grounded in Vico's conception of human nature as inherently and progressively rational. With this in mind, we may return to the question why he thinks that we should accept his substantive account of the development process involved. On the face of it there is no problem about this, since Vico himself explicitly locates it in our capacity for self-reflection. Thus, it is a 'truth which is beyond all possible doubt: that the civil world itself has certainly been made by men, and that its principles therefore can, because they must, be rediscovered within the modifications of our own human mind'. Moreover, the reason why men have concentrated upon the natural sciences rather than a science of humanity is that 'the human mind, immersed and buried in the body, is naturally inclined to have a sense of bodily things, but requires overmuch effort and work to understand itself, like the physical eye, which sees the objects external to itself, but needs a mirror to see itself'.[107] Vico repeats this principle in various statements: 'First men [have a] sense [of things] without [conscious] consideration, then they consider [them] with a perturbed and agitated spirit, finally they reflect [upon them] with a pure mind';[108] or, again: 'The human mind is inclined naturally to see itself through the senses outwardly in the body and with great difficulty to understand itself by means of reflection.'[109]

Some form of the capacity of mind to reflect upon itself is thus involved in Vico's claim to be able to ground the connections in his substantive theory. In this connection, therefore, it is interesting to note that he makes continuous appeals to knowledge which we have, or can gain, of the way in which, in social circumstances, children

[106] *N.S.*[1], 54.   [107] *N.S.*[3], 331; *N.S.*[1], 40.   [108] *N.S.*[3], 218.
[109] *Ibid.*, 236.

mature and undergo a process of development from an imaginative nature, which he assimilates to that of poetic man, to the rational nature of the adults of his own day.

It would, of course, be absurd to suggest that, by any form of self-reflection of this sort, we could come to an understanding of why, say, the first agrarian law must develop into the second and so on. For, for the latter, an interpretation of evidence is required, whereas all that Vico can hope to gain by this sort of argument is knowledge of the necessary principles of the development of the human mind which, in conjunction with evidence, would enable us to confer necessity upon the sequence of development of the various actual laws.

But is it plausible to suggest either that we can gain knowledge of the necessary principles of the development of the human mind by self-reflection, or, if we can, that these must constitute necessary substantive principles of the development of the mind of nations? For both of these claims, it seems, must be acceptable if Vico's conception of a necessary substantive pattern in the history of the nation is correct.

In support of the first claim, it might be pointed out that we can, by reflection, see in our own lives the three stages to which Vico appeals. We can, for example, recollect our first beliefs, full of improbabilities and superstitions, and see how these imaginative conceptions constituted the world for us. Again, we can see how, at a later stage, we are dominated excessively by authority, taken in a very literal sense. Things are taken to be true, for example, merely in virtue of being written, so that on this basis a different world of beliefs arise. Finally, however, we arrive at a stage in which, no matter how we come by our beliefs, we take them as true, in the last analysis, only if they can withstand critical scrutiny.

It might be said, however, that this is basically just a matter of memory and that self-reflection has nothing to do with it. But this can hardly be correct. We may well be able to remember our childhood beliefs, or be able to recollect them by noting those of other children. But merely remembering them, will not, of itself, inform us that they were a product of the imagination and that many of them were, indeed, wholly false. To know that the world of childhood is a world of fantasy, imagination and falsehood, we cannot take it simply on its own terms, as we do when we remember it, but must make judgements upon it, judgements which presuppose conceptions of truth and standards of warrant which are, in the final analysis, susceptible only of a philosophical defence. In a sense, then, the self-reflection which enables us to trace the development of our own nature from the imaginative to the rational, and which teaches us, if Vico is to be believed, that reason is a development of imagination, is itself philosophical. For it requires that we use our capacity to philosophise to explain the process whereby we have come to be able to do so. In Vichian terms, we might say that we use 'pure mind' to explain how it must itself arise from bodily or corporeal mind.

This point seems to me not unconvincing, provided that it is correctly understood. 'Pure mind' or fully developed human rationality, it must be remembered, is for Vico primarily social in character. It consists in the capacity to utilise modes of reasoning and thinking which can come about only in a society, and although it is true that it is individuals who think and reason, the standards which they must meet are those appropriate to, and supported by, the nature of the society. Self-reflection is not therefore mere reflection upon one's individual self – a kind of philosophical introspection, as it were – but reflection upon the development of the rational self as a social entity. One must take oneself as an example, because it is only here that one has access to the subjective side of the self, but it must be an example of a kind which, one has reason to believe, is exemplified in all other individual selves. One cannot simply generalise from oneself to those other selves. Rather what is required is a philosophy of the self as a social product, i.e., a philosophy of the self as a kind.

It must be said that it is doubtful whether Vico really offers an account of this sort. His many remarks about the principles which characterise people at different ages, and about the principles which determine their development through these different ages, have more of the nature of shrewd generalisations than of a systematic philosophy of the developmental phases of the self. Nevertheless, there are some exceptions to this, the most important, perhaps, being his claim that imagination must precede rationality, because only by the use of imagination can we synthesise or construct those beliefs on the basis of our criticism of which we come to develop our rational capacities. Thus we must start, for example, with an imaginative conception of God before we can come to a rational appreciation of Him. The latter, however, is simply one example of the way in which, in general, the imagination must, both logically and historically, precede reason.

It is, perhaps, not unimportant to note here that although Vico does not do much more than point towards the need for a philosophy of the development of the self, many of his generalisations are such as to command an almost instinctive agreement. For this means that he is not merely putting up some wholly *a priori* theory of the self, demanding that we take up an asocial viewpoint, but is drawing upon a content which is available to us as social agents, even if it has not been thought through sufficiently to provide a systematic philosophy of the development of the rational self.

But if this point may seem acceptable, what is to be said of the claim that such a philosophy of the development of the rational self within society can lend support to the principles of the necessary development of a rational society as such? The latter looks much less plausible and, indeed, Vico might well seem guilty of the fallacy of composition in advancing it. Why, for example, should it not be the case that, even if Vico is correct in his account of the development of the individual self within society, entirely different principles determine the development of societies as such?

One consideration which might be advanced in Vico's defence is that we often do talk in terms of a similarity between the two processes. Vico is not alone, for example, in talking of the birth, maturity and decline of a nation, for many other historians have made use of such terms. Nor would the objection that the terms are merely metaphorical be to the point here, for they often serve to indicate a structure which is fundamental to the account offered.[110]

This sort of defence would, however, surely be inadequate. The question is not about what historians do, or have done, in actual practice, but about a certain substantive sequence which must be presupposed in all acceptable interpretations, whether or not it actually has been or ever will be. And Vico in particular could hardly deny this, since his disappointment with the work of other historians

---

[110] In *Metahistory: The Historical Imagination In Nineteenth-Century Europe*, Hayden White has made the much stronger claim that metaphors are essential to the structure of all historical accounts. This, indeed, seems much too strong since he quite correctly denies that the selection of metaphors depends upon rational grounds. In this case, however, one can raise questions neither about the truth of different accounts nor even about their compatibility or incompatibility, since the notion of compatibility can only be used within a context in which one can make sense of the notion of truth. This is to reduce historical works to the status of fictions, a status which Vico would certainly never have accepted.

is well expressed in his impatient assertion that 'we must proceed as if there were no books in the world'.[111]

It might seem that the matter could be resolved by showing that the sequence in question is basic to our conception of human development as such, whether of the individual in society, or of the society itself. But it is not even necessary to try to formulate an argument to support this to see the insufficiency of the suggestion. For even were it agreed that such a sequence is fundamental to our conception of human development, this would provide no reason whatsoever why we should assume, *a priori*, that all nations must develop and, therefore, that this sequence *must* be fundamental to the nature of a nation as such. The crucial point here is that if we take such a sequence to belong to the nature of a nation, we are committed, *a priori*, to the view that nations develop necessarily, and to interpreting all historical evidence in the light of this presupposition. This would have the unfortunate consequence of ruling out any possible falsification of the account, no matter how laboured our interpretation might become.[112] If, on the other hand, we are not to take the sequence to belong to the nature of a nation, but to treat it just as a set of categories to be used for the interpretation of evidence, we would fall into the situation, about which Hegel complained, in which one history followed upon another, without our having the capacity to decide which of two or more incompatible histories were true. The point here would be that, even when sets of categories produced extremely comprehensive and coherent interpretations of evidence, we would not be entitled to conclude that, in addition to being coherent, these interpretations were true, for coherence is a necessary but not a sufficient condition of truth.

It follows, therefore, that Vico has not justified his claim that the 'ideal eternal history' constitutes the nature of nations. For to do so, he must be able to show that all nations must 'develop' in accordance with its specific sequence of eras, whereas, so far, he has been unable to show that any must.

[111] *N.S.*[3], 330.
[112] In 'The Logical Status of Vico's Ideal Eternal History', W. H. Walsh points out that Vico seems more interested in finding confirmations than disconfirmations of his theory. And it is true that in much of his practice he rejects possible falsifying evidence, such as travellers' reports of non-theistic societies, in an extremely high-handed way. But if nothing is to be allowed as at least a potentially falsifying piece of evidence, allegedly 'confirmatory' evidence cannot be confirmatory in any substantial sense.

These difficulties arise on the assumption that Vico is suggesting that we need a substantive theory of the development of human nature for the interpretation of any historical evidence whatsoever, as though, like Hume, he were asking himself how we could come to formulate historical fact at all. On the other hand, a weaker suggestion, to which Vico himself points, is worth exploring, namely, that while the theory of historical development explicated in the 'ideal eternal history' must provide principles leading to a 'continuous and uninterrupted' history of the world, it gains a particular kind of intelligibility because of its incorporation within itself of a theory of the development of the self in society. We do not, in other words, accept the truth of the theory of the historical development of societies because it contains the same necessity which we find in that of the development of the self in society, but we nevertheless find it more intelligible because it incorporates some of the same principles. Thus, if successfully applied, we would accept its results as true in virtue of their greater intelligibility over alternative accounts.

This suggestion involves a connection, therefore, between the intelligibility of the 'ideal eternal history' and that of its truth. It is noticeable that Vico himself talks of some of the claims which become part of the 'ideal eternal history' in terms of a similar distinction. In one passage, for example, having offered his own account of the Publilian Law, he writes:

If we read further into the history of Rome in the light of this hypothesis, we shall find by a thousand tests that it gives support and consistency to all the things therein narrated that have hitherto lacked a common foundation, and a proper and particular connection among themselves ... whereof this hypothesis should be accepted as true. However, if we consider well, this is not so much an hypothesis as a truth meditated in idea which will later be shown with the aid of authority to be the fact ... This hypothesis gives us also the history of all the other cities of the world ... This then is an instance of an ideal eternal history traversed in time by the histories of all nations.[113]

Here Vico refers to something which, in the end, becomes part of an ideal eternal history by means of a series of progressively stronger claims. Initially it is an hypothesis about Rome. Its success in enabling us to construct a consistent and connected history turns it into a true hypothesis. Upon further consideration, it is seen properly as a truth meditated in idea which, with the aid of authority, i.e., with

[113] N.S.³, 114.

the actual material supplied by the philologists, will be shown to be true in fact. Finally, since it is found to be true of all cities, it is an instance of an ideal eternal history.

Interpreted in the light of the general account given earlier, two claims are involved here. On the one hand, the hypothesis advances from applying successfully to one city to applying to all cities. It thus acquires universality because of its success as a universal principle of interpretation. On the other hand, prior to its application to all cities, it becomes a 'truth meditated in idea'. This would mean that, even in its application in a single instance, we find in it a certain persuasiveness, presumably because it contains an intelligibility grounded in the notion of emergent rationality. Or, to put this another way, we cannot, given our notion of emergent rationality, see in what other way the affairs of an emergently rational nation could have proceeded. But this applies only to Rome, and we cannot conclude that the other nations are emergently rational until the same principles are shown to be applicable successfully to them. Emergent rationality then becomes a constitutive principle in their history and thus a part of an ideal eternal history, an instance, i.e., of something which shares the same nature.

The passage thus connects the intelligibility with the truth of an hypothesis. But, it must still be said, it is difficult to see in what way the theory of emergent rationality, which gives the hypothesis its intelligibility, gains any of its special appeal from our prior knowledge of a theory of the development of the self in society. The hypothesis which Vico is here discussing concerns a change in the way in which laws were to be ratified, a change which put law-making in the hands of the plebs and thus changed the Roman state from its 'aristocratic' to its 'popular' form. But what could there be in a theory of the development of the self in society which would give us a particularly intelligible insight into this change? It may be that, in the case of the law, the change can be understood as the realisation that men are by nature equal and that the vaunted heroism of the nobility is a myth. Similarly, there may be in a theory of the social development of the self a stage in which one realises that one is equal, as a person responsible for his own welfare, to all others. But even if this is so, the principles which make this development intelligible to us must be properly grounded. The intelligibility which we find in the case of the theory of the development of the social self cannot rest simply upon the fact that, since we ourselves develop as social selves, we find its principles familiar. For, if mere familiarity were the source of our sense of the superior intelligibility of the principles, we would be unable to distinguish the latter from many other contingent and inessential, but frequent and familiar, features of our experience. There must thus be some special feature involved in the theory of the development of the social self which renders the latter intelligible to us. But if this is so, and if it is the case that the same feature is at work in a theory of the development of the nation in history, then, since it is this feature which we find intelligible, we ought to find the theory of the development of the nation in history intelligible in its own right, without requiring any support from its connection with a different theory involving that feature.

If this is so, Vico cannot claim that the intelligibility of his theory of national development is supported by a theory of the development of the self. The many references which he makes to alleged parallels between the development of the individual and that of the nation may be treated as having heuristic value but not as providing grounds of intelligibility. We may gain helpful ideas about the problematic principles which determine the development of nations from our knowledge of principles which operate in the development of individuals but, in the end, the intelligibility of the theory of national development must stand or fall, independently of any connection which it may have with the development of the self in society.

We must return, therefore, to the criticism advanced earlier, that Vico cannot establish that the 'ideal eternal history' constitutes the nature of nations. For, no matter how attractive his general theory of emergent rationality may be, he can neither establish the necessity for the determinate sequence involved in the 'ideal eternal history' nor show that it is necessary that any nation should have such a nature.[114] In other words, he cannot show that there is a *necessary* sequence in the history of *any* nation, let alone that of all nations.

CONCLUSION

It must be stressed that the failure of Vico's project rests on entirely different grounds from Hegel's failure. First, the Hegelian project required recourse to the implausible notion of the idea of freedom generating its sequence of conceptual phases *a priori* and independently of the historical reality which it informed. Vico, on the other hand,

[114] See above, p. 186.

has not appealed to anything as difficult to accept as the Hegelian notion of reason, producing a more plausible conception of the way in which rationality can arise emergently, under the twin constraints of an increasingly socialised desire for self-preservation and an increasing insight into the false assumptions upon which previous institutional arrangements have depended.

Secondly, Hegel made no attempt to bring the notion of reason to bear upon the constitution of first-order histories. Vico's concern, on the other hand, has all along been with the requirements of first-order history and with the need to introduce some set of structuring principles into historical practice, to free it from producing arbitrary and, ultimately, fictitious results. His failure here stems from the fact that, although he realised that facts are not logically independent and that certain categories must be introduced in order to explain their reciprocal dependencies, he assumed that this could be done only by introducing the concept of a determinate necessary pattern as a presupposition of scientific history. For then he either ruled out the possibility of any falsification of his historical claims or, if he were to abandon the necessity for the presupposition, became unable to show why it, rather than any contenders, should be the preferred pattern or, even, that there should be a preferred pattern at all. There would be no theoretical difficulty, of course, in accepting the pattern which Vico adduced, if this were claimed to be simply an empirical matter. The difficulty relates entirely to its status as a presupposition of history, for then the problem is to find a way of justifying it which does not have the consequence that it is either immune from any possible historical falsification or becomes just one among the many perspectives within which history can be constructed. And Vico himself seems to have been more concerned to guard it from the latter fate than from the former.

It follows from this that, as with Hume and Hegel, Vico is also unable to give a satisfactory ground for his account of what remains constant and what changes in history. This is not to say that he does not give such an account, for, as was noted earlier,[115] he insists that human customs and practices do not change all at once but only by degrees and that they never cease to be affected by the circumstances of their birth. Traces of earlier forms of belief, judgement, custom, language, law, government and so on are, therefore, carried forward into the forms which they take on in later phases of their career. But

[115] See above, pp. 179–80.

although this is an important principle both of historical ontology and methodology for Vico, his incapacity to establish either the necessity for the determinate phases of the 'ideal eternal history', or the necessity for their application to the actual human past, means that his theory is unable to assist in showing, in any actual historical case, what it is that a particular institution or aspect of consciousness receives from the circumstances of its birth, what it is that is carried forward and modified in its subsequent career, and over what span of time such features endure or are modified. In the case of actual historical accounts, the historian is, therefore, left to do the best he can on a purely empirical basis and, according to Vico's criticisms of any historical practice which is not supported by a body of systematic theory, the results are bound to be arbitrary. Things which have changed may well be assumed to have remained constant, while things which have remained constant may well be assumed to have changed. In the light of the incapacity of the 'ideal eternal history' to supply the determinate and necessary guiding principles which scientific history requires, the interpretations involved in first-order historical accounts, and, hence, the results produced, cannot be put upon a defensible foundation. Thus, although an account of which features remain constant and which change, and in what ways, is to be found in the 'ideal eternal history' itself, this provides no answer to the problem of how the historian should think of the relation between what remains constant and what changes when establishing historical knowledge itself.

4

HISTORICAL CONSCIOUSNESS AND HISTORICAL KNOWLEDGE

In the foregoing chapters it has been argued that, despite the many differences between them, Hume, Hegel and Vico shared the belief that knowledge of human history presupposes a theory of human nature or of the development of human nature. According to Hume, knowledge of human history is impossible unless it presupposes the constancy of human nature or of human consciousness and is grounded upon an experimental knowledge of the latter. The advantage of this view is that, since it is the presupposition of constancy *throughout* time which is claimed, knowledge of the specific constants is theoretically available at any historical time. The disadvantage, however, is that, in virtue of this very feature, it rules out *a priori* the possibility of knowledge of any societies which do not share at least a consciousness which is akin, if not identical, to that of the historian's own society and, hence, makes it theoretically impossible to admit the possibility of any fundamental changes or developments in human nature or understanding. In rejecting this, it has not been claimed that we should be committed *a priori* to the existence of the latter, but only that we should not be excluded from it.

Hegel, on the other hand, while agreeing that there is a problem about the presuppositions of historical knowledge, is explicitly opposed to the uniformity of nature thesis. In part this opposition derives from his claim that human nature can be understood only in so far as one recognises that it exists in an internal relation to forms of social consciousness. What people can do is inextricably connected with how they conceive of themselves in their social context and within the limits of what they take that to provide. Given this, therefore, any uniformity of human nature would presuppose a uniformity of consciousness – as, indeed, Hume seems at times to have thought – and, for various reasons, this is a much less plausible thesis to maintain. Against this, Hegel argues for the centrality of the self-development of a rational, social consciousness as something which occurs in and through the historical process, the key to which lies in a grasp of the fundamental substantial principle which emerges through this process. It was argued, however, that despite his claim to have established this principle as the fundamental principle of history, he is unable to show in what way it should be preferred to any contending principles, other than by allowing that our know-ledge of it must be *a priori*. In this case, however, its status must be logically independent of, and prior to, that of the history which it is claimed to inform and, given its strongly developmental character, would eliminate *a priori* the possibility of any constant features in human consciousness. Even if it is granted that spirit cannot exist other than through the activities of determinate societies, it remains the case that the logic of the phases of its self-development must be determinable independently of its actualisation in history. Thus Hegel is unable to meet his own requirement that the facts of history must not be pressed into an *a priori* mould. Indeed, despite his claim that the reason of which he speaks is immanent in history, it transpires that logically it stands upon the same transcendent footing as the concep-tions of providence from which he wants to distance it. His failure to realise this is well illustrated by the fact that the account of history which he actually produces can, at best, only be a second-order account, the alleged rationality of which cannot fail to be vitiated by shortcomings – necessary shortcomings, indeed, according to his own conception of the various forms of history – on the part of the first-order factual accounts which it presupposes.

Vico is shown to be aware of the same problem as Hegel, i.e., of providing a framework for establishing historical knowledge while allowing for the possibility of historical change, but to have a different understanding of it in so far as he believes that the solution must lie in a properly grounded form of first-order history, provided by an account which is at once both an history and a philosophy of the development of human nature. The account which he offers is very much less rationalist than Hegel's. Not only is he prepared to recognise the non-rational nature of the origins of humanity but, more importantly, he postulates an internal connection between the factual and the ideal: 'man as he is' always incorporates an unsuccessful ideal, grounded in communal wisdom, to overcome which man needs only sufficient rationality – a progressive concept of 'man as he should be' – to forge further communal ideals and to accept them on the grounds of (enlightened) self-interest. Nevertheless, successful as this might seem as a way of uniting the factual and the philosophical formally in his vision of universal history, Vico is unable to ground the fundamental substantial principles which he believes to be necessary to the latter, other than by relying upon a dubious analogy between some theory of the development of the self *within* society and his theory that the historical development of society is determined by the development of the concept of the self. He is thus unable to ground his account of the determinate phases of the 'ideal eternal history' and, in consequence, unable to justify the distinction within it between what changes and what remains constant as part of the principles necessary for the interpretation of actual history.

It would appear, therefore, that none of the three theories offers a successful solution to the problem of establishing necessary principles of historical interpretation without, as in Hume's case, eliminating the possibility of the historical development of human nature or, as with Hegel and Vico, either eliminating the possibility of any constancy or determining its limits *a priori*. If this is correct, the fundamental reason for their failure lies in their, largely unconscious, assumption that, if necessary principles are required, they can be gained only by the adoption of an external and, ultimately, ahistorical perspective from which to view history. Thus Hume's proposal that history be a subaltern science, supported by a science of man, the principles of which are experimental and non-historical, rests history upon an ultimately ahistorical source of knowledge. Similarly, Vico's belief that the theory of emergent rationality which is given determinate expression in the 'ideal eternal history' presupposes a theory of the development of the self *in* society is equally ahistorical. Finally, Hegel's inability to avoid an appeal to an *a priori* knowledge of the phases of the self-development of the idea, which is logically prior to the structure of actualised history, rests history upon an equally ahistorical source of knowledge.

THE CONCEPT OF AN HISTORICAL PERSPECTIVE

The primary problem which is here raised is that of finding a framework for understanding history which is not itself ahistorical. I shall conclude, therefore, by discussing how it might be possible to find such a standpoint and what, in very general terms, it ought to include.

It would be helpful first to clarify the notion of an historical standpoint. In one sense, of course, this is simple enough to do. If an ahistorical standpoint is one which involves appeal to ahistorical principles, an historical standpoint can be characterised as one which accepts the historical nature of the principles which it introduces. This means, in effect, that it is a viewpoint in which the historical character and place of the historian, and of his mode of thought, is accepted as a constitutive principle of the history which he produces. This suggestion needs development, however, if it is to be useful for the purpose in hand, for it accords an important role to the notion of the historical, without explaining what this involves. What is required, therefore, is some account of what is specifically 'historical' about the viewpoint.

One sense of historical which might be relevant is that of existing at a particular time. But if this were all that were meant, the suggestion would come down to little more than accepting one of the requirements of metaphysical uniformity, which was discussed earlier. The historian must, it might be argued, be able to place himself in time, in order to be able to place other historical agents in time. But, as we saw, this, though necessary, was insufficient. This can be seen by the fact that, although all three authors discussed knew when they were writing, this knowledge did not prevent them from introducing ahistorical principles into their work. It must be emphasised that it is certainly not being denied that a chronological framework is necessary, if we wish to maintain that our beliefs are about what occurred, or that it makes a considerable difference to the historian what sort of chronological framework is available. It plainly makes a lot of difference to how the historian handles evidence if, like Vico, he believes that the world came into existence a mere six thousand years ago. The point is simply that being in possession of a chronological framework, through which one can place past events in a temporal relationship to oneself, does not, of itself, constitute having an historical viewpoint.

A more promising suggestion is that to have an historical viewpoint is to recognise that consciousness is an historical product and to use this knowledge in the construction of history. This, in a sense, is something which Hegel believed that he partially detected in the attitude of the pragmatic historian and which he tried to develop in a more satisfactory way in his suggestion that in philosophical history we take consciousness as something on behalf of which the most significant conceptual changes in history had occurred. The fact that he was unsuccessful in the way in which he tried to develop this insight should not prevent us from recognising that it has the real merit of introducing an internal relationship between man's knowledge of himself as an historical product and any history which he can justifiably accept.

This is the thesis which I shall try to develop and defend, albeit in a different way from Hegel. I shall proceed, therefore, by considering it in connection with its possible application to the solution of the two main problems which have come forward in the earlier discussion.

EXISTENTIAL HISTORICAL FACTS

The first of these arises in connection with the question of facts about what has existed or been done in the past which, for convenience, I shall refer to as existential historical facts. It was pointed out in the discussion of Hume's claims that he was wrong in his assumption that justified historical beliefs must always be the consequences of valid historical arguments, for, in taking this view, he overlooked the fact that we acquire, as part of our shared cultural inheritance, a number of beliefs which virtually nothing could induce us to abandon. This was stated merely as a matter of fact, but the significance of the distinction was not developed. The position for which I shall argue is that we would not be entitled to accept the conclusions of historical argument as statements of fact if we were not prepared to accept a major part of the body of inherited belief as true in virtue of the fact that that is how we have received it. This is not to deny that there is a distinction between the two kinds of knowledge, but it is to assert that the one presupposes the other and that it is our inherited belief which is constitutive of our sense of our place in history and, therefore, of our primary sense of the determinate structure of the past.

Before attempting to defend this thesis, it is necessary to explain what is involved in the notion of a body of inherited belief. As I shall use that notion, I do not intend that it should be equated solely with beliefs which are transmitted on the basis of oral tradition and in relation to which no documents exist. I shall understand it to refer both to orally transmitted beliefs and to beliefs for which it might seem possible to try to provide an evidential basis by reference to some or other documents which relate to them. In the latter case, however, such beliefs are classified as inherited when, though the documents may exist, our reason for believing a certain interpretation of them is not that the existence of the document compels acceptance of the belief, but that the belief to which that interpretation leads is itself an inherited belief. On this view, we believe a certain fact about, say, Queen Victoria, not because there are documents which can be interpreted so as to support the belief, but because we have inherited that belief and accept a certain interpretation of the documents on the strength of so doing. Thus inherited beliefs can include beliefs for which we may be inclined to cite documentary evidence, but they will be classed as inherited beliefs on the grounds that acceptance of the beliefs in virtue of their inheritance is logically prior to that interpretation of evidence which would be required if it were to lend support to them: we do not accept the belief because there is documentary evidence for it, but we interpret the evidence in that way because we inherit the belief for which it seems to be evidence. It follows that, in such cases, the documents are not the basis of our acceptance of the belief. Their function is the different one of being part of the process whereby transmission of the belief has occurred. A failure to draw this distinction is, I shall argue, one of the reasons why it has been thought that, other than in the case of beliefs which are wholly of oral transmission, all justified historical beliefs rest upon an evidential basis.

The basic reason why priority must be given to inherited historical belief rather than to reasoned historical belief is that, if we were to attempt to give up our inherited belief and to put all of it upon a basis of historical argument, we would have no idea what results we should accept. For our concept of historical reasoning is so dependent upon a set of accepted historical beliefs, which are partially constitutive of our sense of the structure of a determinate past, that, if we had to countenance their possible falsity, we should be left with no idea how to put any others in their place or, therefore, why we should accept the conclusions of historical reasoning as conclusions about the past. It may seem a conceptual possibility that Caesar never existed, but it cannot be an historical possibility. The reason for this is not, however, that all the evidence which we have goes to confirm it, since, as was pointed out in connection with Hume, we can, with appropriate reinterpretations of the premises, reject any *argument* which produces it as a conclusion. The reason is, rather, that the belief is so internal to our inherited conception of the existential past that any attempt to reject it would be destructive of our capacity rationally to accept any alternative beliefs about the past.

At first sight the claim seems both too strong and counter-intuitive. Surely, it will be argued, if it is a conceptual possibility that Caesar never existed, it must be an empirical question whether or not he existed and, hence, one to be decided by the ordinary methods of empirical research, modified, if necessary, to meet the particular needs of establishing facts about a past which is no longer experientially available to us. Such a response has a common-sense plausibility about it and shows, at least, that the general thesis needs considerable defence.

One form which a reply to this objection might take would be to point out that it assigns no theoretical value or importance to the fact that we have inherited a large set of historical beliefs. The reply would not be to the effect that the beliefs are being treated as being of no importance in themselves, but that *the fact of their being inherited* is being treated as being of no importance. It would not be necessary, of course, in asserting this, to deny one's opponent the right to acknowledge the *practical* importance of the inheritance of a body of beliefs. For it would be compatible with the objection that it should allow that the fact of the beliefs' being inherited is of some practical benefit, in so far as it gives us a certain *prima facie* warrant for accepting them and places the immediate burden of proof upon whoever wishes to deny them. But this would, nevertheless, be a purely practical matter for, in the end, our *theoretical* warrant either for accepting or rejecting something as an existential fact would be a matter to be decided by the methods of empirical research.

But this reply would have little force in itself, since it amounts largely to a reassertion of the position which is being opposed. What is required, therefore, is a reason why we must accept the fact of finding ourselves in possession of a set of historical beliefs as a matter of *theoretical*, and not merely, at best, of practical, importance. What is required, in other words, is a defence of the claim that to be in possession of an inheritance of shared historical beliefs is not just a contingent feature of an historical consciousness but something which is, at least in part, constitutive of it. It needs to be shown why it is necessary that, in order for it to be possible to have a conception of history, the past must have impinged upon consciousness in an internal rather than in a purely external way, by providing it with a content of unarguable but necessary belief about the determinate structure of the past.

The suggestion seems implausible if one talks, as I have so far, simply of the existence of a body of indisputable inherited belief. It becomes less so, however, if we ask how the past can impinge upon consciousness in an internal rather than an external manner. For it then seems that this is possible only if there has been a continuing transmission of beliefs about the past over the centuries, as a result of which we find ourselves in possession of a structured view of it. Hume claimed that we needed a transmission of *documents* over the centuries, but, possibly because he confined himself to documents and to evidence, he was unable to see any way in which the historical beliefs about events and occurrences which are arrived at in this way could be internal to consciousness. It would be necessary, indeed, to agree with the conclusion that they are not internal, if one accepted his account of how we acquire – or, rather, should acquire – historical belief. But, as we have seen, this involves acceptance also of an ahistorical view of consciousness, in which no importance is attached to the historically acquired content of the consciousness which is to adjudicate about historical truth. But this is not feasible, not merely because, as a matter of fact, we inherit such a body of belief, but, more fundamentally, because only in this way can we acquire such a view of the determinate structure of the past as is necessary if we are to have any justifiable beliefs about it at all.

It is not the case, of course, that we must accept all elements within this body as being equally certain or incorrigible, nor, indeed, is it the case that we receive it in such a way that we find ourselves equally unable to question any part of it. But what we cannot do – and what would be necessary, if Hume's view were correct – would be somehow to abstract from the *whole* of it and, from such a perspective, subject its component parts, one by one, to some *independent* test of historical truth. For, were we able to adopt such a standpoint, in which we were not prepared to accept that some things are known simply in virtue of the fact that that is how they have come to be received via the mechanisms of historical transmission, there would be no way in which we could situate ourselves in relation to a determinate conception of the past and, therefore, no way in which we could decide which of any beliefs we might construct about the past were a matter of fact or of fiction.

This may not seem obvious if we fasten upon some single fact, such as that Caesar died on the Ides of March. But that is because in this case the fact consists simply in the attribution of a date to an event, and the truth of the dating of events is rarely of sufficient importance to have become constitutive in our conception of the historical past. Even if we were to consider some less determinate assertion, such as that Caesar was assassinated, it might still seem that we are under no theoretical compulsion to accept it. But this will be so only if, in addition, one assumes the logical independence of facts. For then it would seem that we could dispense with this belief without implication for any of our other beliefs. But this is not possible. If we were to believe that Caesar was not assassinated, an enormous range of other implicated facts, both about Caesar and about the Roman history of his time in general, would have to be abandoned. For what would be overlooked, on this view, is the progressive entrenchment which certain facts receive within the body of accepted knowledge, as they are transmitted into the future.

It is important to note how little of this knowledge rests upon evidential reasoning, in any ordinary sense of the term. Rather, it becomes knowledge mainly because of a general confidence in the reliability of the methods whereby information is communicated socially. If we take the case of Caesar's assassination, the first to know it would, no doubt, be those who participated in it or who witnessed it. From there, belief in it would be acquired by public communication, by word of mouth or by seeing or hearing of his funeral cremation and so on. By the time it came to the general constitutional muddle which ensued, or the measures which were eventually taken by Antony and Octavian against Brutus and Cassius, Caesar's death would be so much a presupposition of what was going on in a large part of Roman constitutional life that it would already be beyond the rational possibility of doubt. But these are ways in which it would come to be an item of public knowledge for the Romans, rather than evidence for it. If anyone were to be asked why he believed that Caesar was dead, he might well refer to the way in which he had learnt of it, but this would not, except in the few cases of those who saw his dead body, count as evidence for it. If the question were pressed further, most would simply fall back upon the answer that that was what everybody else believed. In part, of course, this amounts to saying that it becomes an item of knowledge as belief in it becomes more widely accepted and as its effects multiply. But it is not merely a matter of the wider dissemination of the belief. For it also becomes more deeply entrenched within that wider body of belief, and the practices which depend upon it, to a degree which, at a certain point, makes it impossible rationally to question it. After a certain time, belief in the event becomes so constitutive within a communal pattern of interlocking beliefs that there is no way in which doubts about it can rationally be entertained. Thus, if we were not prepared to accept that Caesar was assassinated, relying largely on the fact that, despite a lack of the availability of much evidence for most of the population, it has been transmitted to us as an item of public knowledge for the Romans, we would need, in turn, to disbelieve a very large part of Roman history as we have also received it.

If we thought that it could rationally be doubted, we would accordingly be committed to the need for a dramatic reassessment of our confidence in the reliability of the mechanisms by which this belief arose and has been transmitted to us through the centuries. The whole of this reassessment would, moreover, need to be undertaken from a viewpoint in which, just as we were not prepared to accept the belief that there was, say, a man called Caesar, as true on the strength of the fact that this belief has come down to us as true, so we should not be prepared to accept any other beliefs, such as that there was an Elizabeth I or a Queen Victoria, on the same basis.

We would therefore be committed to the need to put the whole of the beliefs which we have inherited about the past upon a different basis, i.e., upon that of rational historical argument. But, given the under-determination of beliefs by data, there would be no way in which constraints could be introduced into the situation sufficient to justify the conclusion that certain beliefs rather than others were about fact rather than fiction. Hume asserted that the only way in which that distinction could be employed was in virtue of the fact that perception provides us with a material which we both know to exist and from which we can make valid inferences about the determinate past. What he should really have asserted is that we can employ the distinction only because we inherit a set, or sets, of implicated beliefs, and do so in such a way that it is not feasible to entertain the possibility of the falsehood of certain of them without, in so doing, losing our grip on the distinction between determinate fact and fiction in history.

It may seem that there must be a mistake in this line of argument. For, it could be argued, it is not necessary to adopt a methodology which requires a viewpoint which abstracts from the *whole* of historical belief, in order to maintain that any of our beliefs, taken individually, might be false. Or, if the point about the logical dependence of some facts upon other facts is accepted, it could be argued that it is not necessary to adopt such an ahistorical methodology, in order to maintain that any *set* of mutually implicated beliefs might be false. For, rather than adopt a standpoint which makes no assumptions about the past, we can quite properly raise questions about the truth of any belief in an individual occurrence or of any set of mutually implicated beliefs, by provisional acceptance of other beliefs about the past. To put this in terms of Neurath's famous metaphor: we cannot, while sailing in our boat, rebuild the whole thing at once; but we can rebuild it plank by plank, as long as we do not disturb so many planks, at any one time, as to make it unseaworthy. Thus, the objection would be that, while we cannot, indeed, put the whole of our beliefs in question, we can allow some to lie unquestioned in order that, on the basis of these, we can raise questions about the soundness of others.

It is evident, however, that if such a procedure were to be adopted, we could come to conclusions only about the overall coherence of our beliefs. For, if we had no independent reason for accepting the truth of the *unexamined* beliefs, which provide the framework for our investigation of the others, the most that we could do with the latter would be to decide whether or not they cohered with the unexamined beliefs and modify any anomalous beliefs, if we wished, so as to render them coherent with the others. If we were then, in turn, to direct our attention to some of the original unexamined beliefs, the outcome would be the same. The consequences of this are obvious. If we were dealing with a finite set of beliefs, the result would be circular, since the procedure would assume the hypothetical reliability of the very beliefs which, at the end of the process, were pronounced to be unhypothetically reliable in virtue of their coherence with beliefs which presupposed them. It would thus beg the question at issue and provide us with no grounds for believing that we were here dealing with fact rather than fiction. Nor would the position differ significantly if we were dealing with a non-finite set of beliefs. For, at some point, we should have to assess the position as far as it had developed, and take into account the fact that we had started by assuming the reliability of certain beliefs. But the coherence of the rest with these could not establish their reliability, since this was presupposed from the start. It follows that the Neurath metaphor can result, at best, in the view that coherence is the most that we can hope for and, as has been argued earlier, in this case it is difficult to see how we can genuinely separate fact from fiction in history.

It may be objected, however, that, if it is not the case that all beliefs are *in principle* open to empirical assessment, we shall destroy the notion that history is an empirical discipline and be unable to make sense of the actual practice of historians. But neither of these claims would follow. It does not follow, for example, that, because we cannot find a vantage point from which to assess each of them in turn, the beliefs are not themselves empirical. Indeed, it is difficult to see how they could ever have come to be accepted if they were not. All that is being claimed is that *we* are not in a position to establish the truth of each of them *by the same methods* as were involved in their becoming part of our inheritance of true belief. For to reassess the truth of some, we have to take that of others for granted, and the only non-arbitrary way we have of doing this is by accepting as unquestionable those which we have received as unquestionable. This means, of course, that we must accept also that the methods of the acceptance and transmission of historical fact have been, by and large, reliable and that what has come down to us as fact is the product of a basically truth-preserving process. Not all beliefs, however, come down to us in this way. Many are received with much less certainty or as belonging more to the realm of possibility than as something about which we can raise no questions. But this, again, is evidence of the *generally* truth-preserving nature of the processes whereby our concept of our past has been built up. For where, for whatever reason, the truth has remained opaque, it has not become incorporated into the body of belief which we have inherited as unquestionable, and its doubtful status has been preserved. Thus we do not need to accept that all that we have inherited is certain in order to believe that, in virtue of the generally truth-preserving character of these processes of transmission, some of it is certain. Equally, the fact that these processes are only *generally* truth-preserving does not entail that none of our beliefs are certain. There is no direct line of inference from the general character of these processes to the character of specific beliefs which follow from them.

Similarly, it would not follow that we could make no sense of the work of the empirical historian in his search to discover new facts. For it is not the case that, because we have no choice about the acceptance of certain beliefs, we are not free to try to establish many other truths which are outside the set of those which we have inherited. What would be precluded, of course, is that we should accept as true any discoveries which were incompatible with our inherited set. On the other hand, it is also the case that, given our incapacity to find an independent criterion of historical truth, we shall be able fully to warrant claims to truth only for those products of historical reasoning which can, in some or other way, be linked to the inherited set which provides the general structure of our concept of the determinate past. This is the reason why, when, by historical argument, we try to establish facts about parts of history which, for contingent reasons, do not connect in any way with what we have received, the area for disagreement among experts becomes so wide that we are often not justified in accepting any of the many accounts which can be offered as more than plausible hypotheses. But with regard to facts which can be connected to those which are, so to speak, known by transmission, there is scope for the establishment of many new ones, so that the body which we hand on to our successors about our own past may be a much larger body than that which we received. But it will, nevertheless, retain one part of its content in which it overlaps with what we received, and it is in virtue of this that historical belief can be thought of as being factual rather than fictional in character.

A different objection to the suggestion may be that it appears to deny our right to reassess many of the facts of history. To take a trivial example, most of us believe that Guy Fawkes was involved in an attempt to blow up Parliament.[1] Historians, on the other hand, have had serious debates about whether this is true or whether, alternatively, he was falsely accused of such an attempt, with the aim of rounding up a number of prominent Catholics who were thought capable of subversive activities. Thus, it would seem, something which we would claim came to us as part of a shared inheritance of belief may actually be false and can be tested for falsity by the methods of empirical history. But the counter-example does not suffice to disprove the general claim. For, although the traditional

[1] The example may not, perhaps, seem a good one, since from the start there were suspicions that the allegations about the plot may have been spurious. It will suffice, nevertheless, to illustrate the present point.

Guy Fawkes story has been questioned, it is clear that this can be done only against a background of other accepted fact. The suggestion that he was framed makes sense only against the supposition that we know both that he and his potential framers existed. So we are faced once again with the problem that some facts must be accepted if we wish to raise questions about the authenticity of others. And if the argument advanced earlier is correct, we would lose our capacity to have *any* historical beliefs at all if we thought that this required either that we had a methodology whereby we could put them *all* upon an independent foundation of empirical argument or that, starting from the *practical* decision to leave some original set temporarily unquestioned, we could work our way round the rest and eventually put both them and the original set upon such an epistemological basis as to justify belief in the truth of the whole.

HISTORICAL FORMS OF CONSCIOUSNESS

One aspect of what it is, then, to have an historical consciousness is to have a consciousness the content of which is so conditioned by the historical transmission of factual knowledge of determinate activities and events that it is constitutive of it that certain beliefs about the past count as true. The question which must now be investigated is what conditions are required for knowledge of the history of the forms of consciousness and, in particular, what degrees of constancy and change, if any, must be assumed in such an enquiry. In discussing the question of the history of the forms of consciousness, I shall use the latter expression in the way in which Vico and Hegel might have used it, i.e., to refer to conceptions which are fundamental to the different ways in which peoples have thought about themselves and the world in which they lived. Thus the notion of freedom, limited though it was, which dominated the structure of the world of Hegel's oriental despot is a form of consciousness. Similarly, the theological world view of Vico's poetic man, which resulted from the projection of his own image on to the world and which determined the whole social and institutional structure of his way of life, is a form of consciousness.

In what follows I shall argue that it is possible to apply the line of argument which has so far been applied only to existential historical facts to facts about such forms of consciousness. As we have seen, both Hegel and Vico were concerned to find a viewpoint from which they could give a defensible account of the changes, and of the explanation of the changes, which, they claimed, had occurred in the history of the forms of human consciousness. Both failed, it was suggested, because they could not justify the accounts which they offered other than by appealing to some ahistorical principle, which was then logically inappropriate to the task in hand. The present proposal would be that this defect could be overcome by accepting that it is, again, constitutive of an historical consciousness that it finds itself in receipt of a number of beliefs about the forms of its own development, without which it could not establish any further facts about that development or, hence, come to profit from any further reflection upon it.

One feature of this thesis is that we must accept that, if and when forms of consciousness change or remain constant, not merely do they do so but an accompanying series of beliefs is transmitted about the ways in which they have done so. It would not be enough simply to believe that our forms of consciousness have changed, for we could accept this without such recognition giving us any help in knowing which have changed and in what way. It must be the case that as they have changed we have been conscious of the change, and that beliefs about changes and continuities in our forms of consciousness are, therefore, also a part of our shared inheritance of belief. This means, in effect, that we must ascribe to societies a sufficient degree of self-consciousness to be able to be aware of changes in the forms of thought expressed in their different belief systems, and for this awareness, in turn, to be part of the continuing transmission of belief. Thus, to put it rather artificially, each generation must receive a set of beliefs about the way in which different forms of consciousness have or have not changed in the past; each must receive, as part of its inherited constitution, beliefs about its own changing forms.

The basic argument for this is, again, that, unless this is the case, we would have no way of finding an adequate basis for the application of the distinction between fact and fiction to the history of the forms of consciousness. We could, of course, have canons of interpretation. But we would have no right to believe that what we produced through their application was historical truth rather than imaginative phantasy. For, as we have seen, given the under-determination of theory by data, and given the insufficiency of coherence as a criterion of truth, we can produce innumerable different interpretations of equal coherence, between which any choice would be arbitrary.

There arises, therefore, in relation to the history of the forms of consciousness, the same need to introduce constraints upon possible accounts as obtains in the case of existential historical facts and which, as we saw, Hume tried to provide through the uniformity of consciousness thesis, just as did Hegel and Vico by their different theses about the principles of the development of consciousness. The present suggestion would differ from the others in that it would not assume an ahistorical viewpoint but would insist, on the contrary, that the materials for an history of the forms of consciousness must lie within consciousness itself in a way which can be explained only by a certain view about how belief is transmitted.

It is necessary, however, to note an apparent difference between the case of existential historical belief and that of the history of consciousness. It lies in the fact that, in the case of existential historical belief, the belief which is transmitted must be the same belief, whereas, in that of the history of the forms of consciousness, it looks as if it need not and, indeed, if there has been any change in the form of consciousness, as if it could not. We can see this if we return first to the case of Caesar's death. Here, in the case of an event, the belief which the Romans had and that which we have is the same. There is, therefore, no problem in seeing how, via its historical transmission, this belief can become constitutive in our notion of the determinate structure of the human past. But if we turn to some belief about a change in a form of consciousness which has been transmitted through different historical cultures, it may not turn out to be the same belief which will be transmitted because, in the course of transmission, new forms of consciousness can, and often do, produce entirely new ways of thinking about the things believed. Thus some belief held in the Middle Ages – say, that trial by ordeal was just, because God would ensure that only the innocent survived the ordeal – may well have been transmitted to later generations, but that belief would in no way be constitutive of the form of consciousness of those later generations. What they would inherit, once the belief itself had ceased to be accepted, would be the belief that belief in the justice of trial by ordeal was a feature of the consciousness of people who lived in the Middle Ages.

The problem which this difference may appear to introduce is, however, easily overcome. For, it is for this reason that, on this view, it is necessary to accept that a capacity to be conscious of the *history* of its own changing form is an internal feature of an historical consciousness. Such a consciousness must, throughout its development, have the capacity to be aware of changes which take place within its form and, therefore, of how it differs from its preceding form. Thus, in addition to altering in form, it must retain a conception of the development of its own past forms. For, unless such a capacity were to exist throughout its career, there would be no way in which some historian could ever come to justify any account of the ways in which consciousness has and has not changed in the past.

To see that this is so, let us assume that it is false and that we do not inherit any such beliefs about alterations in past forms of consciousness. The historian will then have available to him sets of documents and other sources which require interpretation but which do not, of themselves, supply any of the principles required for that interpretation. He must therefore decide whether to interpret the documents and sources on the assumption that there has been relative constancy in the consciousness of the peoples to whom he is to relate them or whether there have been smaller- or larger-scale changes. If he decides in favour of the first alternative he will, in effect, endorse Hume's choice. If he opts for the second, he will be nearer to Hegel or to Vico, depending upon how he tries to support his decision. But no matter which decision he makes, it will involve an arbitrary choice of principles which will determine *a priori* the results which he produces and will, in the end, produce a set of equally *a priori* beliefs about the history of the forms of consciousness.[2] Thus, it would seem, if we cannot introduce substantial constraints into the situation, involving the concept of an *internal* historical viewpoint, we shall be as unable to justify the distinction between fact and fiction in relation to the history of forms of consciousness as were Hume, Hegel and Vico.

The thesis nevertheless seems open to a number of other objections which must be considered. The first is that we know of many societies which had, and perhaps still have, little or no historical sense at all. Some present-day tribe in the Amazon or many illiterate societies in the past might constitute such cases. The existence of actual or possible ahistorical societies or cultures does not, however, present any real difficulty. For the claim is about the assumptions which must be made if we are to make sense of the notion of an historical

---

[2] This claim, which has already been developed in relation to Hume, Hegel and Vico, is given further support below. See pp. 216–19.

consciousness as an indispensable condition of the concept of historical knowledge. It does not follow from this, however, that consciousness itself is necessarily historical. The claim that if a consciousness is historical, and is therefore capable of possessing historical knowledge, it must necessarily have certain features, does not entail that all consciousness is historical and must have those features. Whether or not a specific consciousness is historical is a purely contingent matter. There may well be many societies which exhibit, or have exhibited, none of the characteristics which are involved in the concept of an historical consciousness, but if there are, it will only follow that they cannot have our sense of an historical past. Their existence cannot, however, constitute a counter-example to what is claimed to be a necessary condition of an historical, as distinct from a non-historical, consciousness.

In this connection, it should be noted that, just as it is contingent whether or not a specific society has an historical consciousness, so also it is contingent how long it has had such a consciousness. The possession of such a consciousness does not imply that it has always been possessed or that it always will be, since, for purely contingent reasons, aspects of any form of knowledge may always be gained or lost. Thus it is possible for a society which has hitherto not had such a consciousness to begin to acquire one, just as it is possible for a society which has had one to lose it. The fact that it is contingent whether or not a society will acquire or lose such a consciousness does not, of course, imply that it is always a matter of chance or accident. Large physical or economic disasters may have such a disruptive effect upon the whole way of life of a society that, if it had such a consciousness, it may well be lost along with many other aspects of its cultural inheritance. But it is also possible that such a consciousness may be lost through a failure to appreciate its benefits sufficiently and to ensure that many of the things which are necessary for its continued existence – books, documents, a reliable mode of transmission of the relevant knowledge, and so on – are maintained. Thus, its continued existence, although contingent, is not always just a matter of sheer chance. The Romans would be an example of a society which had such a consciousness and which lost it, largely as a result of economic breakdown and a consequent incapacity to protect itself from the ravages of nations which neither possessed it nor valued it sufficiently to wish to acquire it. Fortunately, it was not wholly lost. Enough was kept alive in religious institutions to provide a foundation for its reacquisition in the Renaissance. But had enough not endured in that way, there would have been no possibility of its subsequent reacquisition since, if documents alone had survived, with no accompanying transmission of inherited belief, there would have been no possibility of regaining it through historical argument, for the framework of knowledge of the determinate structure of its past changes, which the latter requires, would have been absent.

A more far-reaching objection to the thesis is whether it is possible for a consciousness to possess that combination of the particular kinds of constancy and change which is required. For the proposal entails that it be possible to isolate some parts of a society's consciousness – its inherited beliefs both about existential historical facts and about the ways in which its own modes of thinking have changed – from other parts, such as its religious or scientific beliefs. But, it could be argued, this is impossible, since once fundamental forms of thought change they will bring with them changes in the ways in which we think about everything, historical truth as well as scientific truth.

Such an objection would presuppose, however, an implausibly holistic view of knowledge and of the relation of different bodies of knowledge to one another. We can see this by considering differences within our present body of belief about changes in the forms of consciousness. We believe, for example, both that contemporary natural science is a development of a recognisable form of thought which underlay Greek science and that it is an improvement upon it. We do not, however, find our present form of scientific thinking an insuperable obstacle to understanding the form of Greek scientific thinking nor, indeed, if this were so, would we be able to believe that the one is a development of, and improvement upon, the other. We find ourselves believing the same also of our technology, although its roots go back further. The same is true, again, of our political ideals. We may regret, at times, that our society shows, say, less cohesion than some societies in the past, but if a loss of cohesion is part of the price which must be paid for greater freedom of speech or greater equality of rights, most would think it impossible that it should not be paid. On the other hand, there are areas of belief where the same is not true or, at least, not so obviously true. Religious belief is such an example. We recognise that many of the forms which religious belief takes today are developments of past forms but we do not inherit, with anything like the same conviction, the belief that they are better than their predecessors. It is much less difficult to believe that a truly Christian life, say, requires a return to some form of Christian communism than it is to believe that a better picture of the universe requires a return to Ptolemaic astronomy. The same difference applies also to the arts in general. We see how our present forms of art are developments of earlier forms, without being obliged to believe that they must, more or less in virtue of that fact alone, also be preferred to them.

It is not plausible, therefore, to take a completely holistic view of knowledge in the light of the things which we actually believe. The latter point towards the notion of a plurality of non-isomorphic areas of knowledge. If we accept such a notion, however, it is necessary to diverge further from the assumptions which Hegel and, perhaps to a lesser extent, Vico made about the nature of the historical process. For the Hegelian notion that reason develops itself from its own inner resources carries with it the implication that there is a general parallel progress in all the major areas of consciousness. It is impossible, on this view, that, say, the forms of religion which develop should not be better, in the sense of being more rational, than their predecessors, just as it is impossible that the forms of the state should not develop and become more rational in step with them. For, as we saw, the form of a nation's religion was explicitly stated to determine the form of the state, and this was necessarily so because certain aspects of the self-development of reason, namely, the individual's conception of his relationship to the state, took place within religion. But this was a consequence of Hegel's *a priori* rationalism which led to the view not only that there was a certain necessary relationship between all aspects of the life of a society but that all aspects must develop in conformity with the self-development of the same underlying principle. Thus, just as Hume made it impossible for there to be any major developments of consciousness, Hegel made it impossible for there not to be such developments. Whereas, in a properly conceived science of history, it ought to be accepted that it is a contingent matter whether or not, and how uniformly, there have been such changes.

In Vico's case, things may not appear so straightforward. As we saw, although he claimed that there is an overall pattern in the practices of a society and in its forms of government, legislation, language and so on, which he traced to a shared social consciousness, he also recognised that practices based on old forms of consciousness can live on for a long time in a new era because, as he asserts, it is contrary to human nature to abandon old habits and practices at a stroke.[3] He thus allowed for a certain degree of pluralism within a basically holistic conception of consciousness. Not all religious practices, for example, need conform to the pattern which a generally shared social consciousness requires. Nor need all language do so. The poetic language of the first era can live on, in a form which we now think of as metaphor, into the age of rational man, where it can co-exist with the much more abstract and technical forms of language which are appropriate to the consciousness of rational man.

But his recognition of these features was insufficient to save him from the same difficulty as arises for Hegel. For the allowance which he made for them must be understood in the context of the basically ahistorical theory which is fundamental to his account of the changing forms of consciousness in history, which deprives it of its theoretical value. For, if an ahistorical principle determines the sequence of changing forms of consciousness in history, it cannot be a contingent matter which aspects of the consciousness, life and institutions of a nation change and which live on in an old form. The latter must be built into the general theoretical framework. Hence, in so far as Vico himself used the proviso to explain certain things in his own interpretations of actual histories, which seemed to deviate from the demands of the 'ideal eternal history', he was working in a way which was incompatible with his overall theory. His procedure as an historian was thus, according to his own conception, arbitrary.

A further difficulty which must now be considered is whether, despite its emphasis upon the operation of the contingent in history – or, more relevantly in the present context, in the development of an historical consciousness – the present proposal leaves any more room than is to be found in the theories of Hegel and Vico for the contingent to operate in the manner required. How can it be the case, it may be asked, that it is a contingent matter that our beliefs about the development of, say, the concept of equality, are as they are, if the suggestion is that we are in possession of a set of beliefs about that development which are so internal to our way of thinking about it that we are unable to question it? But this question rests upon a confusion. Part of what is being claimed is that our consciousness is itself historically conditioned and that, in consequence of this fact, we

[3] See above, pp. 179–80.

find ourselves in possession of certain beliefs which we cannot but accept as true. It does not follow from this, however, that we cannot have acquired those beliefs as a result of the operation of contingent factors in the past. For the claim that we cannot have a coherent notion of the history of consciousness unless we accept that we have an historical consciousness does not rule out the possibility that it is a contingent fact that we have such a consciousness or that it should have the content or form which it has. There is no incoherence in the conjunction of the claims that we cannot have an historical consciousness unless we have acquired a series of beliefs which are so constitutive within that consciousness as to be beyond question by that consciousness, that it is contingent that we have such a consciousness, and that it is contingent what its contents and form are. The assertion that it is necessary that, if we have an historical consciousness, we must have been historically conditioned does not entail that we are *necessarily* historically conditioned. Had various features about our nature and psychological capacities differed from what they are *in fact*, had we not had a capacity, say, to remember and transmit beliefs, we certainly would not have been historically conditioned or, hence, have had an historical consciousness. The mistake is similar to that which has occasionally been made with regard to the *Cogito*. From the fact that I cannot now doubt that I exist, it does not follow that it is necessary that I should have existed. Similarly, from the fact that I cannot now doubt certain beliefs which I have, it does not follow that it is necessary that I should have had those beliefs.

THE EXISTENCE AND LOCATION OF HISTORICAL CONSCIOUSNESS

It cannot be denied, however, that the thesis gives rise to a certain sense of mystery, in so far as it may not be so clear that the relevant beliefs, particularly about the development of the forms of consciousness, exist as, say, that beliefs about the state of the economy exist, or, if they exist, where they exist. Indeed, it seems quite plausible to deny that there are any beliefs about the development of our own consciousness which are received in such a way that we cannot question them.

In addressing the problem of the existence of an historical consciousness, it is necessary to begin by noting, as will probably be obvious, that I have so far spoken as though there is one recognisable set of beliefs, with an historically fixed content, shared by all of us. But this is plainly not the case. There may well be some beliefs which are shared by all of us, but there will certainly be others which are held only by certain parts of the community, or of certain communities, the existence of which is to be explained by the particular line of transmission available within that part of the community. A simple example of this would be our beliefs about what has or has not gone wrong with the economic situation in Great Britain since the Second World War, which differ in the minds of supporters of the different political parties, largely as a result of what they have been brought up to believe. Similarly, it is almost impossible for anybody brought up in post-war Britain not to believe that Britain, with help from the USA, saved national autonomy and freedom in Western Europe from total extinction by the Nazis, but this belief is by no means universally accepted in all other countries in Western Europe.

After making this allowance, however, it is necessary to remember that, although it would be possible for the thesis to be examined in its wider application to different people and different groups of people, it has been introduced in answer to a specific problem which relates to the activities of historians. For although all of us may be affected in various ways by our historical conditioning, it is historians who are faced with the problem of trying to construct defensible interpretations of the development of various aspects of consciousness, whether at the social or more narrowly construed cultural level. The question of the existence of the beliefs in question should therefore be understood as the question whether historians, as a result of the historical development of their discipline, find themselves in receipt of certain beliefs about changes and constancies in consciousness in the past which establish parameters within which they can carry out research which can be thought of as satisfying the conditions of knowledge in relation to the past.

Put in this way, it seems incontestable that there exists within the community of historians such a set of beliefs. The claim is not that there is an inherited set of beliefs which all historians share but rather that historical research is carried out within a coherent framework provided by what has been inherited and built up within history as an ongoing discipline, the different parts of which have been transmitted to historians interested in different areas of consciousness and culture. The historical consciousness which is in question is not a property of any individual historian as such, but of historians as a community and as a community which has developed historically, i.e., of historians of society, economics, art, religion, politics, philosophy and so on. So, to take a political example, while one historian will know that it is impossible to deny the growth of nationalism in Western Europe in the nineteenth century, another will know that it is impossible to assert it there in the twelfth century. If they have been narrowly trained, it is possible that the one may know something which the other does not. But it is a consequence of the interdependence of belief within the community that the one will not be able to maintain as a serious historical thesis something which implies the falsity of what the other must accept as true.

This point could be expressed by saying that, although historians of consciousness are involved in a research programme, it is a programme bounded by parameters which lie within beliefs inherited by the community of historians as a whole. Vico saw the task of the historian as involving the production of a continuous and coherent narrative. This, indeed, probably lay at the root of his search for an over-arching ideal narrative, in the light of which to interpret evidence consistently and, thus, to produce the required historical narrative. On the view which is here under discussion, it may well be the case that no such historical narrative exists as a totality, because of the division of labour among historians, but the theoretical possibility of it must exist merely in virtue of the way in which the community itself has developed historically. Thus the function of the over-arching truth, for which both Vico and Hegel sought, is fulfilled not by some external theory, in the light of which the historian might try to interpret the evidence and establish the truth, but by the historical development within historians, as a community, of a body of belief without which they could not operate as historians.

It may well be said that this would give us no guarantee that we shall produce even short-term histories, let alone universal histories, with the continuity and coherence for which Vico sought. But this point, if meant as an objection, could be turned on its head. For it is no part of the historian's task to find continuity and coherence where they never existed. It must, surely, be an open question what degrees of continuity or coherence are to be found in the changing beliefs and practices of any particular historical society, given the many contingencies by which it may be affected in its career. Thus, no history of a society ought to be bound by some *a priori* conception of what

degree of coherence and continuity it ought to exhibit. The introduction of such an ahistorical constraint as this would again require
the historian to adopt a viewpoint which is external to the historical
consciousness of which he is a part and would deprive him of the
context of determinate beliefs about the past necessary for his further
historical work. It does not follow from this, of course, that the history
produced will display no degree of coherence or continuity whatsoever, for, if the arguments presented earlier are correct, the
historian should be in receipt of a body of belief which accurately
reflects such coherence and continuity as its subject possessed. But it
will be a contingent matter what these degrees are.

It follows from this that the beliefs in question exist within the
consciousness of the community of historians, rather than, for
example, in sets of documents or books to be found in museums and
libraries. This does not mean, of course, that there is no need for
documents or books for, as mentioned earlier, the transmission of
beliefs about the truth or falsity of what is asserted in documents and
books is one of the main methods of the transmission of belief. But
they will not be, as, for example, Sir Karl Popper has claimed in the
case of objective knowledge, constituted by the evidence and the
theories to be found in museums and libraries. For nothing can count
as evidence until it has received interpretation and, if the earlier
argument is correct, we cannot justify a preference for any particular
theory of interpretation if we are required to abstract from, and
disregard, the contents of a consciousness which has developed
historically.

This point may be illustrated by reference to one of the arguments
which Popper has adduced to support what is, in effect, a counter-
position. In 'Epistemology Without a Knowing Subject',[4] he invites us
to undertake two thought experiments. In the first, we are to imagine
a situation in which all our machines, tools and subjective learning,
including our knowledge of the use of machines and tools, are
destroyed, but in which our libraries and our capacity to learn from
them survive. In the second, we are to imagine a situation in which
all that was destroyed in the first case is still destroyed but in which,
in addition, all libraries are also destroyed, so that our capacity to
learn from them is rendered useless. The conclusion which Popper
draws from consideration of the two experiments is that, in the first

[4] Karl R. Popper, *Objective Knowledge: An Evolutionary Approach* (Oxford, Oxford
   University Press, 1972; reprinted 1974), pp. 107–8.

case, after much difficulty, our world of knowledge can be re-established, but that, in the second case, our civilisation would not re-emerge for many millennia – presumably, though he does not say this, after something like the same length of time which it has taken to emerge in the first place. The point of the thought experiment is to enable us to see that the world of 'problems, conjectures, theories, arguments, journals, and books' constitutes an objective sphere of knowledge from which, were it to survive in some major catastrophe in which we were to lose all our subjective learning and retain only our capacity to learn from books, we could, after the application of a properly based methodology, reconstitute our original body of subjective knowledge.

The position which Popper here advances is similar to that described earlier as epistemological neutralism, which would commit us to accepting the results of a methodology in which nothing was assumed and, hence, no outcome was precluded. For what he is proposing, in effect, is that in a situation in which we started with no inherited beliefs whatsoever, except perhaps a command of the languages in which the books in which our former learning was expressed were written, we could reconstruct that learning. Thus, if this proposal were to be applied to the history of the forms of consciousness, it would constitute a counter-position, in so far as it would deny the need for us to inherit beliefs about the development of our own historical consciousness as a basis for distinguishing between fact and fancy in the history of consciousness.

There are two weaknesses, however, in this argument. The first is that the requirement that we have the capacity to learn from the books is by no means as innocent as it looks. For the languages in which books are written require interpretation and, if the foregoing argument is correct, this would not be possible had we not inherited a considerable knowledge of the history of the languages in which they had been written. A medieval Latin charter can no more be understood as though it had been written in classical Latin – which would, in any case, itself be in need of interpretation – than can a sonnet by Donne as though it were written in modern English. To have access to the languages which we would need to know, in order to exercise our capacity to learn from the books in question, we would need a grasp of the history of the languages in which they had been written. But we could not achieve that in a situation in which all our subjective learning was lost and had to be reconstructed by the use of a neutral methodology which made use of no inherited learning. The import-ance of this point can be seen if we consider the enormous difference between what we know about, say, many aspects of the culture and practice of the Romans and of the Etruscans. It is difficult not to believe that this is to be explained by the difference between the historical circumstances by which the Romans, and their language, are related to us and those by which the Etruscans are related to us. For this is such that, with regard to the Romans, we have inherited a vast knowledge of their language, literature and practices, whereas, with the Etruscans, for reasons which are well known, we have inherited almost nothing. In the latter case, therefore, we are almost in the state posited in Popper's hypothesis, and the difficulties in coming to any reliable knowledge of Etruscan culture and practice provide a strong counter-example to his claim.

The second weakness in Popper's argument, which has impli-cations for the first, is that it offers no adequate solution to the problem which is constituted by the theoretical infinity of the number of interpretative hypotheses which may be adduced. For no matter how many unsatisfactory hypotheses were eliminated by the applica-tion of Popper's falsification procedures, an infinity of further hypo-theses would remain to be tested, while it would be nothing more than an accident that we had tested those which we had. For if we had no inherited beliefs, acquired in such a way as to be constitutive of our consciousness, we could introduce no substantial constraints, such as the latter supplies, into the interpretative situation and would, therefore, be in no position to exercise a rational choice between the many possible interpretative strategies which would survive any purely formal methodological tests. Popper has rightly drawn attention to the fact that research is social in character and is pursued by a community of scholars. It is unfortunate that, in this argument at least, he has lost sight of the equally important fact that it is also historical in character and that the only reason which we have for proceeding with our present theories rather than others is that they spring from a tradition of knowledge without belief in the reliability of which we would be unable to find any justifiable starting place in our enquiries. In a sense, then, his proposal, if it were applied to historical knowledge, would require a vantage point which, because it lacked an internal connection with any substantial content whatsoever, was as ahistorical as those of the thinkers examined earlier. For the same reason, therefore, it must be rejected.

It is no part of this response to Popper's claim to deny the necessity for books and for remains from the past. The need for this has already been made clear by the claim that, given the nature of our cognitive processes, books and documents are a necessary part of the way in which belief is transmitted. Were our cognitive capacities different – were we, for example, endowed with memories of a quite different capacity and a quite different standard of reliability – our methods of transmission of belief would no doubt also be different. But, given the way they are, were there no documents or other remnants from the past round which to organise the transmission of belief, we might well not have many of the historical beliefs which we have. Equally, however, neither could we have them if that were all that there was. What we need, in addition, is a continuing transmission of beliefs about the truth or falsity of what is asserted in these documents and remnants, received by us as part of our present way of thinking. Were this to be absent, there is no way in which we could begin to have a sense of a determinate historical past, other than the limited view which memory and oral tradition might allow. Thus the relation between the documents and remnants which endure and our beliefs about them is internal and not, as Popper's theory implies, external. This is not to say that some artefact which comes to us in the context of a continuing tradition of belief about our past could not exist without being part of such a tradition. But it is to say that should it do so, it would no longer be a part of historical knowledge and that, if everything which comes to us in the former way were to come in the latter, as is the suggestion in Popper's thought experiment, we could have no historical knowledge and no knowledge of the historical nature of our own consciousness. The idea that we could regain the whole of our present historical knowledge on the basis of evidence which can be offered for it, but in the absence of the beliefs about it which we have inherited as part of our own understanding of our position in the history of consciousness, is based upon a mistaken conception of the relation between an historical consciousness and historical knowledge.

THE LIMITS OF CONSTANCY AND CHANGE

At this point it would be useful to turn to a further criticism of the main thesis which would be most likely to emanate from a Popperian viewpoint – its apparent conservatism. For it looks as though the implication is that the historian already knows much – perhaps too much – of what he is supposed to discover and establish, a consequence with which Hegel was charged and for which he was criticised. This criticism would impinge differently upon the thesis as it applies to the history of events and to the history of consciousness, but I shall disregard the former here, since it has already been discussed earlier in the chapter.[5]

One should note first that the parallel with Hegel is misleading. The objection to his thesis about the self-development of reason was not just that the philosophical historian seemed to need, in advance of his account of world history, the principles of that very knowledge which only a philosophical history was supposed to be able to provide, but that what he needed, in advance of it, was an *a priori* knowledge of those substantial principles, and that there was no way in which this knowledge could be grounded or justified. It will be obvious, however, that, while it is certainly part of the present thesis that the historian cannot proceed without some unchallengeable knowledge of the development of consciousness in the past, there is nothing *a priori* about this knowledge or its source. It has constantly been emphasised that the knowledge in question is that which is acquired by a form of consciousness in virtue of the fact that that consciousness has itself been historically conditioned, that is to say, conditioned by contingent features of the process by which it has been produced and of which it is a part. To assert that the historian does not work in an epistemological void and that some of the principal materials for his work are to be found within the consciousness which he shares with other historians is not to assert that he requires some *a priori* knowledge of the history which he is to produce.

Nor, indeed, is it clear that there is anything more than an apparent conservatism about the thesis. For it does not follow from the claim that the historian cannot avoid taking into account certain beliefs, shared by him and others who are products of the same cultural tradition, that there is nothing left for him to do. His position will be precisely the same as that of earlier historians. Like them, he may, as a result of the operation of various factors within his own times, come to have certain beliefs about the kind of history which should be written, which may differ from those of his predecessors and be either not reflected or only partially reflected in the historical accounts which are available. If there has been some major change in

[5] See above, pp. 203–4.

consciousness, this may result in a major reassessment of the history of some aspect of consciousness, since he may find himself in considerable disagreement with the assumptions of the predecessors whose work he has received. Dependent upon the nature of the change, it may well, indeed, involve the more or less complete abandonment of a certain kind of account as being based upon presuppositions which are now held to be false or partial or unacceptable in some or other way. Examples of this might be the development of economic history which took place once economics had emancipated itself from philosophy or the growth of feminist history which is currently occurring under the influence of changing beliefs about the nature of women and their place in society. The latter, for example, started as if it were largely a matter of attending to previously overlooked aspects of the past. It is now developing into a new genre as it is coming to be realised that what is required is a new framework within which to write histories in which women are viewed not under traditional categories but in quite different relations to almost the whole range of activities, interests and attitudes to be found in social life. If, on the other hand, there have been only slight shifts in outlook in a certain area of interest, the historian's work will consist in something more like a re-presentation of the kind of accounts earlier available, with some up-dating to take cognisance of new empirical discoveries. This will result in some relatively minor changes of detail to the overall picture which is theoretically available, rather than, as in the former case, the production of an almost totally new kind of account.

It may seem, nevertheless, that to admit the possibility of major reinterpretations of the history of consciousness, governed by conceptions which have arisen as a result of some major change in a form of consciousness, is incompatible with an insistence upon the necessity to accept as true our inherited beliefs about the history of the forms of consciousness. For, it could be argued, should such major changes occur, their effect will be so to transform our knowledge of the history of consciousness as to render what we have received irrelevent and dispensable. But this again does not follow. For although such major reinterpretations may alter our conception of the history of consciousness, they cannot be developed and applied unless they can be linked to what we have inherited as providing the factual basis for all histories of consciousness. Thus, when developed, they do not dispense with the need for the latter, any more than the enormous

range of discoveries about existential historical fact made by
reasoned historical research dispenses with the need for a body of
inherited historical belief. The advent of feminist history, for example,
does not mean that our inherited 'non-feminist' beliefs about women
in the past can be disregarded. In their absence, there would again be
no way of retaining our knowledge of the historical nature of our own
standpoint, including the new feminist viewpoint. We would simply
lose this knowledge and, in so doing, lose our capacity to deal with
the problems engendered by the under-determination of theory by
data, which have already been discussed. Thus new histories of
aspects of consciousness are possible, but only those can be accepted
which are compatible with what we have inherited. If this means that
some new conceptions must be relegated to the category of historical
fiction, this can hardly be regarded as a criticism of the thesis, since a
major argument for it is its capacity to distinguish between this and
historical fact.

It may be thought that, in laying such stress upon the importance
of the historian's own historical position, one is doing no more than
subscribe to Croce's dictum that all history is contemporary history.
But this would be a misunderstanding. The claim that all history is
contemporary history is often construed in such a way as to carry the
implication not only that each age must write its own history from
the perspective of its own interests but that it must also necessarily
differ from what went before. But that is certainly not an implication
of the present thesis. Whether any new history will be different in kind
from earlier history is, as has been stressed above, a contingent
matter. It is certainly true that the historian must have access to a
basis of various kinds of historical belief, which comes to him as
given, and without acceptance of which he would be unable to
partake seriously in current historical research. But this entails
neither that what is produced must differ from former historical
accounts nor that it must be the same. Whether and to what degree it
is the same in kind as earlier accounts will depend upon similarities in
and differences between the consciousness of contemporary historians and that of earlier historians, and that is an entirely contingent matter.

It does not follow from this, however, that there are no *a priori*
conditions concerning the degrees of constancy or change in the
contents of consciousness over time required for the writing of
histories of consciousness. For, if the present suggestion is correct and

such histories are possible only if there has been a continuing historical transmission of socially based knowledge, those conditions in virtue of which such a mode of transmission is made possible must themselves be *a priori* conditions of the possibility of historical knowledge of the sort which we have. But these are, in fact, relatively uninteresting and amount to little more than the presupposition of metaphysical uniformity and of the psychological features required for the acquisition and transmission of knowledge. Thus if there were to be a massive change in our metaphysical conception of the universe – were we, for example, no longer to have the conception of individual agents, whose activities were undertaken in the light of beliefs which they held about individuatable items in the universe – then we would certainly be unable to have historical knowledge, for we would be unable to understand anything inherited which presupposed the earlier conception. Similarly, were there to be some massive transformation of human psychological capacities – were memory, say, to be so weakened that the social production and transmission of knowledge became impossible – we would again be unable to understand what we inherited as a form of knowledge at all. But these are conditions both of knowledge of our activities as agents and of our being as agents. In their absence both would be destroyed and it would be idle to speculate what might replace them. They may well be *a priori* conditions of history, therefore, but they are conditions of a wholly unproblematic character and amount to little more than insisting that historical knowledge is about human beings as we currently understand them to be.

It is not the case, however, that, when these relatively uncontroversial constraints have been acknowledged, there are no further *limiting* conditions for the writing of histories of consciousness, but only that there is no way of determining what these limits are, other than by attending to the historical situation of the consciousness of historians themselves. Thus, histories can be written, as prescribed by Hume, on the basis of a belief in a massive uniformity of consciousness over time. Alternatively they can be written, as advocated by Hegel and Vico, on the basis of a belief in massive changes in its content over time. There is nothing *a priori* unacceptable about any of these different approaches, except the crucial assumption that they are *a priori* necessary conditions of historical knowledge. If we find it difficult now to accept Hume's assumptions about massive uniformity, this is not because there is anything ultimately incoherent in the suggestion. His mistake was, rather, to advance, as a condition of the production of *any history whatsoever*, a thesis which could be justified, at best, only as a condition of the production of history in his own time. The difficulty which we now find with his assumptions or, alternatively, those of Hegel and Vico is, therefore, a consequence of the purely contingent development of our own historical consciousness, as a result of which we find ourselves unable to abandon a rather different set of beliefs.

HISTORICAL CONSCIOUSNESS AND HISTORICAL KNOWLEDGE

It is possible now to summarise some of the general historical and philosophical conclusions which emerge from the argument of this book. First, Hume, Hegel and Vico were correct in thinking that historians work within a set of presuppositions about the nature of, and methods proper to, their subject. They were correct, moreover, in holding that there must be, among these, some criterion by which we could distinguish fact from phantasy about the past. They were wrong, however, each in his different way, in thinking that this could be provided by appeal to something which was external to history as a discipline or, if they did not actually assert this, in offering solutions which implied it. They were correct also in believing that it is necessary to have a view as to what is constant and what can change in the course of history. But they were incorrect, again, in offering solutions which failed to respect the autonomy of history as a discipline, because they failed to connect the latter to a complete acceptance of the historical nature of man. Thus they came to conclusions in which, as in the case of Hume, massive constancy was an *a priori* presupposition and, in the case of Hegel and Vico, massive change was an *a priori* presupposition.

In contrast to their various claims, it has been argued, first, that the distinction between fact and fiction in history, although necessary, requires no philosophical underpinning, other than that which is supplied by a thoroughgoing acceptance of the autonomy of history as a discipline and of the particular, and historical, way in which it comes to acquire its content. There is no way in which the 'facts' of history can be distinguished from mere fancy other than by an appreciation of the way in which we have come to acquire belief in them and of the constitutive place which they occupy in our thinking

HISTORICAL CONSCIOUSNESS   225

about the past, or by historical reasoning which accepts a core of inherited belief as imposing a constraint upon what, in virtue of that reasoning, can be accepted as factual. This thesis about the autonomy of history as a mode of knowledge does, however, produce three philosophical requirements. The first is that of metaphysical uniformity, which, it has been argued, is a necessary condition of any statements of fact whatsoever and, hence, of those which are proper to history. The second is that of the uniformity of the structure, and hence of the conditions of the understanding, of human action, without which the presupposition of metaphysical uniformity would be insufficient to support our conception of historical fact. For it would be of no assistance to us to know that historical agents in the past lived in a world the general characteristics of which we can understand, if we could not also see how their activities in it were explicable in terms of their beliefs. The third is that of the conditions under which socially engendered knowledge can be transmitted, to provide that body of factual belief which constitutes the core of our notion of the determinate structure of the past.

In discussing the question of the degrees of constancy and change permissible in history, the emphasis has been wholly upon what can change or must remain constant in human consciousness. Here again, it has been argued, the relationship between these cannot be subject to any *a priori* constraints other than those given above. For, once further *a priori* constraints are introduced, they destroy the contingent character of aspects of the past and require that they be replaced by ahistorical determinants deriving from theories for which it is impossible to provide any justification. It has not, however, been argued that historians do not operate a distinction between what has changed or remained constant in consciousness throughout history. But the lines of demarcation between the two are given with the historical consciousness which historians themselves inherit as a result of our contingent development as historical beings. Any attempt to establish *a priori* determinants of the *contents* of an historical consciousness must therefore inevitably involve a denial of its essentially historical nature.

It does not follow from this that the historian is some sort of prisoner of the past and that there is neither need nor room for the production of new views of the history of consciousness or of other forms of history more generally. The beliefs about changes in the forms of consciousness which historians inherit are not monolithic sets of unquestionable beliefs, but sets received with different degrees of certainty and entrenchment. There are limits within which the historian must think as an historian, but these fall well short of determining what he must think throughout the whole range of his activities as an historian. In relation to the latter, indeed, they provide something like an Archimedean point, but one which is internal rather than external to the world of knowledge to which it provides indispensable support. There is scope, indeed, for the historian to think about different aspects of the past with the ambitions which Hegel and Vico entertained, i.e., in such a way as to find in them patterns of development of a generality sufficient to be of philosophical significance. But in so doing, he must remain faithful to the concept of historical consciousness as being itself historically conditioned, if what is produced is to be a genuine form of knowledge. The expectations which Vico and Hegel had of philosophical history thus remain legitimate, although, for the reasons given, they must be based upon a more pluralistic view of knowledge than those which they advocated. More importantly, however, they must be pursued within a conception which more fully recognises the historical character of history as a form of knowledge.

BIBLIOGRAPHY

Anscombe, G. E. M. 'Hume and Julius Caesar', in *From Parmenides to Wittgenstein: Collected Philosophical Papers*, Vol. I, Oxford, Basil Blackwell, 1981

Avineri, Shlomo. *Hegel's Theory of the Modern State*, Cambridge, Cambridge University Press, 1972

Badaloni, Nicola. *Introduzione a G. B. Vico*, Milan, Feltrinelli, 1961

Beard, Charles. 'That Noble Dream', *American Historical Review*, 41 (1935)
'Written History as an Act of Faith', *American Historical Review*, 39 (1934)

Becker, Carl L. 'What Are Historical Facts?', *Western Political Quarterly*, 8 (1955)

Bedani, Gino. *Vico Revisited: Orthodoxy, Naturalism and Science in the 'Scienza Nuova'*, Oxford, Berg, 1989

Berlin, Isaiah. 'Comment on Professor Verene's Paper' in *Vico and Contemporary Thought*, ed. Giorgio Tagliacozzo, Michael Mooney and Donald Phillip Verene, London, Macmillan Press, 1980
Vico and Herder: Two Studies in the History of Ideas, London, Hogarth Press, 1976

Berry, Christopher J. *Hume, Hegel and Human Nature*, The Hague, Martinus Nijhoff, 1982

Black, J. B. *The Art of History*, London, Methuen, 1926

Cantelli, Gianfranco. *Mente corpo linguaggio*, Florence, G. C. Sansoni Editore Nuova, 1986

Collingwood, R. G. *The Idea of History*, Oxford, Clarendon Press, 1946; reprinted in Oxford Paperbacks 1961

Croce, Benedetto. *La filosofia di G. B. Vico*, Bari, Laterza, 1911. Translated by R. G. Collingwood as *The Philosophy of Giambattista Vico*, London, Howard Latimer, 1913

Dray, William. *Perspectives on History*, London, Routledge & Kegan Paul, 1980
Philosophy of History, Englewood Cliffs, N.J., 1964

228 BIBLIOGRAPHY

Elton, G. R. *The Practice of History*, The Fontana Library, London, Collins, 1969

Flew, Anthony. *David Hume: Philosopher of Moral Science*, Oxford, Basil Blackwell, 1986

Forbes, Duncan. *Hume's Philosophical Politics*, Cambridge, Cambridge University Press, 1975

Haddock, B. A. *An Introduction to Historical Thought*, London, Edward Arnold, 1980

'Vico's Discovery of the True Homer: A Case Study in Historical Reconstruction', *Journal of the History of Ideas*, 40 (1979)

Vico's Political Thought, Swansea, Mortlake Press, 1986

Hegel, G. W. F. *Hegel's Logic*, Part I of the *Encyclopaedia of the Philosophical Sciences*, translated by William Wallace, 3rd edn, Oxford, Oxford University Press, 1975

Hegel's Philosophy of Right, translated by T. M. Knox, Oxford, Oxford University Press, 1967, reprinted 1973

Lectures on the History of Philosophy, translated by Elisabeth S. Haldane and Frances H. Simson, London, Kegan Paul, Trench, Trubner, 1892–5

Lectures on the Philosophy of World History, translated by H. B. Nisbet, Cambridge, Cambridge University Press, 1975

Hempel, Carl G. 'The Function of General Laws in History', *Journal of Philosophy*, 39 (1942)

Hume, David. *Enquiries Concerning the Human Understanding and Concerning the Principles of Morals*, ed. L. A. Selby-Bigge, 1893; reprinted Oxford, Clarendon Press, 1955

A Treatise of Human Nature, ed. L. A. Selby-Bigge, 1888; reprinted London, Oxford University Press, 1960

Ilting, K.-H. 'Hegel's Concept of the State and Marx's Early Critique' in *The State and Civil Society: Studies in Hegel's Political Philosophy*, ed. Z. A. Pelczynski, Cambridge, Cambridge University Press, 1984

Jones, Peter. *Hume's Sentiments: Their Ciceronian and French Context*, Edinburgh, Edinburgh University Press, 1982

Kaufmann, Walter. *Hegel: Reinterpretation, Texts and Commentary*, London, Weidenfeld & Nicolson, 1966

Kemp Smith, Norman. *The Philosophy of David Hume*, London, Macmillan, 1941

Livingston, Donald W. *Hume's Philosophy of Common Life*, Chicago, University of Chicago Press, 1984

Löwith, Karl. *Meaning in History*, Chicago, University of Chicago Press, 1949

McCullagh, C. Behan. *Justifying Historical Descriptions*, Cambridge, Cambridge University Press, 1984

Mandelbaum, Maurice. *History, Man and Reason: A Study in Nineteenth Century Thought*, Baltimore, the Johns Hopkins University Press, 1971

Manuel, Frank. *The Eighteenth Century Confronts the Gods*, Cambridge, Mass., Harvard University Press, 1959

Mure. G. R. G. *An Introduction to Hegel*, Oxford, Clarendon Press, 1940

Murphey, Murray G. *Our Knowledge of the Historical Past*, Indianapolis, Bobbs-Merrill, 1973

Murray, Michael. *Modern Philosophy of History*, The Hague, Martinus Nijhoff, 1970

Noxon, James. *Hume's Philosophical Development: A Study of his Methods*, Oxford, Clarendon Press, 1973

O'Brien, George Dennis. 'Does Hegel Have a Philosophy of History?', *History and Theory*, Vol. 10, No. 3 (1971), *Hegel on Reason and History: A Contemporary Interpretation*, Chicago, University of Chicago Press, 1975

Pares, Richard. *King George III and the Politicians*, Oxford, Clarendon Press, 1953

Passmore, John. *Hume's Intentions*, 3rd edn, London, Duckworth, 1980

Piovani, Pietro. 'Vico without Hegel' in *Vico: An International Symposium*, ed. Giorgio Tagliacozzo and Hayden V. White, Baltimore, the Johns Hopkins University Press, 1969

Plant, Raymond. *Hegel: An Introduction*, 2nd edn, Oxford, Basil Blackwell, 1983

Pompa, Leon. 'Imagination in Vico', in *Vico: Past and Present*, ed. Giorgio Tagliacozzo, Atlantic Highlands, N.J., Humanities Press, 1981
  Vico: Selected Writings, Cambridge, Cambridge University Press, 1982
  Vico: A Study of the 'New Science', 2nd edn, Cambridge, Cambridge University Press, 1990

Popper, Karl R. *Objective Knowledge: An Evolutionary Approach*, Oxford, Oxford University Press, 1972; reprinted 1974

Stace, W. T. *The Philosophy of Hegel*, London, Macmillan, 1924

Strawson, P. F. *Individuals: An Essay in Descriptive Metaphysics*, London, Methuen, 1959

Stroud, Barry. *Hume*, London, Routledge & Kegan Paul, 1977

Taylor, Charles. *Hegel*, Cambridge, Cambridge University Press, 1975

Vaughan, Frederick. '*La Scienza Nuova*: Orthodoxy and the Art of Writing', *Forum Italicum*, Vol. 2, No. 4 (1968)
  The Political Philosophy of Giambattista Vico, The Hague, Martinus Nijhoff, 1972

Verene, Donald Phillip. 'Vico's Philosophy of Imagination' in *Vico and Contemporary Thought*, ed. Giorgio Tagliacozzo, Michael Mooney and Donald Phillip Verene, London, Macmillan Press, 1980
  Vico's Science of Imagination, Ithaca, Cornell University Press, 1981

Vico, Giambattista. *The Autobiography of Giambattista Vico*, translated by Max Harold Fisch and Thomas Goddard Bergin, Great Seal Books, New York, Cornell University Press, 1963

The New Science of Giambattista Vico, translated by Thomas Goddard Bergin and Max Harold Fisch, revised edn, Ithaca, Cornell University Press, 1968

Walsh, W. H. 'The Constancy of Human Nature' in *Contemporary British Philosophy*, Fourth Series, ed. H. D. Lewis, London, George Allen & Unwin, 1976

An Introduction to Philosophy of History, Hutchinson's University Library, London, Hutchinson, 1951

'The Logical Status of Vico's Ideal Eternal History' in *Giambattista Vico's Science of Humanity*, ed. Giorgio Tagliacozzo and Donald Phillip Verene, Baltimore, the Johns Hopkins University Press, 1976

Whelen, Frederick G. *Order and Artifice in Hume's Political Philosophy*, Princeton, Princeton University Press, 1985

White, Hayden. *Metahistory: The Historical Imagination in Nineteenth-Century Europe*, Baltimore, the Johns Hopkins University Press, 1973

'The Tropics of History: The Deep Structure of the *New Science*' in *Giambattista Vico's Science of Humanity*, ed. Giorgio Tagliacozzo and Donald Phillip Verene, Baltimore, the Johns Hopkins University Press, 1976

Wilkins, Burleigh Taylor. *Hegel's Philosophy of History*, Ithaca, Cornell University Press, 1974

Winch, Peter. *The Idea of a Social Science and its Relations to Philosophy*, London, Routledge & Kegan Paul, 1958

INDEX

Alexander the Great, 46, 49
anachronism, conceptual, 141, 141n,
    176–7
Anaxagoras, 83–4, 117n
Anscombe, G. E. M., 26n
Antony, 200
Archimedes, 226
Aristotle, 86, 86n
Avineri, Shlomo, 68n, 96n, 97n

Badaloni, Nicola, 134n, 144n
barbarism of reflection, Vico's, *see*
    reflection
Beard, Charles, 2n
Becker, Carl L., 2n
Bedani, Gino, 134n, 144n
belief, historically situated, 51–3, 58–9,
    61, 65, 76–7
Berecynthia, 144n
Bergin, Thomas Goddard, 137n, 155n
Berlin, Isaiah, 134n, 140n, 141n,
    154n
Berry, Christopher J., 15, 68n, 102n
Black, J. B., 15
Brutus, 200
Budé, Guillaume, 4n

Caesar, Julius, 25, 26, 26n, 27, 27n,
    28, 32, 34, 70, 72, 99, 104, 197–8,
    200–1, 207
Cantelli, Gianfranco, 144n
Cassius, 200
causes, invariance of the operation of,
    35–7; *see also* historical belief, Hume's
    causal account of; human nature
Charlemagne, 96n

Collingwood, R. G., 3n, 15, 67n, 68n,
    133n
consciousness, historical, 12, 65–6;
    internally related to historical fact,
    195–219
consciousness, Hume's theory of the
    constancy of, 10, 49–57, 59–60,
    64–5, 192, 223; Hegel's criticisms of,
    70–1, 77
consciousness, social, the primacy of,
    63–6, 73, 83, 87, 91, 130, 170–1
Croce, Benedetto, 133n, 161–2, 222
Cujas, Jacques, 4n
Curtius Rufus, Quintus, 46, 49
Cybele, 144n

Descartes, 135, 176
Dewey, John, 78
dialectic, as the self-determining idea,
    107–17; *see also* idea, the logical
    priority of the
Dray, William H., 2n, 68n

Elizabeth I, Queen, 200
epistemological neutralism, 10, 57–9,
    61, 107n, 217
Elton, G. R., 2n

fact, objective, metaphysical conditions
    of, 37–40; *see also* historical fact;
    uniformity, metaphysical
Fawkes, Guy, 204–5
Fisch, Max Harold, 137n, 155n
Flora, 145n
Forbes, Duncan, 16, 43n, 44n, 68n,
    72n, 117n, 124n